"A word to the wise is enough."
—Poor Richard

The model for *Poor Charlie's Almanack* is, of course, Ben Franklin's *Poor Richard's Almanack*. Franklin, as many know, was a polymath. Born in Boston and a leader of the American Revolution, he was a journalist, publisher, author, philanthropist, abolitionist, public servant, scientist, librarian, diplomat, and inventor.

Using the pseudonym of "Poor Richard," Franklin published his *Almanack* from 1733 to 1758. Its content varied, including not only many Franklin aphorisms that became famous but also calendars, weather forecasts, astronomical information, and astrological data. The *Almanack* was hugely popular in the American colonies, selling about 10,000 copies per year.

Poor Richard's maxims ranged widely in topic and were typically laced with humor. Some samples include:

- *"No nation was ever ruined by trade."*

- *"Drive thy Business, or it will drive thee."*

- *"He that falls in love with himself will have no rivals."*

- *"Where there's Marriage without Love, there will be Love without Marriage."*

- *"Necessity never made a good bargain."*

- *"Three may keep a secret, if two of them are dead."*

- *"There is no little enemy."*

- *"It's difficult for an empty sack to stand upright."*

Poor Charlie's
Almanack

—Abridged—

The Wit and Wisdom of
CHARLES T. MUNGER

Foreword By *WARREN E. BUFFETT*
Edited by Peter D. Kaufman

Attempts have been made to identify the owners of
any copyrighted materials appearing in this book. The
editor and publisher extend their apologies for any
errors or omissions and encourage any copyright owners
inadvertently missed to contact them.

For information write:

The Donning Company Publishers
184 Business Park Drive, Suite 206
Virginia Beach, VA 23462

Dwight Tompkins, Project Director
Steve Mull, General Manager
Pamela Koch, Editor
Scott Rule, Designer

Original illustrations and caricatures by Ed Wexler

Library of Congress
Cataloging-in-Publication Data

Poor Charlie's almanack : the wit and wisdom of Charles
T. Munger / edited by Peter D. Kaufman.
    p. cm.
  Includes index.
  ISBN 1-57864-303-1 (original hardcover : alk. paper)
  ISBN-10 1-57864-338-4 (abridged)
  ISBN-13 978-1-57864-338-7 (abridged)
  1. Investments--Decision making. 2. Investments-
-Humor. 3. Berkshire Hathaway Inc.--History. 4.
Munger, Charles T., 1924- I. Kaufman, Peter D. II.
Title.
  HG4515.M86 2005
  332.6'02'07--dc22

            2005000483

Printed in the United States of America
by Walsworth Publishing Company
Marceline, Missouri

To obtain a copy of the unabridged edition of "Poor
Charlie's Almanack: The Wit and Wisdom of Charles T.
Munger," go online to:

www.poorcharliesalmanack.com

"A Lesson on Elementary, Worldly Wisdom as it Relates to
Investment Management and Business"; "Worldly Wisdom,
Revisited: Lesson #2"; and "Worldly Wisdom, Revisited: Lesson
#2, Part 2"; appearing on pages 57-107, and 111-165 respectively,
are copyright *Outstanding Investor Digest* and www.oid.com, and
quoted by permission.

2005©www.AlanLevenson.com

Shelby Cullom Davis   Shelby M. C. Davis   Christopher C. Davis   Andrew A. Davis

Editor's Foreword
to the Abridged Edition of
Poor Charlie's Almanack

by Peter D. Kaufman

Chris Davis asked me if I would produce, for distribution by Davis Advisors, an abridged version of *Poor Charlie's Almanack* featuring four of the ten talks contained in the original. I immediately got Charlie's okay and we agreed to provide the abridged books at cost, provided Davis Advisors made an appropriate donation to the Huntington Library.

Agreeing to this project was easy. Both Charlie and I admire the Davis family, three successful generations of which are caricatured above. Davis Advisors, started by Shelby M.C. Davis and now headed by Chris Davis, has had a successful record of investment management, now involving well over $50 billion in assets. Charlie and I like the fact that the Davis family "eats its own cooking"—that is, a very substantial part of the Davis family's wealth is invested in mutual funds managed by Davis Advisors. Our decision was also made easy by the philosophy of the Davis family and firm, whose ideas and practices are quite similar to Charlie's. Consider the following quotations:

> *"You make most of your money in a bear market, you just don't realize it at the time."*
>
> —Shelby Cullom Davis

> *"Our investment process is founded on two essential questions: 'What kind of businesses do we want to own?' and 'How much should we pay for them?'"*
>
> —Christopher C. Davis and Kenneth Charles Feinberg

> *"As we like to say, "Nothing focuses the mind more on researching companies than having one's own money on the line."*
>
> —Shelby M.C. Davis

> *"Investors repeatedly abandon a sensible wealth-building strategy just because it is not generating short-term results, and almost without fail, give up on it at precisely the wrong time."*
>
> —Christopher C. Davis

Kenneth Charles Feinberg
Portfolio Manager

Finally, for reasons that should be readily apparent, Charlie identifies strongly with the patriarch of this family, Shelby Cullom Davis, who from a start near zero left behind $800 million—plus a considerable reputation as a curmudgeon. Charlie, something of one himself, advised Wesco annual meeting attendees in May that, **"if you get my book and don't like it, you can always give it to a more intelligent friend."**

And so, we are pleased to bring you *Poor Charlie's Almanack Abridged*, which by the way boasts one small advantage over the original. Out of his high regard for the Davises, Charlie agreed to append some brief comments to each of the four selected talks. These postscripts follow each of the four selections.

> *"Both Charlie and I are great admirers of the Davis family, and welcome this opportunity to share our book with their friends."*

Contents

A word about the style and layout of the book: Charlie is enormously curious about nearly everything he bumps into in life. Accordingly, as we ourselves bumped into people, places, and subjects mentioned by Charlie in his talks, we supplemented his text with related information, photographs, and other graphics. The "sidebars" peppered throughout the talks, for example, serve to explain concepts, add a supporting voice, or emphasize an important Munger idea. We hope these sidebars will not only inform, but also amuse and even encourage you to further pursue these subjects on your own.

Foreword: Buffett on Munger

by Warren E. Buffett

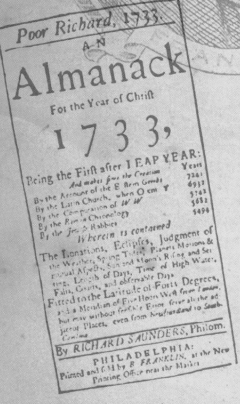

From 1733 to 1758, Ben Franklin dispensed useful and timeless advice through *Poor Richard's Almanack*. Among the virtues extolled were thrift, duty, hard work, and simplicity.

Subsequently, two centuries went by during which Ben's thoughts on these subjects were regarded as the last word. Then Charlie Munger stepped forth.

Initially a mere disciple of Ben's, Charlie was soon breaking new ground. What Ben had recommended, Charlie demanded. If Ben suggested saving pennies, Charlie raised the stakes. If Ben said be prompt, Charlie said be early. Life under Ben's rules began to look positively cushy compared with the rigor demanded by Munger.

Moreover, Charlie consistently practiced what he preached (and, oh, how he preached). Ben, in his will, created two small philanthropic funds that were designed to teach the magic of compound interest. Early on, Charlie decided

"PARTNERS"

that this was a subject far too important to be taught through some posthumous project. Instead, he opted to become a living lesson in compounding, eschewing frivolous (defined as "any") expenditures that might sap the power of his example. Consequently, the members of Charlie's family learned the joys of extended bus trips while their wealthy friends, imprisoned in private jets, missed these enriching experiences.

In certain areas, however, Charlie has not sought to improve on Ben's thinking. For example, Ben's "Advice on the Choice of a Mistress" essay has left Charlie in the "I have nothing to add" mode that is his trademark at Berkshire annual meetings.

As for myself, I'd like to offer some "Advice on the Choice of a Partner." Pay attention.

There was only one partner who fit my bill of particulars in every way—Charlie.

Look first for someone both smarter and wiser than you are. After locating him (or her), ask him not to flaunt his superiority so that you may enjoy acclaim for the many accomplishments that sprang from his thoughts and advice. Seek a partner who will never second-guess you nor sulk when you make expensive mistakes. Look also for a generous soul who will put up his own money and work for peanuts. Finally, join with someone who will constantly add to the fun as you travel a long road together.

All of the above is splendid advice. (I've never scored less than an A in self-graded exams.) In fact, it's so splendid that I set out in 1959 to follow it slavishly. And there was only one partner who fit my bill of particulars in every way—Charlie.

In Ben's famous essay, he says that only an older mistress makes sense, and he goes on to give eight very good reasons as to why this is so. His clincher: "…and, lastly, they are so grateful."

Charlie and I have now been partners for forty-five years. I'm not sure whether he had seven other reasons for selecting me. But I definitely meet Ben's eighth criterion. I couldn't be more grateful.

Two Views of Charles T. Munger

Q and A with Warren Buffett

OK, the first question is how, when, and where did you first meet Charlie Munger?

Well, I first met Charlie in 1959 when the Davis family got me together with him. Dr. Davis previously had often mistaken me for Charlie, and I wanted to find out whether that was a compliment or an insult. So, when Charlie came home to Omaha in 1959, the Davises arranged for us to go to dinner; in fact, I think we had a small little private room with a few Davises in attendance. Sometime during the evening, when Charlie started rolling on the floor laughing at his own jokes, I knew I had met a kindred spirit.

What was your first impression?

My first impression was that I had run into somebody that had a lot of similarities to me. I've been known to roll on the floor laughing at my own stuff, too, and to try to dominate the conversation. Charlie was a little more successful at that than I've ever been, but he's been great to study under.

This is great. Now, here's your big one. What are the secrets of his success?

Well, one time, some attractive woman sat next to Charlie and asked him what he owed his success to, and, unfortunately, she insisted on a one-word answer. He had a speech prepared that would have gone on for several hours. But, when forced to boil it down to one word, he said that he was "rational." You know, he comes equipped for rationality, and he applies it in business. He doesn't always apply it elsewhere, but he applies it in business, and that's made him a huge business success.

What other character traits do you think have contributed to his success?

I think actually it really does come out of Ben Franklin that he admires so much. I mean, there is honesty and integrity, and always doing more than his share and not complaining about what the other person does. We've been associated for forty years, and he's never second-guessed anything I've done. We've never had an argument. We've disagreed on things, but he's a perfect partner.

What would you say are his most unusual characteristics?

I would say everything about Charlie is unusual. I've been looking for the usual now for forty years, and I have yet to find it. Charlie marches to his own music, and it's music like virtually no one else is listening to. So, I would say that to try and typecast Charlie in terms of any other human that I can think of, no one would fit. He's got his own mold.

Last question, what effect do you think Nancy has had on his life?

I would have to say that Charlie is not looking for anyone to have an effect on him, but that Nancy has done a remarkable job in spite of that fact. I would hate to be a marriage broker with Charlie as a client.

Wendy Munger conducted this interview with Warren Buffett in November of 1998.

And Bill Gates Has His Say:

"Ben Franklin once said, 'I cannot conceive otherwise than that He, the Infinite Father, expects or requires no worship or praise from us, but that He is even infinitely above it.'

"I think the same can be said of Charlie Munger—despite any accolades from me or others in this book he will still be his own best critic as well as the person who appreciates his own jokes the most.

"Warren told me before I met Charlie that he was the most amazing business partner a man could have. He also warned me not to expect to get a word in edgewise when talking to Charlie because even at a cocktail party Charlie would hold his hand up to prevent others from starting to speak while he took a drink.

"He also warned me that Charlie might not be the best person to choose as a boat captain, relating a story where he managed to sink a boat in a totally calm lake with no other traffic by going full speed in reverse with a low transom on the stern.

"Charlie exceeded even the high expectations that Warren set. He is truly the broadest thinker I have ever encountered. From business principles to economic principles to the design of student dormitories to the design of a catamaran he has no equal.

"Our most memorable correspondence was about stock options and their power to distort business results. Our longest correspondence was a detailed discussion on the mating habits of naked mole rats and what the human species might learn from them.

"Charlie has the ability to capture knowledge with simple descriptions. When discussing the intelligence of offspring, he refers to the 'genetic lottery.' When discussing venture capitalists who defend stock options, he deems them 'no better than the piano player in a whorehouse.' When discussing the deleterious effects on efficiency of cost-plus contracts, he likes to say 'even the mule knew to slow down.'

"This book capturing Charlie's wisdom is long overdue."

The Munger Approach to Life, Learning, and Decision Making

"Take a simple idea and take it seriously."
—*Munger*

Despite being largely self-taught, Ben Franklin was spectacularly successful in such diverse fields as journalism, publishing, printing, philanthropy, public service, science, diplomacy, and inventing. Much of Franklin's success was due to the essential nature of the man—most especially his appetite for hard work but also his insatiable curiosity and patient demeanor. Above all, he possessed a quick and willing mind that enabled him to easily master each new field of endeavor he chose to undertake. It is not surprising that Charlie Munger considers Franklin his greatest hero, for Munger is also largely self-taught and shares many of Franklin's unique characteristics. Like Franklin, Charlie has made himself into a grandmaster of preparation, patience, discipline, and objectivity. He has parlayed these attributes into great success in both his personal and business endeavors, especially in his investing.

Business as an Ecosystem

"When we try to pick out anything by itself, we find it hitched to everything else in the universe."
—John Muir

"I find it quite useful to think of a free market economy—or partly free market economy—as sort of the equivalent of an ecosystem. Just as animals flourish in niches, people who specialize in some narrow niche can do very well.

"This is a very unfashionable way of thinking because early in the days after Darwin came along, people like the robber barons assumed that the doctrine of the survival of the fittest authenticated them as deserving power. But the truth is that it is a lot like an ecosystem. And you get many of the same results.

"In business we often find that the winning system goes almost ridiculously far in maximizing and/or minimizing one or a few variables—like the discount warehouses of Costco."

To Charlie, successful investing is simply a byproduct of his carefully organized and focused approach to life. Warren Buffett once said, "Charlie can analyze and evaluate any kind of deal faster and more accurately than any man alive. He sees any valid weakness in sixty seconds. He is a perfect partner." Why does Buffett proffer such high praise? The answer lies in the markedly original approach Munger applies to life, learning, and decision making—the principal subject of this overview.

A word to the wise before we begin: Given the complexity of Charlie's approach, what follows is not intended as a "how-to" lesson for the aspiring investor. Instead, it is a general overview of "how he seems to do it." Our goal here is to present the basic outline of Charlie's approach to prepare you for the voluminous details that follow in the rest of the book. If you are anxious to get to the heart of the matter, his investment advice and the "Four Talks" sections—presented verbatim in Charlie's own words—are the best source for exacting "how-to" advice on a broad range of topics. Here we will content ourselves with a presentation of the general thought processes Charlie employs when considering an investment, followed by an outline of his guiding investment principles.

Munger's "Multiple Mental Models" Approach to Business Analysis and Assessment

"You must know the big ideas in the big disciplines and use them routinely—all of them, not just a few. Most people are trained in one model—economics, for example—and try to solve all problems in one way. You know the old saying: 'To the man with a hammer, the world looks like a nail.' This is a dumb way of handling problems."

Charlie's approach to investing is quite different from the more rudimentary systems used by most investors. Instead of making a superficial stand-alone assessment of a company's financial information, Charlie conducts a comprehensive analysis of both the internal workings of the investment candidate as well as the larger, integrated "ecosystem" in which it operates. He calls the tools he uses to conduct this review "Multiple Mental Models." These models, discussed at length in several of the Talks, serve as a framework for gathering, processing, and acting on information. They borrow from and neatly stitch together the analytical tools, methods, and formulas from such traditional disciplines as history, psychology,

"You have to realize the truth of biologist Julian Huxley's idea that, 'Life is just one damn relatedness after another.' So you must have the models, and you must see the relatedness and the effects from the relatedness."

physiology, mathematics, engineering, biology, physics, chemistry, statistics, economics, and so on. The unassailable logic of Charlie's "ecosystem" approach to investment analysis: *Just as multiple factors shape almost every system, multiple models from a variety of disciplines, applied with fluency, are needed to understand that system.* As John Muir observed about the interconnectedness of nature, "When we try to pick out anything by itself, we find it hitched to everything else in the universe."

A Latticework of Mental Models

"Simplicity is the end result of long, hard work, not the starting point."
—Frederick Maitland

"I've long believed that a certain system—which almost any intelligent person can learn—works way better than the systems that most people use. What you need is a latticework of mental models in your head. And, with that system, things gradually get to fit together in a way that enhances cognition.

"However, my particular approach seldom seems to get through, even to people of immense ability. Things usually die after going to the 'Too-Hard' pile."
—Munger

Charlie seeks to discover the universe hitched to each of his investment candidates by gaining a firm grasp on all, or at least most, of the relevant factors comprising both its internal and external environment. When properly collected and organized, his Multiple Mental Models (about one hundred in number, he estimates) provide a context or "latticework" that leads to remarkable insights as to the purpose and nature of life. More pertinent to our purpose here, his models supply the analytical structure that enables him to reduce the inherent chaos and confusion of a complex investment problem into a clarified set of fundamentals. Especially important examples of these models include the redundancy/backup system model from engineering, the compound interest model from mathematics, the breakpoint/tipping-moment/autocatalysis models from physics and chemistry, the modern Darwinian synthesis model from biology, and cognitive misjudgment models from psychology.

A Willingness to Change His Mind

"Faced with the choice between changing one's mind and proving there is no need to do so, almost everyone gets busy on the proof."

—John Kenneth Galbraith

Charlie has developed an unusual additional attribute—a willingness, even an eagerness, to identify and acknowledge his own mistakes and learn from them. As he once said, "If Berkshire has made a modest progress, a good deal of it is because Warren and I are very good at destroying our own best-loved ideas. Any year that you don't destroy one of your best-loved ideas is probably a wasted year."

Charlie likes the analogy of looking at one's ideas and approaches as "tools." "When a better tool (idea or approach) comes along, what could be better than to swap it for your old, less useful tool? Warren and I routinely do this, but most people, as Galbraith says, forever cling to their old, less useful tools."

Famously willing to change his mind, Thomas Alva Edison (1847–1931) found "10,000 ways that won't work" in his ultimately successful pursuit of the incandescent bulb.

The net result of this broad-spectrum analysis is a heightened understanding for how the many factors affecting an investment candidate blend and link to one another. Sometimes this understanding reveals the existence of second order, "ripple," or "spillover" effects. Other times the factors employed combine to create enormous "*lollapalooza-level results*," good or bad. By applying this framework,

Charlie lives in a different world from most investors when it comes to investment analysis. His approach accepts the reality that investment problems are inherently complex, and in a manner more in keeping with the rigors of scientific inquiry than conventional "investing," he attacks them with a staggering degree of preparation and broad-based research.

Charlie's "Big Ideas from the Big Disciplines" approach to investment evaluation is certainly unique in the business world—as is its origin. Not finding any existing approach adequate to the task, Charlie painstakingly created his own largely self-taught system. The "self-taught" statement is no exaggeration; he once said, "To this day, I have never taken any course, anywhere, in chemistry, economics, psychology, or business." And yet these disciplines—especially psychology—form the foundation upon which his system is built.

It is this signature approach, backed by Charlie's formidable intellect, temperament, and decades of relevant experience, that have made him the virtuoso of business pattern recognition so valued by Buffett. Like a chess grandmaster, through logic, instinct, and intuition, he determines the most promising investment "moves," all the while projecting the illusion that the insight came easily, even simply. But make no mistake: This "simplicity" comes only at the end of a long journey toward understanding—not at the beginning. His clarity is hard won: the product of a lifetime of studying the patterns of human behavior, business systems, and a myriad of other scientific disciplines.

Charlie counts preparation, patience, discipline, and objectivity among his most fundamental guiding principles. He will not deviate from these principles, regardless of group dynamics, emotional itches, or popular wisdom that "this time

An Acceptance for Reality

"I'm afraid that's the way it is. If there are twenty factors and they interact some, you'll just have to learn to handle it—because that's the way the world is. But you won't find it that hard if you go at it Darwin-like, step by step with curious persistence. You'll be amazed at how good you can get."

—Munger

2005 © www.AlanLevenson.com

"Perhaps the most valuable result of all education is the ability to make yourself do the thing you have to do, when it ought to be done, whether you like it or not. It is the first lesson that ought to be learned and however early a man's training begins, it is probably the last lesson that he learns thoroughly."

—Thomas Henry Huxley
Darwin's self-apponited
advocate or "bulldog"

Patience Escalier, Van Gogh, 1888, oil on canvas, private collection (Niarchos)

Patience: The Art of "Waiting Without Tiring of Waiting"

"Look at those hedge funds—you think they can wait? They don't know how to wait! In my personal portfolio, I have sat for years at a time with $10 to $12 million in treasuries or municipals, just waiting, waiting...."

"As Jesse Livermore said, 'The big money is not in the buying and selling...but in the waiting.'"

around it's different." When faithfully adhered to, these traits result in one of the best-known Munger characteristics: *not buying or selling very often.* Munger, like Buffett, believes a successful investment career boils down to only a handful of decisions. So when Charlie likes a business, he makes a very large bet and typically holds the position for a long period (see Warren Buffett's analysis of the original 1962–1975 Munger partnership on page 32). Charlie calls it "sit on your ass investing" and cites its benefits: "You're paying less to brokers, you're listening to less nonsense, and if it works, the tax system gives you an extra one, two, or three percentage points per annum." In his view, a portfolio of three companies is plenty of diversification. Accordingly, Charlie is willing to commit uncommonly high percentages of his investment capital to individual "focused" opportunities. Find a Wall Street organization, financial advisor, or mutual fund manager willing to make that statement!

Given Charlie's record of success, not to mention Buffett's endorsement, why aren't his investment practices more routinely emulated by others? Perhaps the answer is that, for most people, Charlie's multidisciplinary approach is simply too hard. Further, few investors share Charlie's willingness to appear foolish by not following "the herd." Religious in his objectivity, Charlie is content to swim imperturbably against the tide of popular

LEMMING
(*Dicrostonyx groenlandicus*)

Charlie on Honesty:
2004 Wesco Meeting

"Ability will get you to the top, but it takes character to keep you there."

"Trickery and treachery are the practices of fools that have not the wits enough to be honest."

"Louis Vincenti, who used to sit in the chair I occupy today, used to say, 'If you tell the truth, you don't have to remember your lies.' So we try and keep it simple by telling it like it is at all times. Having so many longtime loyal shareholders means that we have never given a damn whether any quarter's earnings were up or down—at least we don't care in terms of their effect on shareholders. We prefer profits to losses, obviously. But we're not willing to manipulate in any way just to make some quarter look a little better. And that's a very different ethos from the standard.

"And in terms of intellectual content, I think this place tries harder to be rational than most places. And I think it tries harder than most places to be ethical—meaning to tell the truth and to not be abusive. Now with 175,000 employees, or something like that, at Berkshire, I'll bet as I sit here at least one of them is doing something that I would very much regret. However, despite the presence of some human failing, we've had an amazingly low amount of litigation or scandal or anything of that sort over a vast number of decades. And people notice that.

"We think there should be a huge area between what you're willing to do and what you can do without significant risk of suffering criminal penalty or causing losses. We believe you shouldn't go anywhere near that line. You ought to have an internal compass. So there should be all kinds of things you won't do even though they're perfectly legal. That's the way we try to operate.

"I don't think we deserve a lot of credit for that because we early understood that we'd make more money that way. And since we understood it so well, I'm not sure that we're entitled to credit for such morality as we have.

"Of course, it is hard to know your own motivations. But I'd like to believe that we'd all behave well even if it didn't work so well financially. And every once in a while, we get an opportunity to behave that way. But more often we've made extra money out of morality. Ben Franklin was right for us. He didn't say honesty was the best morals, he said it was the best policy."

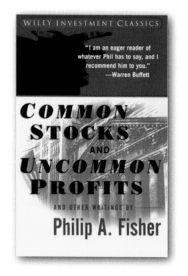
opinion—indefinitely, if necessary—which is a rare attribute in the average investor. And while this behavior can at times appear simply stubborn or contrarian, that is not the defining characteristic. Charlie is simply content to trust his own judgment even when it runs counter to the wisdom of the herd. This "lone-wolf" aspect of Charlie's temperament is a rarely appreciated reason why he consistently outperforms the larger investment community. Indeed, if temperament chiefly arises from inborn tendencies, it may be that hard work, intellect, and experience, regardless of their intensity, are by themselves insufficient to make a great investor like Charlie Munger. As we shall witness throughout the remainder of this book, the right kind of genetically predetermined "wiring" is needed as well.

At the 2004 Berkshire Hathaway annual meeting, a young shareholder asked Buffett how to succeed in life. After Buffett shared his thoughts, Charlie chimed

"When Warren lectures at business schools, he says, 'I could improve your ultimate financial welfare by giving you a ticket with only twenty slots in it so that you had twenty punches—representing all the investments that you get to make in a lifetime. And once you'd punched through the card, you couldn't make any more investments at all. Under those rules, you'd really think carefully about what you did, and you'd be forced to load up on what you'd really thought about. So you'd do so much better.'"

in: "Don't do cocaine. Don't race trains. And avoid AIDS situations." Many would dismiss his seemingly flippant answer as merely humorous (which it certainly was), but in fact it faithfully reflects both his general views on avoiding trouble in life and his particular method for avoiding missteps in investing.

Often, as in this case, Charlie generally focuses first on what to avoid—that is, on what NOT to do—before he considers the affirmative steps he will take in a given situation. "All I want to know is where I'm going to die, so I'll never go there" is one of his favorite quips. In business as in life, Charlie gains enormous advantage by summarily eliminating the unpromising portions of "the chess board," freeing his time and attention for the more productive regions. Charlie strives to reduce complex situations to their most basic, unemotional fundamentals. Yet, within this pursuit of rationality and simplicity, he is careful to avoid what he calls "physics envy," the common human craving to reduce enormously complex systems (such as those in economics) to one-size-fits-all Newtonian formulas. Instead, he faithfully honors Albert Einstein's admonition, "A scientific theory should be as simple as possible, but no simpler." Or in his own words, "What I'm against is being very confident and feeling that you know, for sure, that your particular action will do more good than harm. You're dealing with highly complex systems wherein everything is interacting with everything else."

Another Benjamin—Graham, not Franklin—played a significant role in forming Charlie's investing outlook. One of the most enduring concepts in Graham's *The Intelligent Investor* is Mr. Market. Usually, Mr. Market is a temperate and reasonable fellow, but some days he is gripped by irrational fear or greed. Graham cautioned the investor to carefully use his own, unemotional judgment of value instead of relying on the often manic-depressive behavior of the financial markets. Similarly, Charlie recognizes that even among the most competent and motivated of people, decisions are not always made on a purely rational basis. For this reason, he considers the psychological factors of human misjudgment some of the most important mental models that can be applied to an investment opportunity:

"Personally, I've gotten so that I now use a kind of two-track analysis. First, what are the factors that really govern the interests involved, rationally considered? And second, what

The Influence of Ben Graham

Mr. Market

"In the short run, the market is a voting machine. But in the long run, it is a weighing machine."

Valuation

"Investment is most successful when it is most businesslike."

"Investors should purchase stocks like they purchase groceries—not like they purchase perfume."
—Ben Graham

Paradox

"It's not the bad ideas that do you in, it's the good ideas. And you may say, 'That can't be so. That's paradoxical.' What he [Graham] meant was that if a thing is a bad idea, it's hard to overdo. But where there is a good idea with a core of essential and important truth, you can't ignore it. And then it's so easy to overdo it. So the good ideas are a wonderful way to suffer terribly if you overdo them."
—Munger

are the subconscious influences where the brain at a subconscious level is automatically forming conclusions in various ways—which, by and large, are useful—but which often malfunction? One approach is rationality—the way you'd work out a bridge problem, by evaluating the real interest, the real probabilities, and so forth. And the other is to evaluate the psychological factors that cause subconscious conclusions—many of which are wrong." (For more specifics on this topic see Talk Four, in which Charlie applies mental models from the field of psychology to illustrate twenty-five common causes of human misjudgment.)

Obviously, the methods described to this point can't be learned in a university classroom or on Wall Street. They were developed by Charlie, from scratch, to satisfy his own exacting requirements. They probably deserve a title of their own, something like: "Quickly Eliminate the Big Universe of What Not to Do, Follow Up with a Fluent, Multidisciplinary Attack on What Remains, Then Act Decisively When, and Only When, the Right Circumstances Appear." Is it worth the effort to develop and adhere to such an approach? Charlie seems to think so: "It's kind of fun to sit there and outthink people who are way smarter than you are because you've trained yourself to be more objective and more multidisciplinary. Furthermore, there is a lot of money in it, as I can testify from my own personal experience."

The Two-Track Analysis

"Generally, stocks are valued in two ways. One is the way that wheat is valued—in terms of its perceived practical utility to the user of the wheat. The second way is the way that Rembrandts are valued. And to some extent, Rembrandts are valued highly because they've gone up in price in the past."

"To us, investing is the equivalent of going out and betting against the pari-mutuel system. We look for a horse with one chance in two of winning and which pays you three to one. You're looking for a mispriced gamble. That's what investing is. And you have to know enough to know whether the gamble is mispriced. That's value investing."

"We're emphasizing the knowable by predicting how certain people and companies will swim against the current. We're not predicting the fluctuation in the current."

Talk about the difficulty of swimming against the current!
The Alcatraz Sharkfest Swim mimics the feat the Anglin brothers and Frank Lee Morris pulled off in their successful escape from Alcatraz on the night of June 12, 1962. This swim is not for novices; the event pits experienced swimmers against brutal currents and frigid water temperatures.

An Investing Principles Checklist

"No wise pilot, no matter how great his talent and experience, fails to use his checklist."

We have now examined Charlie's approach to thinking in general and to investing in particular. In keeping with our intent to observe "how he seems to do it," we will recap his approach by using the "checklist" methodology he advocates. Note, however, that the following principles are most certainly not employed by Charlie in a one-by-one or one-time fashion as the checklist format might seem to imply. Nor can they necessarily be prioritized in terms of any apparent or relative importance. Rather, each must be considered as part of the complex whole or gestalt of the investment analysis process, in much the same way that an individual tile is integral to the larger mosaic in which it appears.

- ■ Risk—All investment evaluations should begin by measuring risk, especially reputational
  - Incorporate an appropriate margin of safety
  - Avoid dealing with people of questionable character
  - Insist upon proper compensation for risk assumed
  - Always beware of inflation and interest rate exposures
  - Avoid big mistakes; shun permanent capital loss
- ■ Independence—"Only in fairy tales are emperors told they are naked"
  - Objectivity and rationality require independence of thought
  - Remember that just because other people agree or disagree with you doesn't make you right or wrong—the only thing that matters is the correctness of your analysis and judgment
  - Mimicking the herd invites regression to the mean (merely average performance)

Compound Interest

"…'tis the stone that will turn all your lead into gold…. Remember that money is of a prolific generating nature. Money can beget money, and its offspring can beget more."

—Benjamin Franklin

"If you took our top fifteen decisions out, we'd have a pretty average record. It wasn't hyperactivity, but a hell of a lot of patience. You stuck to your principles and when opportunities came along, you pounced on them with vigor."

"There are worse situations than drowning in cash and sitting, sitting, sitting. I remember when I wasn't awash in cash—and I don't want to go back."

—Munger

Invert,
Always Invert

Know What to Avoid

"The 'Munger System of Avoiding Dumb Stuff' will alone, strictly adhered to, allow you to prevail over your 'betters,' no matter how smart they are."

■ Preparation—"The only way to win is to work, work, work, work, and hope to have a few insights"

- Develop into a lifelong self-learner through voracious reading; cultivate curiosity and strive to become a little wiser every day

- More important than the will to win is the will to prepare

- Develop fluency in mental models from the major academic disciplines

- If you want to get smart, the question you have to keep asking is "why, why, why?"

■ Intellectual humility—Acknowledging what you don't know is the dawning of wisdom

- Stay within a well-defined circle of competence

- Identify and reconcile disconfirming evidence

- Resist the craving for false precision, false certainties, etc.

- Above all, never fool yourself, and remember that you are the easiest person to fool

"Understanding both the power of compound interest and the difficulty of getting it is the heart and soul of understanding a lot of things."

■ Analytic rigor—Use of the scientific method and effective checklists minimizes errors and omissions

- Determine value apart from price; progress apart from activity; wealth apart from size

- It is better to remember the obvious than to grasp the esoteric

- Be a business analyst, not a market, macroeconomic, or security analyst
- Consider totality of risk and effect; look always at potential second order and higher level impacts
- Think forwards and backwards—Invert, always invert
- ■ Allocation—Proper allocation of capital is an investor's number one job
  - Remember that highest and best use is always measured by the next best use (opportunity cost)
  - Good ideas are rare—when the odds are greatly in your favor, bet (allocate) heavily
  - Don't "fall in love" with an investment—be situation-dependent and opportunity-driven
- ■ Patience—Resist the natural human bias to act
  - "Compound interest is the eighth wonder of the world" (Einstein); never interrupt it unnecessarily
  - Avoid unnecessary transactional taxes and frictional costs; never take action for its own sake
  - Be alert for the arrival of luck
  - Enjoy the process along with the proceeds, because the process is where you live
- ■ Decisiveness—When proper circumstances present themselves, act with decisiveness and conviction
  - Be fearful when others are greedy, and greedy when others are fearful
  - Opportunity doesn't come often, so seize it when it does
  - Opportunity meeting the prepared mind: that's the game

Mispriced Bets

"It's not given to human beings to have such talent that they can just know everything about everything all the time. But it is given to human beings who work hard at it—who look and sift the world for a misplaced bet—that they can occasionally find one."

Thomas Carlyle
(1795–1881)

"The task of a man is not to see what lies dimly in the distance, but to do what lies clearly at hand."

"How do some people get wiser than other people? Partly it is inborn temperament. Some people do not have a good temperament for investing. They're too fretful; they worry too much. But if you've got a good temperament, which basically means being very patient, yet combine that with a vast aggression when you know enough to do something, then you just gradually learn the game, partly by doing, partly by studying. Obviously, the more hard lessons you can learn vicariously, instead of from your own terrible experiences, the better off you will be. I don't know anyone who did it with great rapidity. Warren Buffett has become one hell of a lot better investor since the day I met him, and so have I. If we had been frozen at any given stage, with the knowledge hand we had, the record would have been much worse than it is. So the game is to keep learning, and I don't think people are going to keep learning who don't like the learning process."

■ Change—Live with change and accept unremovable complexity

- Recognize and adapt to the true nature of the world around you; don't expect it to adapt to you
- Continually challenge and willingly amend your "best-loved ideas"
- Recognize reality even when you don't like it—especially when you don't like it

■ Focus—Keep things simple and remember what you set out to do

- Remember that reputation and integrity are your most valuable assets—and can be lost in a heartbeat
- Guard against the effects of hubris and boredom
- Don't overlook the obvious by drowning in minutiae
- Be careful to exclude unneeded information or slop: "A small leak can sink a great ship"
- Face your big troubles; don't sweep them under the rug

Since human beings began investing, they have been searching for a magic formula or easy recipe for instant wealth. As you can see, Charlie's superior performance doesn't come from a magic formula or some business-school-inspired system. It comes from what he calls his "constant search for better methods of thought," a willingness to "prepay" through rigorous preparation, and from the extraordinary outcomes of his multidisciplinary research model. *In the end, it comes down to Charlie's most basic guiding principles, his fundamental philosophy of life: Preparation. Discipline. Patience. Decisiveness.* Each attribute is in turn lost without the other, but together they form the dynamic critical mass for a cascading of positive effects for which Munger is famous (the "lollapalooza").

Finally, a word or two on why this overview of Charlie's investment philosophy has focused so much on the subject of "what to buy" and so little on "when to sell." The answer, in Charlie's own words, serves as a wonderful summation of the "Munger School" of highly-concentrated, focused investing described here:

"We're partial to putting out large amounts of money where we won't have to make another decision. If you buy something because it's undervalued, then you have to think about selling it when it approaches your calculation of its intrinsic value. That's hard. But, if you can buy a few great companies, then you can sit on your ass. That's a good thing."

Like his hero, Benjamin Franklin, Charlie Munger painstakingly developed and perfected unique approaches to personal and business endeavors. Through these methods, and the development and maintenance of sound, lifelong habits, he has achieved extraordinary success.

"And so these complex, aging prodigies carefully tend their compound interest machine, a joint creation of two exceptional personalities. Others may try to duplicate Berkshire Hathaway, but they won't be able to duplicate these two exceptional minds."

—Robert Lenzner and David S. Fondiller

Sir William Osler
(1849–1919)

"The very first step towards success in any occupation is to become interested in it."

Sir William Osler, a Canadian physician, has been called "The Father of Modern Medicine." An outspoken advocate of "pluralism," like Charlie, he constantly warned of the dangers of specialization: "The incessant concentration of thought upon one subject, however interesting, tethers a man's mind in a narrow field."

Osler studied and taught at McGill University in Montreal, Quebec, where he obtained his medical degree. Later he became the first Professor of Medicine at Johns Hopkins University in Baltimore. A physician who made himself into a literary man, Osler was a voracious reader, a prolific author, and a great collector of books (at his death, his personal library numbered 8,000 volumes). His most famous work is the *Principles and Practice of Medicine*, which appeared in many editions and translations for over fifty years.

Investment Advice

The Importance of Temperament, Patience, and Curiosity

[One of the key elements to successful investing is having the right] temperament—most people are too fretful; they worry too much. Success means being very patient, but aggressive when it's time. And the more hard lessons you can learn vicariously rather than through your own hard experience, the better.

I think there's something to be said for developing the disposition to own stocks without fretting. [But] temperament alone won't do it. You need a lot of curiosity for a long, long time.

You need to have a passionate interest in why things are happening. That cast of mind, kept over long periods, gradually improves your ability to focus on reality. If you don't have that cast of mind, you're destined for failure even if you have a high I.Q.

Focus Investing

Our investment style has been given a name—focus investing—which implies ten holdings, not one hundred or four hundred.

Our game is to recognize a big idea when it comes along, when one doesn't come along very often. Opportunity comes to the prepared mind.

The idea that it is hard to find good investments, so concentrate in a few, seems to me to be an obviously good idea. But ninety-eight percent of the investment world doesn't think this way. It's been good for us—and you—that we've done this.

What's funny is that most big investment organizations don't think like this. They hire lots of people, evaluate Merck vs. Pfizer and every stock in the S&P 500, and think they can beat the market. You can't do it.

We have this investment discipline of waiting for a fat pitch.

If I was offered the chance to go into a business where people would measure me against benchmarks, force me to be fully invested, crawl around looking over my shoulder, etc., I would hate it. I would regard it as putting me into shackles.

Very few people have adopted our approach. Focus investing is growing somewhat, but what's really growing is the unlimited use of consultants to advise on asset allocation, to analyze other consultants, an so forth. Maybe two percent of people will come into our corner of the tent, and the rest of the ninety-eight percent will believe what they've been told [e.g., that markets are totally efficient].

Misteaching Investing

Beta and modern portfolio theory and the like—none of it makes any sense to me. We're trying to buy businesses with sustainable competitive advantages at a low, or even a fair, price.

How can professors spread this [nonsense that a stock's volatility is a measure of risk]? I've been waiting for this craziness to end for decades. It's been dented, but it's still out there.

Warren once said to me, "I'm probably misjudging academia generally [in thinking so poorly of it] because the people that interact with me have bonkers theories."

Waiting for a Fat Pitch

Harmon Killebrew (b. 1936) played for the Washington Senators, Minnesota Twins, and Kansas City Royals over his twenty-two-year career. Famous for his ability to put fat pitches deep into the bleachers, the Hall of Fame slugger hit 573 career home runs. At the time of his election to the Hall of Fame in 1984, he ranked fifth on the all-time home run list and was second only to Babe Ruth among American League players.

"Don't gamble. Take all your savings and buy some good stock and hold it till it goes up, then sell it. If it don't go up, don't buy it."

—Will Rogers

Diversification

The idea of excessive diversification is madness.

We don't believe that widespread diversification will yield a good result. We believe almost all good investments will involve relatively low diversification.

If you took our top fifteen decisions out, we'd have a pretty average record. It wasn't hyperactivity, but a hell of a lot of patience. You stuck to your principles, and when opportunities came along, you pounced on them with vigor.

Berkshire in its history has made money betting on sure things.

Sit-on-Your-Ass Investing

If you buy something because it's undervalued, then you have to think about selling it when it approaches your calculation of its intrinsic value. That's hard. But if you buy a few great companies, then you can sit on your ass. That's a good thing.

We're partial to putting out large amounts of money where we won't have to make another decision.

What Is a Better Business?

There are two kinds of businesses: The first earns twelve percent, and you can take the profits out at the end of the year. The second earns twelve percent, but all the excess cash must be reinvested—there's never any cash. It reminds me of the guy who sells construction equipment—he looks at his used machines, taken in as customers bought new ones, and says, "There's all of my profit, rusting in my yard." We hate that kind of business.

See's Candy: Case Study of a Better Business

If See's Candy [when we were buying it] had asked for $100,000 more [Buffett chimed in, "$10,000 more"], Warren and I would have walked—that's how dumb we were.

Ira Marshall said you guys are crazy—there are some things you should pay up for, like quality businesses and people. You are underestimating quality. We listened to the criticism and changed our mind. This is a good lesson for anyone: the ability to take criticism constructively and learn from it. If you take the indirect lessons we learned from See's, you could say Berkshire was built on constructive criticism.

Canadian Charles See came to Los Angeles in 1921 and, using his mother's recipes, started a high-quality confection business. An image of his mother, Mary See, also became the company's icon. See's grew from one shop to twelve by the mid-1920s— and then kept growing throughout California. In 1972, in a transaction initiated by Robert T. Flaherty (now a Wesco Financial director), See's was purchased by Blue Chip Stamps, now wholly-owned by Berkshire Hathaway. Today, See's Candies are sold in more than two hundred shops and in certain foreign locations, such as Hong Kong and Tokyo.

N. Gregory Mankiw, on the economics faculty at Harvard University, is also a research associate of the National Bureau of Economic Research and an adviser to the Federal Reserve Bank of Boston and the Congressional Budget Office. His popular textbooks have been translated into other languages, including German, as this book indicates.

Cost of Capital and Opportunity Costs

Obviously, consideration of costs is key, including opportunity costs. Of course, capital isn't free. It's easy to figure out your cost of borrowing, but theorists went bonkers on the cost of equity capital. They say that if you're generating a one hundred percent return on capital, then you shouldn't invest in something that generates an eighty percent return on capital. It's crazy.

Value of Forecasts

People have always had this craving to have someone tell them the future. Long ago, kings would hire people to read sheep guts. There's always been a market for people who pretend to know the future. Listening to today's forecasters is just as crazy as when the king hired the guy to look at the sheep guts. It happens over and over and over.

IPOs

It is entirely possible that you could use our mental models to find good IPOs to buy. There are countless IPOs every year, and I'm sure that there are a few cinches that you could jump on. But the average person is going to get creamed. So if you think you're talented, good luck.

IPOs are too small for us, or too high tech—we won't understand them. So, if Warren's looking at them, I don't know about it.

The once high-flying eToys built on its "successful" IPO to secure a market capitalization of almost $10 billion. The California-based company has since filed for bankruptcy. It closed its "brick-and-mortar-free" doors in 2001.

"The Greek orator was clearly right about an excess of optimism being the normal human condition, even when pain or the threat of pain is absent. Witness happy people buying lottery tickets or believing that credit-furnishing, delivery-making grocery stores were going to displace a great many superefficient cash-and-carry supermarkets."

—From Talk Four: "The Psychology of Human Misjudgment"

Charlie Munger Investment Partnership Results

"Table 5 is the record of a friend of mine who is a Harvard Law graduate, who set up a major law firm. I ran into him in about 1960 and told him the law was fine as a hobby but he could do better. He set up a partnership quite the opposite of Walter's (Walter J. Schloss, another superinvestor profiled in the article). His portfolio was concentrated in very few securities and, therefore, his record was much more volatile but it was based on the same discount-from-value approach. He was willing to accept greater peaks and valleys of performance, and he happens to be a fellow whose whole psyche goes toward concentration, with the results shown. Incidentally, this record belongs to Charlie Munger, my partner for a long time in the operation of Berkshire Hathaway. When he ran his partnership, however, his portfolio holdings were almost completely different from mine and the other fellows mentioned earlier."

[Excerpt from "The Superinvestors of Graham-and-Doddsville," by Warren E. Buffett]

Table 5 -- Charles Munger

Year	Mass. Inv. Trust (%)	Investors Stock (%)	Lehman (%)	Tri-Cont. (%)	Dow (%)	Over-all Partnership (%)	Limited Partners (%)
Yearly Results (1)							
1962	-9.8	-13.4	-14.4	-12.2	-7.6	30.1	20.1
1963	20.0	16.5	23.8	20.3	20.6	71.7	47.8
1964	15.9	14.3	13.6	13.3	18.7	49.7	33.1
1965	10.2	9.8	19.0	10.7	14.2	8.4	6.0
1966	-7.7	-9.9	-2.6	-6.9	-15.7	12.4	8.3
1967	20.0	22.8	28.0	25.4	19.0	56.2	37.5
1968	10.3	8.1	6.7	6.8	7.7	40.4	27.0
1969	-4.8	-7.9	-1.9	0.1	-11.6	28.3	21.3
1970	0.6	-4.1	-7.2	-1.0	8.7	-0.1	-0.1
1971	9.0	16.8	26.6	22.4	9.8	25.4	20.6
1972	11.0	15.2	23.7	21.4	18.2	8.3	7.3
1973	-12.5	-17.6	-14.3	-21.3	-13.1	-31.9	-31.9
1974	-25.5	-23.6	-30.3	-27.6	-23.1	-31.5	-31.5
1975	32.9	33.3	30.8	35.4	44.4	73.2	73.2
Compound Results (2)							
1962	-9.8	-13.4	-14.4	-12.2	-7.6	30.1	20.1
1962-3	8.2	0.9	6.0	5.6	11.5	123.4	77.5
1962-4	25.4	15.3	20.4	19.6	32.4	234.4	136.3
1962-5	38.2	26.6	43.3	32.4	51.2	262.5	150.3
1962-6	27.5	14.1	39.5	23.2	27.5	307.5	171.3
1962-7	53.0	40.1	78.5	54.5	51.8	536.5	273.0
1962-8	68.8	51.4	90.5	65.0	63.5	793.6	373.7
1962-9	60.7	39.4	86.9	65.2	44.5	1046.5	474.6
1962-70	61.7	33.7	73.4	63.5	57.1	1045.4	474.0
1962-71	76.3	56.2	119.5	100.1	72.5	1336.3	592.2
1962-72	95.7	79.9	171.5	142.9	103.9	1455.5	642.7
1962-73	71.2	48.2	132.7	91.2	77.2	959.3	405.8
1962-74	27.5	10.3	62.2	38.4	36.3	625.6	246.5
1962-75	69.4	47.0	112.2	87.4	96.8	1156.7	500.1
Average Annual Compounded Rate	**3.8**	**2.8**	**5.5**	**4.6**	**5.0**	**19.8**	**13.7**

Discipline and Patience

Ted Williams' Seventy-Seven-Cell Strike Zone

"It takes character to sit there with all that cash and do nothing.
I didn't get to where I am by going after mediocre opportunities."
—Munger

"In making investments, I have always believed that you must act with discipline whenever you see something you truly like. To explain this philosophy, Buffett/Munger like to use a baseball analogy that I find particularly illuminating, though I myself am not at all a baseball expert. Ted Williams is the only baseball player who had a .400 single-season hitting record in the last seven decades. In the *Science of Hitting*, he explained his technique. He divided the strike zone into seventy-seven cells, each representing the size of a baseball. He would insist on swinging only at balls in his 'best' cells, even at the risk of striking out, because reaching for the 'worst' spots would seriously reduce his chances of success. As a securities investor, you can watch all sorts of business propositions in the form of security prices thrown at you all the time. For the most part, you don't have to do a thing other than be amused. Once in a while, you will find a 'fat pitch' that is slow, straight, and right in the middle of your sweet spot. Then you swing hard. This way, no matter what natural ability you start with, you will substantially increase your hitting average."

—Li Lu of LL Investment Partners

How to Be Happy, Get Rich, and Other Advice

Tips on How to Be Happy and Successful

If all you succeed in doing in life is getting rich by buying little pieces of paper, it's a failed life. Life is more than being shrewd in wealth accumulation.

A lot of success in life and business comes from knowing what you want to avoid: early death, a bad marriage, etc.

Just avoid things like AIDs situations, racing trains to the crossing, and doing cocaine. Develop good mental habits.

Ulysses and the Sirens,
Herbert James Draper (British, 1863–1920), oil on canvas, private collection

Avoid evil, particularly if they're attractive members of the opposite sex.

If your new behavior earns you a little temporary unpopularity with your peer group, then the hell with them.

Be Satisfied with What You Have

Here's one truth that perhaps your typical investment counselor would disagree with: If you're comfortably rich and someone else is getting richer faster than you by, for example, investing in risky stocks, so what?! Someone will always be getting richer faster than you. This is not a tragedy.

Look at Stanley Druckenmiller [who ran one of George Soros' funds, which suffered large losses in speculative tech and biotech stocks]: He always had to be the best and couldn't stand that others were beating him by investing in these sectors.

Soros couldn't bear to see others make money in the technology sector without him, and he got killed. It doesn't bother us at all [that others are making money in the tech sector].

Beware of Envy

The idea of caring that someone is making money faster [than you are] is one of the deadly sins. Envy is a really stupid sin because it's the only one you could never possibly have any fun at. There's a lot of pain and no fun. Why would you want to get on that trolley?

How to Get Rich

[A young shareholder asked Charlie how to follow in his footsteps, and Charlie brought down the house by saying:]

We get these questions a lot from the enterprising young. It's a very intelligent question: You look at some old guy who's rich and you ask, "How can I become like you, except faster?"

Madwoman (Obsession of Envy),
Theodore Gericault (1791–1824),
oil on canvas, Musée des Beaux-Arts,
Lyon, France

Spend each day trying to be a little wiser than you were when you woke up. Discharge your duties faithfully and well. Step by step you get ahead, but not necessarily in fast spurts. But you build discipline by preparing for fast spurts…. Slug it out one inch at a time, day by day. At the end of the day—if you live long enough—most people get what they deserve.

How to Find a Good Spouse

What's the best way to get a good spouse? The best single way is to deserve a good spouse because a good spouse is by definition not nuts.

The Importance of Reading

In my whole life, I have known no wise people (over a broad subject matter area) who didn't read all the time—none, zero. You'd be amazed at how much Warren reads—and at how much I read. My children laugh at me. They think I'm a book with a couple of legs sticking out.

I am a biography nut myself. And I think when you're trying to teach the great concepts that work, it helps to tie them into the lives and personalities of the people who developed them. I think you learn economics better if you make Adam Smith your friend. That sounds funny, making friends among the eminent dead, but if you go through life making friends with the eminent dead who had the right ideas, I think it will work better in life and work better in education. It's way better than just being given the basic concepts.

Reduce Material Needs

Most people will see declining returns [due to inflation]. One of the great defenses if you're worried about inflation is not to have a lot of silly needs in your life—you don't need a lot of material goods.

Philanthropy

[Warren and I] feel that those of us who have been very fortunate have a duty to give back. Whether one gives a lot as one goes along as I do, or a little and then a lot [when one dies] as Warren does, is a matter of personal preference. I would hate to have people ask me for money all day long. Warren couldn't stand it.

Avoid Debt

Once you get into debt, it's hell to get out. Don't let credit card debt carry over. You can't get ahead paying eighteen percent.

The Decline of Public Schools

You could argue that [the decline of public schools] is one of the major disasters in our lifetime. We took one of the greatest successes in the history of the earth and turned it into one of the greatest disasters in the history of the earth.

Japan's Recession

Anyone has to be flabbergasted by Japan's recession, which has endured for ten years, despite interest rates below one percent. The government is playing all the monetary games, but it's not working. If you had described this situation to Harvard economists, they would have said it's impossible. Yet at the same time, there's an asset bubble in Hong Kong. *Why? Because Japan and China are two vastly different cultures. The Chinese are gamblers.*

This is a classic example of why, to be a successful investor, one must draw from many disciplines. Imagine an economist standing up at a meeting of economists and giving my explanation. It wouldn't be politically correct! But the tools of economics don't explain what's going on.

Mental Models

The Importance of Multiple Mental Models

You must know the big ideas in the big disciplines and use them routinely—all of them, not just a few. Most people are trained in one model—economics, for example—and try to solve all problems in one way. You know the old saying: To the man with a hammer, the world looks like a nail. This is a dumb way of handling problems.

You need a different checklist and different mental models for different companies. I can never make it easy by saying, "Here are three things." You have to derive it yourself to ingrain it in your head for the rest of your life.

You can't learn those one hundred big ideas you really need the way many students do—where you learn 'em well enough to bang 'em back to the professor and get your grade, and then you empty them out as though you were emptying a bathtub so you can take in more water next time. If that's the way you learn the one hundred big models you're going to need, [you'll be] an "also ran" in the game of life. You have to learn the models so that they become part of your ever-used repertoire.

By the way, there's no rule that you can't add another model or two even fairly late in life. In fact, I've clearly done that. I got most of the big ones quite early [however].

The happier mental realm I recommend is one from which no one willingly returns. A return would be like cutting off one's hands.

Charlie's oft-used diagnosis of narrow specialization:

"To the man with a hammer, the world looks like a nail."

The Ethos of Not Fooling Yourself

It is ridiculous the way a lot of people cling to failed ideas. Keynes said, "It's not bringing in the new ideas that's so hard. It's getting rid of the old ones."

The ethos of not fooling yourself is one of the best you could possibly have. It's powerful because it's so rare.

Common (and Uncommon) Sense

Organized common (or uncommon) sense—very basic knowledge—is an enormously powerful tool. There are huge dangers with computers. People calculate too much and think too little.

Part of [having uncommon sense] is being able to tune out folly, as opposed to recognizing wisdom. If you bat away many things, you don't clutter yourself.

We read a lot. I don't know anyone who's wise who doesn't read a lot. But that's not enough: You have to have a temperament to grab ideas and do sensible things. Most people don't grab the right ideas or don't know what to do with them.

The Earth: Flat or Round?

As early as AD 140, Ptolemy produced a map that depicted the Earth as a globe. The Mediaeval church rejected the Greek idea, calling it heresy: the earth was flat—above the Earth was Heaven, below was Hell, and in between lived Man and Woman. For many hundreds of years sailors feared losing sight of land, and sea voyages hugged coastlines. But beginning in the 14th-century, exploration of the oceans began in earnest—islands, countries and continents were discovered. Many explorers completed voyages of discovery—Marco Polo, Christopher Columbus, and Vasco Da Gama. The known world expanded with every voyage until it became obvious to all who wanted to see it that the Earth was indeed a sphere. Finally the Victoria, the only surviving ship of Ferdinand Magellan's fleet, circumnavigated the world and put the issue to rest.

Provenance unknown, illustration from the dust-jacket, Daniel Boorstin's *The Discoverers*, attributed to a 16th century woodcut by the Bettmann Archive.

The more basic knowledge you have, the less new knowledge you have to get. The guy who plays chess blindfolded [a chess master comes to Omaha during Berkshire's annual meeting weekend and, in an exhibition, plays multiple players blindfolded]—he has a knowledge of the board, which allows him to do this.

Henry E. Singleton
(1916–1999)

Business and Chess Master

Singleton was co-founder of Teledyne, Inc. and chief executive of the Los Angeles-based conglomerate for three decades. He attended the Naval Academy, then transferred to MIT where he received Bachelor's, Master's, and Ph.D. degrees in Electrical Engineering. An enormously skilled chess player, he was only 100 points below the Grandmaster level and could play without looking at the board.

From 1963 to 1990, Teledyne returned an astounding 20.4 percent compound annual return to shareholders—a period in which the S&P 500 returned 8.0 percent. Adroitly repurchasing 90 percent of Teledyne's outstanding shares primarily between 1972 and 1984, Singleton built a record as a manager and capital allocator with few peers in modern business history.

Sharing Buffett's admiration for Henry E. Singleton, Charlie wonders, "Given the man's talent and record, have we learned enough from him?"

"Henry Singleton has the best operating and capital deployment record in American business...if one took the 100 top business school graduates and made a composite of their triumphs, their record would not be as good as Singleton's."

—Warren Buffett, 1980

Four Talks

C harlie Munger is not the least bit shy when it comes to offering both frank criticism and constructive advice. When he sets his sights on an issue—be it a corrupt business practice, an academic failing, or a financial scandal—he lets loose with both barrels. Which is not to say he spends all his time focused on life's failings. He is equally at home discussing the values of lifelong learning or the joys of a successful marriage. But whatever the topic, Charlie is apt to tell it like it is, which is exactly what he has done in over two decades of public speaking. Here then are four of Charlie's best talks, including a special compilation he prepared exclusively for *Poor Charlie's Almanack*. Enjoy.

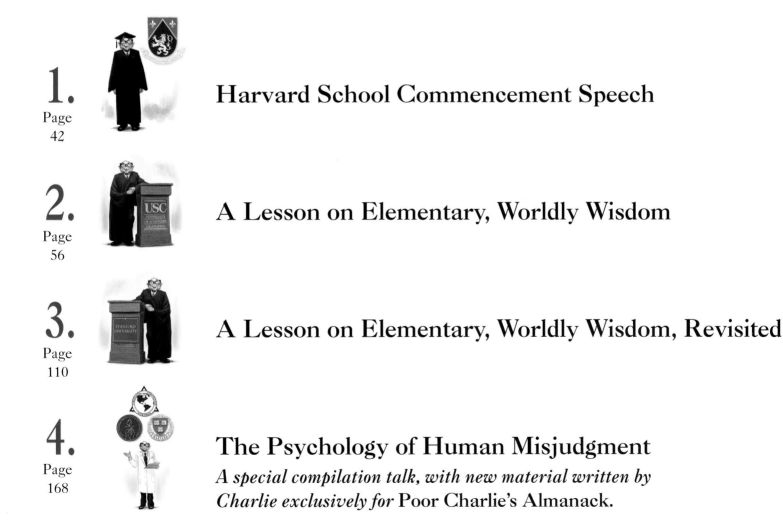

POSSUNT QUIA POSSE VIDENTUR

I n a vow that students the world over may hope he renounces, Charlie delivered "the one and only graduation speech I will ever make" in 1986 at the Harvard School in Los Angeles. The occasion was the graduation of Philip Munger, the last of five Munger family sons to matriculate at this prep school (originally an all-boys institution and now the coeducational school called Harvard-Westlake).

Despite Charlie's self-effacing protestations about then lacking "significant public-speaking experience," he demonstrates imposing rhetorical talents in this short speech. We also get a good taste of both Charlie's value system and wit. Most graduation speakers choose to lay out a prescription for attaining a happy life. Charlie, using the inversion principle he recommends in the speech, compellingly makes the opposite case by setting forth what a graduate may do to reach a state of misery.

For those of you who want to remain unenlightened and mirthless, do not, under any circumstances, read this selection.

Harvard School Commencement Speech
June 13, 1986

Now that Headmaster Berrisford has selected one of the oldest and longest-serving trustees to make a commencement speech, it behooves the speaker to address two questions in every mind:

1) Why was such a selection made?

2) How long is the speech going to last?

I will answer the first question from long experience alongside Berrisford. He is seeking enhanced reputation for our school in the manner of the man who proudly displays his horse that can count to seven. The man knows that counting to seven is not much of a mathematical feat, but he expects approval because doing so is creditable, considering the performer is a horse.

The second question, regarding the length of the speech, I am not going to answer in advance. It would deprive your upturned faces of lively curiosity and obvious keen anticipation, which I prefer to retain, regardless of source.

Marcus Tullius Cicero
(106–43 BC)

A poet, philosopher, rhetorician, and humorist, Cicero was also one of Rome's great orators. Cicero viewed public service to be a Roman citizen's highest duty. He defended those unjustly accused by dictatorial leaders and brought down corrupt governments. Late in life, he led the Senate's unsuccessful battle against Antony, for which he paid with his life in 43 BC. The illustration is *Young Cicero Reading,* c. 1464, Vincenzo Foppa, Wallace Collection, London.

But I will tell you how my consideration of speech length created the subject matter of the speech itself. I was puffed up when invited to speak. While not having significant public-speaking experience, I do hold a black belt in chutzpah, and I immediately considered Demosthenes and Cicero as role models and anticipated trying to earn a compliment like Cicero gave when asked which was his favorite among the orations of Demosthenes. Cicero replied:

"The longest one."

However, fortunately for this audience, I also thought of Samuel Johnson's famous comment when he addressed Milton's poem *Paradise Lost* and correctly said, "No one ever wished it longer." And that made me consider which of all the twenty Harvard School graduation speeches I had heard that I had wished longer. There was only one such speech, given by Johnny Carson, specifying Carson's prescriptions for guaranteed misery in life. I, therefore, decided to repeat Carson's speech but in expanded form with some added prescriptions of my own. After all, I am much older than Carson was when he spoke and have failed and been miserable more often and in more ways than was possible for a charming humorist speaking at a younger age. I am plainly well qualified to expand on Carson's theme.

What Carson said was that he couldn't tell the graduating class how to be happy, but he could tell them from personal experience how to guarantee misery. Carson's prescription for sure misery included:

1. Ingesting chemicals in an effort to alter mood or perception;

2. Envy; and

3. Resentment.

I can still recall Carson's absolute conviction as he told how he had tried these things on occasion after occasion and had become miserable every time.

It is easy to understand Carson's first prescription for misery—ingesting chemicals. I add my voice. The four closest friends of my youth were highly intelligent, ethical, humorous types, favored in person and background. Two are long dead, with alcohol a contributing factor, and a third is a living alcoholic—if you call that living.

Carson said he couldn't tell the graduating class how to be happy, but he could tell them from personal experience how to guarantee misery.

While susceptibility varies, addiction can happen to any of us through a subtle process where the bonds of degradation are too light to be felt until they are too strong to be broken. And yet, I have yet to meet anyone, in over six decades of life, whose life was worsened by fear and avoidance of such a deceptive pathway to destruction.

Envy, of course, joins chemicals in winning some sort of quantity prize for causing misery. It was wreaking havoc long before it got a bad press in the laws of Moses. If you wish to retain the contribution of envy to misery, I recommend that you never read any of the biographies of that good Christian, Samuel Johnson, because his life demonstrates in an enticing way the possibility and advantage of transcending envy.

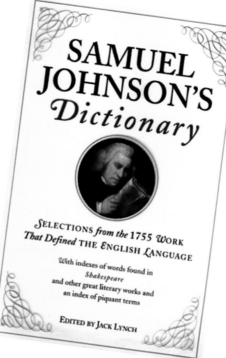

Samuel Johnson
(1709–1784)

Samuel Johnson, English author and the leading literary scholar and critic of his time, was celebrated for his brilliant and witty conversation. Johnson's first work of lasting importance, and the one that permanently established his reputation, was his *Dictionary of the English Language* (1755). James Boswell's famous biography of Johnson presents his life, his sharp comments, and wit in exhaustive and fascinating detail.

John Milton
(1608–1674)

One of the greatest poets of the English language, John Milton was best known for his epic poem *Paradise Lost* (1667). His powerful prose and the eloquence of his poetry had an immense influence, especially on eighteenth-century verse. Milton also published pamphlets defending civil and religious rights. To Samuel Johnson's point about Milton's long-windedness, *Paradise Lost* runs to twelve "books" and thousands of lines.

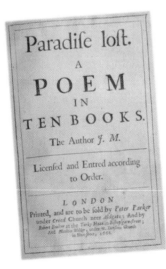

Resentment has always worked for me exactly as it worked for Carson. I cannot recommend it highly enough to you if you desire misery. Johnson spoke well when he said that life is hard enough to swallow without squeezing in the bitter rind of resentment.

For those of you who want misery, I also recommend refraining from practice of the Disraeli compromise, designed for people who find it impossible to quit resentment cold turkey. Disraeli, as he rose to become one of the greatest prime ministers, learned to give up vengeance as a motivation for action, but he did retain some outlet for resentment by putting the names of people who wronged him on pieces of paper in a drawer. Then, from time to time, he reviewed these names and took pleasure in noting the way the world had taken his enemies down without his assistance.

> *Johnson spoke well when he said that life is hard enough to swallow without squeezing in the bitter rind of resentment.*

> *Addiction can happen to any of us through a subtle process where the bonds of degradation are too light to be felt until they are too strong to be broken.*

Well, so much for Carson's three prescriptions. Here are four more prescriptions from Munger:

First, be unreliable. Do not faithfully do what you have engaged to do. If you will only master this one habit, you will more than counterbalance the combined effect of all your virtues, howsoever great. If you like being distrusted and excluded from the best human contribution and company, this prescription is for you. Master this one habit, and you will always play the role of the hare in the fable, except that instead of being outrun by one fine turtle, you will be outrun by hordes and hordes of mediocre turtles and even some mediocre turtles on crutches.

I must warn you that if you don't follow my first prescription, it may be hard to end up miserable even if you start disadvantaged. I had a roommate in college who was and is severely dyslexic. But he is perhaps the most reliable man I have ever known. He has had a wonderful life so far, outstanding wife and children, chief executive of a multibillion dollar corporation. If you want to avoid a conventional, main-culture, establishment result of this kind, you simply can't count on your other handicaps to hold you back if you persist in being reliable.

I cannot here pass by a reference to a life described as "wonderful so far," without reinforcing the "so far" aspects of the human condition by repeating the remark of Croesus, once the richest king in the world. Later, in ignominious captivity, as he prepared to be burned alive, he said: "Well now do I remember the words of the historian Solon: 'No man's life should be accounted a happy one until it is over.'"

My second prescription for misery is to learn everything you possibly can from your own experience, minimizing what you learn vicariously from the good and bad experience of others, living and dead. This prescription is a sure-shot producer of misery and second-rate achievement.

You can see the results of not learning from others' mistakes by simply looking about you. How little originality there is in the common disasters of mankind—drunk driving deaths, reckless driving maimings, incurable venereal

Croesus
(about 546 BC)

Croesus, legendary for his huge wealth, was king of Lydia from 560 BC until his defeat by the Persians in about 547 BC. Upon capture, Croesus supposedly threw himself upon a funeral pyre.

diseases, conversion of bright college students into brainwashed zombies as members of destructive cults, business failures through repetition of obvious mistakes made by predecessors, various forms of crowd folly, and so on. I recommend as a memory clue to finding the way to real trouble from heedless, unoriginal error the modern saying: "If at first you don't succeed, well, so much for hang gliding."

The other aspect of avoiding vicarious wisdom is the rule for not learning from the best work done before yours. The prescription is to become as non-educated as you reasonably can.

Perhaps you will better see the type of nonmiserable result you can thus avoid if I render a short historical account. There once was a man who assiduously mastered the work of his best predecessors, despite a poor start and very tough time in analytical geometry. Eventually, his own work attracted wide attention, and he said of his work:

"If I have seen a little farther than other men, it is because I stood on the shoulders of giants."

The bones of that man lie buried now, in Westminster Abbey, under an unusual inscription:

**Franklin on
Vicarious Learning**

"If you will not hear reason, she will surely rap your knuckles."

"They that won't be counseled, can't be helped."

"Experience keeps a dear school, but fools will learn in no other and scarce in that; for it is true, we may give advice, but we cannot give conduct."

Sir Isaac Newton
(1642–1727)

At birth in Lincolnshire, England, Newton was so tiny and frail that he was not expected to live. Yet he lived into his eighties. During his young adulthood, Newton made tremendous discoveries in general mathematics, algebra, geometry, calculus, optics, and celestial mechanics. Most famous among these discoveries was his description of gravity. The publication of his book *The Mathematical Principles of Natural Philosophy* in 1687 marked the peak of Newton's creative career.

"Here lie the remains of all that was mortal in Sir Isaac Newton."

My third prescription to you for misery is to go down and stay down when you get your first, second, or third severe reverse in the battle of life. Because there is so much adversity out there, even for the lucky and wise, this will guarantee that, in due course, you will be permanently mired in misery. Ignore at all cost the lesson contained in the accurate epitaph written for himself by Epictetus: "Here lies Epictetus, a slave, maimed in body, the ultimate in poverty, and favored by the gods."

"Invert, always invert," Jacobi said. He knew that it is in the nature of things that many hard problems are best solved when they are addressed backward.

My final prescription to you for a life of fuzzy thinking and infelicity is to ignore a story they told me when I was very young about a rustic who said, "I wish I knew where I was going to die, and then I'd never go there." Most people smile (as you did) at the rustic's ignorance and ignore his basic wisdom. If my experience is any guide, the rustic's approach is to be avoided at all cost by someone bent on misery. To help fail, you should discount as mere quirk, with no useful message, the method of the rustic, which is the same one used in Carson's speech.

What Carson did was to approach the study of how to create X by turning the question backward, that is, by studying how to create non-X. The great algebraist, Jacobi, had exactly the same approach as Carson and was known for his constant repetition of one phrase: "Invert, always invert." It is in the nature of things, as Jacobi knew, that many hard problems are best solved only when they are addressed backward. For instance, when almost everyone else was trying to revise the electromagnetic laws of Maxwell to be consistent with the motion laws of Newton, Einstein discovered special relativity as he made a 180-degree turn and revised Newton's laws to fit Maxwell's.

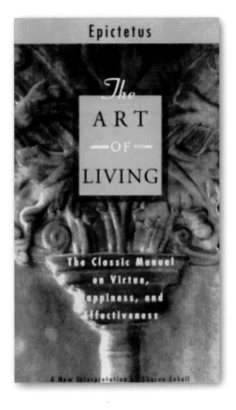

Epictetus
(55–135)

Even though he was born a slave in Hierapolis and endured a permanent physical disability, Epictetus maintained that all human beings are perfectly free to control their own lives and to live in harmony with nature. After intense study of the traditional Stoic curriculum of logic, physics, and ethics, Epictetus spent his entire career teaching philosophy and promoting a daily regime of rigorous self-examination. He eventually gained his freedom but was exiled from Rome by Domitian in 89.

It is my opinion, as a certified biography nut, that Charles Robert Darwin would have ranked near the middle of the Harvard School graduating class of 1986. Yet he is now famous in the history of science. This is precisely the type of example you should learn nothing from if bent on minimizing your results from your own endowment.

Darwin's result was due in large measure to his working method, which violated all my rules for misery and particularly emphasized a backward twist in that he always gave priority attention to evidence tending to disconfirm whatever cherished and hard-won theory he already had. In contrast, most people early achieve and later intensify a tendency to process new and disconfirming information so that any original conclusion remains intact. They become people of whom Philip Wylie observed: "You couldn't squeeze a dime between what they already know and what they will never learn."

The life of Darwin demonstrates how a turtle may out-run the hares, aided by extreme objectivity, which helps the objective person end up like the only player without a blindfold in a game of Pin the Tail on the Donkey.

The life of Darwin demonstrates how a turtle may outrun a hare, aided by extreme objectivity, which helps the objective person end up like the only player without a blindfold in a game of Pin the Tail on the Donkey.

Charles Darwin
(1809–1882)

Charles Darwin was a British naturalist whose teachings on evolution by natural selection revolutionized the science of biology. His *On the Origin of Species* sold out immediately and was heavily attacked because it did not support the depiction of creation given in the Bible.

If you minimize objectivity, you ignore not only a lesson from Darwin but also one from Einstein. Einstein said that his successful theories came from "Curiosity, concentration, perseverance, and self-criticism." And by self-criticism, he meant the testing and destruction of his own well-loved ideas.

Finally, minimizing objectivity will help you lessen the compromises and burden of owning worldly goods because objectivity does not work only for great physicists and biologists. It also adds power to the work of a plumbing contractor in Bemidji. Therefore, if you interpret being true to yourself as requiring that you retain every notion of your youth, you will be safely underway, not only toward maximizing ignorance, but also toward whatever misery can be obtained through unpleasant experiences in business.

It is fitting that a backward sort of speech end with a backward sort of toast, inspired by Elihu Root's repeated accounts of how the dog went to Dover, "leg over leg." To the class of 1986:

Gentlemen, may each of you rise by spending each day of a long life aiming low.

Elihu Root
(1845–1937)

Elihu Root, born in New York and the son of a mathematics professor, became one of the most brilliant administrators in American history. By age thirty, he had established himself as a prominent lawyer specializing in corporate affairs. Shifting to public service, Root distinguished himself as secretary of war, secretary of state, U.S. senator, and ambassador to Russia. In the interest of worldwide peace, he originated many treaties of arbitration. He was awarded the Nobel Peace Prize in 1912.

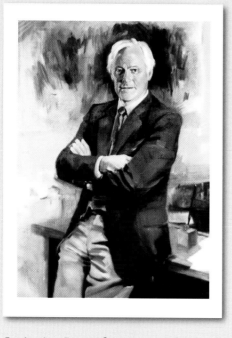

Invitation Letter from Harvard School

This is the original letter from Headmaster Berrisford of the Harvard School inviting Charlie to speak at the graduation ceremony the following June. Note Charlie's reply at the bottom of the letter.

HARVARD SCHOOL

3700 Coldwater Canyon Road
Post Office Box 1037
North Hollywood, California 91604
Telephone 818 • 980-6692

Christopher Berrisford
Headmaster

September 13, 1985

Mr. Charles T. Munger
P.O. Box 55007
Los Angeles, California 90057

Dear Charlie:

We discovered last June that a Commencement Speaker who knew the School well, and who had a command of the language, was a much better contributor to our celebrations than a distinguished citizen with a mastery of platitudes.

Last year I spent time and energy chasing two or three distinguished politicians in the hope that their presence at our Commencement exercises would add a little luster to the proceedings. I was wrong. Nat Reynolds did us proud; the politicians were as evasive as you might suppose.

I am anxious to settle the issue for next year in good time and I believe that we should henceforth stay with those that know Harvard and should avoid outsiders. Since this year sees the last Munger (of the present generation, at least) graduating from Harvard School and since you must know more about Harvard than anyone who is not an alumnus - and probably more than most who are - I would like to invite you with as much persuasion as I can muster to be Harvard's Commencement Speaker for the Class of 1986.

Jim Maloney set a precedent when he spoke at Tom's graduation. Would you be kind enough to follow his lead and perform the same function for Philip's graduating class?

This invitation has been on my mind for awhile, but it was brought back to my immediate attention because, in sorting through papers left over from last year, I came across the Berkshire Hathaway Report to which you contributed. I re-read your section and what Warren Buffet had to say, envying the clarity of insight that you both show and the capacity you have to say what is on your mind succinctly, precisely and eloquently. What better credentials could there be for a Commencement Speaker?

My colleagues at the School enthusiastically support this invitation. We all hope you will accept.

Best wishes,

Christopher Berrisford

cc: Dr. Norman F. Sprague, III

Chris 9/16/85

Will do.

Charlie

BERKSHIRE HATHAWAY INC.

CHARLES T. MUNGER
VICE CHAIRMAN OF THE BOARD

July 7, 1986

Mr. Johnny Carson
NBC-National Broadcasting
  Company, Inc.
3000 W. Alameda Avenue
Burbank, CA. 91523

Dear Mr. Carson:

This year at my son's graduation from Harvard School I repeated
the graduation speech you made when your son graduated. There
were some additions of my own, and I, of course, gave due credit
to the Carson original.

I thought you might be amused by the educational influence you
have had, on and through me, and I therefore enclose a copy of
my expanded version of your speech.

I also enclose a copy of Berkshire Hathaway's 1986 annual report,
which may possibly interest you because of our recent acquisition
of a large stock position in the ABC television network, which,
unfortunately, has no equivalent of Johnny Carson.

Best regards,

Charles Munger

Charles T. Munger

CTM/mek
Enclosures
bcc: Warren E. Buffett
     Thomas S. Murphy

P.O. BOX 55007, LOS ANGELES, CA 90055

JOHNNY CARSON

August 6, 1986

Mr. Charles T. Munger
Berkshire Hathaway Inc.
P.O. Box 55007
Los Angeles, Ca. 90055

Dear Charles:

Thanks for your kind letter and the copy of your
speech to the Harvard school graduates. I am
happy I was able to furnish a small framework for
you to expand on.

All Good Wishes,

Johnny Carson

Johnny Carson

JC/daw

Johnny (John William) Carson
(1925–2005)

Born in Corning, Iowa, Johnny Carson became famous as America's late-night king of comedy. He had a popular radio show in Omaha for years and claimed the city as his hometown. For thirty years, from 1962 to 1992, he entertained millions as host of NBC television's *The Tonight Show*. His show featured thousands of authors, filmmakers, actors, singers—and stand-up comedians, of course, many of whose careers he launched.

Talk One Revisited

As I review in 2005 this talk made in 1986, I would not revise a single idea. If anything, I now believe even more strongly that (1) reliability is essential for progress in life and (2) while quantum mechanics is unlearnable for a vast majority, reliability can be learned to great advantage by almost anyone.

Indeed, I have often made myself unpopular on elite college campuses by dwelling on this reliability theme. What I say is that McDonald's is one of our most admirable institutions. Then, as signs of shock come to surrounding faces, I explain that McDonald's, providing first jobs to millions of troubled teenagers over the years, has successfully taught most of them the one lesson they most need: to show up reliably if they are to work effectively. Then I usually go on to say that if the elite campuses were as successful as McDonald's in teaching sensibly, we would have a better world.

If

Avoiding Life's Pitfalls
a la Kipling

If you can keep your head when all about you
Are losing theirs and blaming it on you,
If you can trust yourself when all men doubt you
But make allowance for their doubting too,
If you can wait and not be tired by waiting,
Or being lied about, don't deal in lies,
Or being hated, don't give way to hating,
And yet don't look too good, nor talk too wise…

If you can talk with crowds and keep your virtue,
Or walk with kings—nor lose the common touch,
If neither foes nor loving friends can hurt you;
If all men count with you, but none too much,
If you can fill the unforgiving minute
With sixty seconds' worth of distance run,
Yours is the Earth and everything that's in it,
And—which is more—you'll be a Man, my son!

Excerpted from the poem "If"

W ell-known because it was published in *Outstanding Investor Digest* (May 5, 1995), this talk was given in 1994 to Professor Guilford Babcock's business class at the University of Southern California. Charlie ranges in the talk from education systems to psychology to the importance of possessing both common and uncommon sense. Dissecting business management, he brilliantly describes psychological impacts that can damage or benefit a firm. He also presents an outstanding set of principles for investment, business management, and—most importantly from Charlie's perspective—decision making in everyday life.

Your time investment in reading this talk will be paid back quickly via the effect it will have on your own decision-making abilities.

A Lesson on Elementary, Worldly Wisdom as It Relates to Investment Management and Business

The University of Southern California Marshall School of Business, April 14, 1994

I am going to play a minor trick on you today—because the subject of my talk is the art of stock picking as a subdivision of the art of worldly wisdom. That enables me to start talking about worldly wisdom—a much broader topic that interests me because I think all too little of it is delivered by modern educational systems, at least in an effective way.

And, therefore, the talk is sort of along the lines that some behaviorist psychologists call "Grandma's Rule"—after the wisdom of Grandma when she said that you have to eat the carrots before you get the dessert.

Eat Your Carrots

The iron fist of "Grandma's Rule" dictates the course of Charlie's lecture on Worldly Wisdom and Investment Management at the Marshall School of Business, USC.

The carrot part of this talk is about the general subject of worldly wisdom, which is a pretty good way to start. After all, the theory of modern education is that you need a general education before you specialize. And I think, to some extent, before you're going to be a great stock picker, you need some general education.

The talk is sort of along the lines that some behaviorist psychologists call "Grandma's Rule"—after the wisdom of Grandma when she said that you have to eat the carrots before you get the dessert.

So, emphasizing what I sometimes waggishly call remedial worldly wisdom, I'm going to start by waltzing you through a few basic notions.

What is elementary, worldly wisdom? Well, the first rule is that you can't really know anything if you just remember isolated facts and try and bang 'em back. If the facts don't hang together on a latticework of theory, you don't have them in a usable form.

You've got to have models in your head. And you've got to array your experience—both vicarious and direct—on this latticework of models. You may have noticed students who just try to remember and pound back what is remembered. Well, they fail in school and fail in life. You've got to hang experience on a latticework of models in your head.

What are the models? Well, the first rule is that you've got to have multiple models—because if you have just one or two that you're using, the nature of human psychology is such that you'll torture reality so that it fits your models, or at least you'll think it does. You become the equivalent of a chiropractor, who, of course, is the great boob in medicine.

It's like the old saying, "To the man with only a hammer, every problem looks like a nail." And, of course, that's the way the chiropractor goes about practicing medicine. But that's a perfectly disastrous way to think and a perfectly disastrous way to operate in the world. So you've got to have multiple models.

And the models have to come from multiple disciplines—because all the wisdom of the world is not to be found in one little academic department. That's why poetry professors, by and large, are so unwise in a worldly sense. They don't have enough models in their heads. So you've got to have models across a fair array of disciplines.

You may say, "My God, this is already getting way too tough." But, fortunately, it isn't that tough—because eighty or ninety important models will carry about ninety percent of the freight in making you a worldly-wise person. And, of those, only a mere handful really carry very heavy freight.

Poetry professors, by and large, are so unwise in a worldly sense. They don't have enough models in their heads. So you've got to have models across a wide array of disciplines.

So let's briefly review what kind of models and techniques constitute this basic knowledge that everybody has to have before they proceed to being really good at a narrow art like stock picking.

First there's mathematics. Obviously, you've got to be able to handle numbers and quantities—basic arithmetic.

And the great useful model, after compound interest, is the elementary math of permutations and combinations. And that was taught in my day in the sophomore year in high school. I suppose by now, in great private schools, it's probably down to the eighth grade or so.

**Pierre de Fermat
and Blaise Pascal**

Invited by French aristocrat Chevalier de Méré to help resolve a gambling dispute in the mid-seventeenth century, mathematicians Pierre de Fermat and Blaise Pascal laid the foundations for probability theory in a series of letters.

De Méré's question concerned bets on rolls of a die that at least one "6" would appear during four rolls. From experience, he knew he would win more often than lose at this game. As a diversion, he changed the game to a bet that he would get a total of 12, or a double "6," on twenty-four rolls of two dice. The new game was less profitable than the old one. He asked the mathematicians to determine why this change occurred.

The basic neural network of the brain is there through broad genetic and cultural evolution. And it's not Fermat/Pascal. It uses a very crude, shortcut-type of approximation.

It's very simple algebra. And it was all worked out in the course of about one year in correspondence between Pascal and Fermat. They worked it out casually in a series of letters.

It's not that hard to learn. What is hard is to get so you use it routinely almost every day of your life. The Fermat/Pascal system is dramatically consonant with the way that the world works. And it's fundamental truth. So you simply have to have the technique.

Many educational institutions—although not nearly enough—have realized this. At Harvard Business School, the great quantitative thing that bonds the first-year class together is what they call "decision tree theory." All they do is take high school algebra and apply it to real life problems. And the students love it. They're amazed to find that high school algebra works in life.

By and large, as it works out, people can't naturally and automatically do this. If you understand elementary psychology, the reason they can't is really quite simple: The basic neural network of the brain is there through broad genetic and cultural evolution. And it's not Fermat/Pascal. It uses a very crude, shortcut-type of approximation. It's got elements of Fermat/Pascal in it. However, it's not good.

So you have to learn in a very usable way this very elementary math and use it routinely in life—just the way if you want to become a golfer, you can't use the natural swing that broad evolution gave you. You have to learn to have a certain grip and swing in a different way to realize your full potential as a golfer.

If you don't get...elementary probability into your repertoire...you go through a long life like a one-legged man in an ass-kicking contest.

If you don't get this elementary, but mildly unnatural, mathematics of elementary probability into your repertoire, then you go through a long life like a one-legged man in an ass-kicking contest. You're giving a huge advantage to everybody else.

One of the advantages of a fellow like Buffett, whom I've worked with all these years, is that he automatically thinks in terms of decision trees and the elementary math of permutations and combinations.

C. F. Braun Company

The C. F. Braun Company, a petrochemical engineering and construction firm, rose to prominence in the San Gabriel Valley in the early to mid-twentieth century. Along with competitors such as Fluor, Bechtel, and Parsons, Braun designed and built plants throughout the world. In the early 1980s, Braun was purchased by Santa Fe International, ably led by Ed Shannon.

Obviously, you have to know accounting. It's the language of practical business life. It was a very useful thing to deliver to civilization. I've heard it came to civilization through Venice, which, of course, was once the great commercial power in the Mediterranean. However, double-entry bookkeeping was a hell of an invention.

And it's not that hard to understand.

But you have to know enough about it to understand its limitations—because although accounting is the starting place, it's only a crude approximation. And it's not very hard to understand its limitations. For example, everyone can see that you have to more or less just guess at the useful life of a jet airplane or anything like that. Just because you express the depreciation rate in neat numbers doesn't make it anything you really know.

In terms of the limitations of accounting, one of my favorite stories involves a very great businessman named Carl Braun who created the C. F. Braun Engineering Company. It designed and built oil refineries—which is very hard to do. And Braun would get them to come in on time and not blow up and have efficiencies and so forth. This is a major art.

And Braun, being the thorough Teutonic type that he was, had a number of quirks. And one of them was that he took a look at standard accounting and the way it was applied to building oil refineries, and he said, "This is asinine."

So he threw all of his accountants out, and he took his engineers and said, "Now, we'll devise our own system of accounting to handle this process." And, in due time, accounting adopted a lot of Carl Braun's notions. So he was a formidably willful and talented man who demonstrated both the importance of accounting and the importance of knowing its limitations.

He had another rule, from psychology, which, if you're interested in wisdom, ought to be part of your repertoire—like the elementary mathematics of permutations and combinations.

His rule for all the Braun Company's communications was called the five Ws—you had to tell who was going to do what, where, when, and why. And if you wrote a letter or directive in the Braun Company telling somebody to do something, and you didn't tell him why, you could get fired. In fact, you *would* get fired if you did it twice.

You might ask why is that so important? Well, again, that's a rule of psychology. Just as you think better if you array knowledge on a bunch of models that are basically answers to the question, why, why, why, if you always tell people why, they'll understand it better, they'll consider it more important, and they'll be more likely to comply. Even if they don't understand your reason, they'll be more likely to comply.

If you always tell people why, they'll understand it better, they'll consider it more important, and they'll be more likely to comply.

So there's an iron rule that just as you want to start getting worldly wisdom by asking why, why, why in communicating with other people about everything, you want to include why, why, why. Even if it's obvious, it's wise to stick in the why.

Which models are the most reliable? Well, obviously, the models that come from hard science and engineering are the most reliable models on this Earth. And engineering quality control—at least the guts of it that matters to you and me and people who are not professional engineers—is very much based on the elementary mathematics of Fermat and Pascal.

It costs so much, and you get so much less likelihood of it breaking if you spend this much. It's all elementary high school mathematics. And an elaboration of that is what Deming brought to Japan for all of that quality-control stuff.

I don't think it's necessary for most people to be terribly facile in statistics. For example, I'm not sure that I can even pronounce the Gaussian distribution, although

W. Edwards Deming
(1900–1993)

Born in Iowa but raised in Wyoming from an early age, W. Edwards Deming grew up in a four-room tarpaper shack. A serious student despite his impoverishment, he earned a Ph.D. in mathematical physics from Yale. He took a job in the Department of Agriculture, but eventually developed a love for statistical analysis. During World War II, wanting to help the war effort, Deming sought to apply statistics to manufacturing. American companies essentially ignored his ideas. Following the war, Deming went to Japan to teach Japanese managers, engineers, and scientists how to build quality into their manufacturing. Only after Japanese manufacturing skill became apparent to the rest of the world (in the 1980s) did Deming gain fame in his home country. The Deming prize for quality was first awarded in Japan but is now recognized internationally. The Japanese poster reads "Factory Safety Leads to Efficiency."

I know what it looks like and I know that events and huge aspects of reality end up distributed that way. So I can do a rough calculation.

But if you ask me to work out something involving a Gaussian distribution to ten decimal points, I can't sit down and do the math. I'm like a poker player who's learned to play pretty well without mastering Pascal.

And, by the way, that works well enough. But you have to understand that bell-shaped curve at least roughly as well as I do.

And, of course, the engineering idea of a backup system is a very powerful idea. The engineering idea of breakpoints—that's a very powerful model, too. The notion of a critical mass—that comes out of physics—is a very powerful model.

All of these things have great utility in looking at ordinary reality. And all of this cost-benefit analysis—hell, that's all elementary high school algebra. It's just been dolled up a little bit with fancy lingo.

And you can demonstrate that point quite simply: There's not a person in this room viewing the work of a very ordinary professional magician who doesn't see a lot of things happening that aren't happening and not see a lot of things happening that are happening.

I suppose the next most reliable models are from biology/physiology because, after all, all of us are programmed by our genetic makeup to be much the same.

And then when you get into psychology, of course, it gets very much more complicated. But it's an ungodly important subject if you're going to have any worldly wisdom.

And the reason why is that the perceptual apparatus of man has shortcuts in it. The brain cannot have unlimited circuitry. So someone who knows how to take advantage of those shortcuts and cause the brain to miscalculate in certain ways can cause you to see things that aren't there.

Now you get into the cognitive function as distinguished from the perceptual function. And there, you are equally—more than equally in fact—likely to be misled. Again, your brain has a shortage of circuitry and so forth—and it's taking all kinds of little automatic shortcuts.

So when circumstances combine in certain ways—or more commonly, your fellow man starts acting like the magician and manipulates you on purpose by causing you cognitive dysfunction—you're a patsy.

And so just as a man working with a tool has to know its limitations, a man working with his cognitive apparatus has to know its limitations. And this knowledge, by the way, can be used to control and motivate other people.

The mind of man at one and the same time is both the glory and the shame of the universe.

"...all human beings, as we meet them, are commingled out of good and evil."

—Dr. Jekyll, reflecting on mankind, from Robert Louis Stevenson's *Dr. Jekyll and Mr. Hyde*

So the most useful and practical part of psychology—which I personally think can be taught to any intelligent person in a week—is ungodly important. And nobody taught it to me, by the way. I had to learn it later in life, one piece at a time. And it was fairly laborious. It's so elementary though that, when it was all over, I just felt like a total horse's ass.

And yeah, I'd been educated at Caltech and the Harvard Law School and so forth. So very eminent places miseducated people like you and me.

The elementary part of psychology—the psychology of misjudgment, as I call it—is a terribly important thing to learn. There are about twenty little principles.

And they interact, so it gets slightly complicated. But the guts of it is unbelievably important.

Terribly smart people make totally bonkers mistakes by failing to pay heed to it. In fact, I've done it several times during the last two or three years in a very important way. You never get totally over making silly mistakes.

There's another saying that comes from Pascal that I've always considered one of the really accurate observations in the history of thought. Pascal said, "The mind of man at one and the same time is both the glory and the shame of the universe."

Two Tracks of Another Kind

The famed James J. Hill Stone Arch Bridge, Minneapolis, Minnesota, is the only railway structure on which the legendary "empire-builder" Hill allowed his name to be inscribed. The $6.5 million span was completed in 1883 for Hill's Great Northern Railroad franchise, today the Burlington Northern Santa Fe. Your editor considers Hill, along with Andrew Carnegie, Harvey Firestone, and Les Schwab, to be among the best self-made operators who can be studied by young businesspeople.

And that's exactly right. It has this enormous power. However, it also has these standard misfunctions that often cause it to reach wrong conclusions. It also makes man extraordinarily subject to manipulation by others. For example, roughly half of the army of Adolf Hitler was composed of believing Catholics. Given enough clever psychological manipulation, what human beings will do is quite interesting.

I now use a kind of two-track analysis.

Personally, I've gotten so that I now use a kind of two-track analysis. First, what are the factors that really govern the interests involved, rationally considered? And second, what are the subconscious influences where the brain at a subconscious level is automatically doing these things—which, by and large, are useful but which often misfunction?

One approach is rationality—the way you'd work out a bridge problem: by evaluating the real interests, the real probabilities, and so forth. And the other is to evaluate the psychological factors that cause subconscious conclusions—many of which are wrong.

Now we come to another somewhat less reliable form of human wisdom—microeconomics. And here, I find it quite useful to think of a free market economy—or partly free market economy—as sort of the equivalent of an ecosystem.

Just as animals flourish in niches, similarly, people who specialize in the business world—and get very good because they specialize—frequently find good economics that they wouldn't get any other way.

This is a very unfashionable way of thinking because early in the days after Darwin came along, people like the robber barons assumed that the doctrine of the survival of the fittest authenticated them as deserving power—you know, "I'm the richest. Therefore, I'm the best. God's in his heaven, etc."

And that reaction of the robber barons was so irritating to people that it made it unfashionable to think of an economy as an ecosystem. But the truth is that it is a lot like an ecosystem. And you get many of the same results.

Just as in an ecosystem, people who narrowly specialize can get terribly good at occupying some little niche. Just as animals flourish in niches, similarly, people who specialize in the business world—and get very good because they specialize—frequently find good economics that they wouldn't get any other way.

And once we get into microeconomics, we get into the concept of advantages of scale. Now we're getting closer

USA
37

PELICAN ISLAND NATIONAL WILDLIFE REFUGE
1903-2003   2003

to investment analysis—because in terms of which businesses succeed and which businesses fail, advantages of scale are ungodly important.

For example, one great advantage of scale taught in all of the business schools of the world is cost reductions along the so-called experience curve. Just doing something complicated in more and more volume enables human beings, who are trying to improve and are motivated by the incentives of capitalism, to do it more and more efficiently.

In 1907, Henry Ford announced his goal for the Ford Motor Company: to create "a motor car for the great multitude." At that time, automobiles were expensive, custom-made machines. Ford installed the first moving assembly line in 1913, launching American industry mass production.

The very nature of things is that if you get a whole lot of volume through your operation, you get better at processing that volume. That's an enormous advantage.

The very nature of things is that if you get a whole lot of volume through your operation, you get better at processing that volume. That's an enormous advantage. And it has a lot to do with which businesses succeed and fail.

Let's go through a list—albeit an incomplete one—of possible advantages of scale. Some come from simple geometry. If you're building a great circular tank, obviously, as you build it bigger, the amount of steel you use in the surface goes up with the square and the cubic volume goes up with the cube. So as you increase the dimensions, you can hold a lot more volume per unit area of steel.

And there are all kinds of things like that where the simple geometry—the simple reality—gives you an advantage of scale.

For example, you can get advantages of scale from TV advertising. When TV advertising first arrived—when talking color pictures first came into our living rooms—it was an unbelievably powerful thing. And in the early days, we had three networks that had whatever it was—say ninety percent of the audience.

Am I going to take something I don't know and put it in my mouth—which is a pretty personal place, after all—for a lousy dime?

Well, if you were Procter & Gamble, you could afford to use this new method of advertising. You could afford the very expensive cost of network television because you were selling so damn many cans and bottles. Some little guy couldn't. And there was no way of buying it in part. Therefore, he couldn't use it. In effect, if you didn't have a big volume, you couldn't use network TV advertising—which was the most effective technique.

So when TV came in, the branded companies that were already big got a huge tailwind. Indeed, they prospered and prospered and prospered until some of them got fat and foolish, which happens with prosperity—at least to some people.

And your advantage of scale can be an informational advantage. If I go to some remote place, I may see Wrigley chewing gum alongside Glotz's chewing gum. Well, I know that Wrigley is a satisfactory product whereas I don't know anything about Glotz's. So if one is forty cents and the other is thirty cents, am I going to take something I don't know and put it in my mouth—which is a pretty personal place, after all—for a lousy dime?

Be Healthy-Happy-Wise Enjoy Delicious Double Mint Gum

WRIGLEY'S DOUBLE MINT CHEWING GUM

Aid Teeth Breath—Digestion Daily . . . *Millions Do*

Jack Welch on Management

Jack Welch
(b. 1935)

"From 1981 to 1995, we said we were going to be "the most competitive enterprise in the world" by being No. 1 or No. 2 in every market—fixing, selling, or closing every underperforming business that couldn't get there. There was no doubt what this mission meant or entailed."

"Before you are a leader, success is all about growing yourself. When you become a leader, success is all about growing others."

"What you measure is what you get. What you reward is what you get."

"The consistent lesson I've learned over the years is that I have been in many cases too cautious. Almost everything should have been done faster."

"Give a project visibility. Put great people on it and give them plenty of money. This continues to be the best formula for success."

"Finding great people happens in all kinds of ways, and I've always believed, 'Everyone you meet is another interview.'"

"A cardinal rule of business: never allow anyone to get between you and your customers or suppliers. Those relationships take too long to develop and are too valuable to lose."

"Don't kid yourself. It is the way it is."

So, in effect, Wrigley, simply by being so well known, has advantages of scale—what you might call an informational advantage.

Another advantage of scale comes from psychology. The psychologists use the term "social proof." We are all influenced—subconsciously and, to some extent, consciously—by what we see others do and approve. Therefore, if everybody's buying something, we think it's better. We don't like to be the one guy who's out of step.

Again, some of this is at a subconscious level, and some of it isn't. Sometimes, we consciously and rationally think, "Gee, I don't know much about this. They know more than I do. Therefore, why shouldn't I follow them?"

The social proof phenomenon, which comes right out of psychology, gives huge advantages to scale—for example, with very wide distribution, which of course is hard to get. One advantage of Coca-Cola is that it's available almost everywhere in the world.

Well, suppose you have a little soft drink. Exactly how do you make it available all over the Earth? The worldwide distribution setup—which is slowly won by a big enterprise—gets to be a huge advantage.... And if you think about it, once you get enough advantages of that type, it can become very hard for anybody to dislodge you.

There's another kind of advantage to scale. In some businesses, the very nature of things is to sort of cascade toward the overwhelming dominance of one firm. The most obvious one is daily newspapers. There's practically no city left in the United States, aside from a few very big ones, where there's more than one daily newspaper.

And, again, that's a scale thing. Once I get most of the circulation, I get most of the advertising. And once I get most of the advertising and circulation, why would anyone want the thinner paper with less information in it? So it tends to cascade to a winner-take-all situation. And that's a separate form of the advantages of scale phenomenon.

Similarly, all these huge advantages of scale allow greater specialization within the firm. Therefore, each person can be better at what he does.

And these advantages of scale are so great, for example, that when Jack Welch came into General Electric, he just said, "To hell with it. We're either going to be #1 or #2 in every field we're in or we're going to be out. I don't care how many people I have to fire and what I have to sell. We're going to be #1 or #2 or out."

The Saturday Evening Post and all those things are gone. What we have now is Motocross—which is read by a bunch of nuts who like to participate in tournaments where they turn somersaults on their motorcycles.

That was a very tough-minded thing to do, but I think it was a very correct decision if you're thinking about maximizing shareholder wealth. And I don't think it's a bad thing to do for a civilization either, because I think that General Electric is stronger for having Jack Welch there.

And there are also disadvantages of scale. For example, we—by which I mean Berkshire Hathaway—are the largest shareholder in Capital Cities/ABC. And we had trade publications there that got murdered—where our competitors beat us. And the way they beat us was by going to a narrower specialization.

We'd have a travel magazine for business travel. So somebody would create one which was addressed solely at corporate travel departments. Like an ecosystem, you're getting a narrower and narrower specialization.

Brad Lackey wows the crowd with a feet-up, full-power slide at the Luxemburg Grand Prix, 1982. Lackey was the first American to win an international motocross championship. He was closely associated for many years with CZ, a premier Czechoslovakian motorcycle. (The editor of this book used to be one of these motocross nuts.)

Well, they got much more efficient. They could tell more to the guys who ran corporate travel departments. Plus, they didn't have to waste the ink and paper mailing out stuff that corporate travel departments weren't interested in reading. It was a more efficient system. And they beat our brains out as we relied on our broader magazine.

That's what happened to the *Saturday Evening Post* and all those things. They're gone. What we have now is *Motocross*—which is read by a bunch of nuts who like to participate in tournaments where they turn somersaults on their motorcycles. But they care about it. For them, it's the principal purpose of life. A magazine called *Motocross* is a total necessity to those people. And its profit margins would make you salivate.

Just think of how narrowcast that kind of publishing is. So occasionally, scaling down and intensifying gives you the big advantage. Bigger is not always better.

The great defect of scale, of course, which makes the game interesting—so that the big people don't always win—is that as you get big, you get the bureaucracy. And with the bureaucracy comes the territoriality—which is again grounded in human nature.

The big people don't always win...as you get big, you get the bureaucracy.

And the incentives are perverse. For example, if you worked for AT&T in my day, it was a great bureaucracy. Who in the hell was really thinking about the shareholder or anything else? And in a bureaucracy, you think the work is done when it goes out of your in-basket into somebody else's in-basket. But, of course, it isn't. It's not done until AT&T delivers what it's supposed to deliver. So you get big, fat, dumb, unmotivated bureaucracies.

They also tend to become somewhat corrupt. In other words, if I've got a department and you've got a department and we kind of share power running this thing, there's sort of an unwritten rule: "If you won't bother me, I won't bother you, and we're both happy." So you get layers of management and associated costs that nobody needs. Then, while people are justifying all these layers, it takes forever to get anything done. They're too slow to make decisions, and nimbler people run circles around them.

Television was dominated by one network— CBS—in its early days.

The constant curse of scale is that it leads to big, dumb bureaucracy— which, of course, reaches its highest and worst form in government where the incentives are really awful. That doesn't mean we don't need governments—because we do. But it's a terrible problem to get big bureaucracies to behave.

So people go to stratagems. They create little decentralized units and fancy motivation and training programs. For example, for a big company, General Electric has fought bureaucracy with amazing skill. But that's because they have a combination of a genius and a fanatic running it. And they put him in young enough so he gets a long run. Of course, that's Jack Welch.

But bureaucracy is terrible.... And as things get very powerful and very big, you can get some really dysfunctional behavior. Look at Westinghouse. They blew billions of dollars on a bunch of dumb loans to real estate developers. They put some guy who'd come up by some career path—I don't know exactly what it was, but it could have been refrigerators or something—and all of a sudden, he's loaning

During the 1960s, CBS was a formidable power in network television, boasting such popular weekly series as *The Wild, Wild West*, which aired 104 episodes from 1965 to 1969.

Sam Walton. Mike Wimmer. 2005.
Oil on canvas. 2nd floor near rotunda,
Oklahoma State Senate. Sponsored by
The Wal-Mart Foundation.

money to real estate developers building hotels. It's a very unequal contest. And, in due time, they lost all those billions of dollars.

CBS provides an interesting example of another rule of psychology—namely, Pavlovian association. If people tell you what you really don't want to hear—what's unpleasant—there's an almost automatic reaction of antipathy. You have to train yourself out of it. It isn't foredestined that you have to be this way. But you will tend to be this way if you don't think about it.

Television was dominated by one network—CBS—in its early days. And Paley was a god. But he didn't like to hear what he didn't like to hear, and people soon learned that. So they told Paley only what he liked to hear. Therefore, he was soon living in a little cocoon of unreality and everything else was corrupt—although it was a great business.

So the idiocy that crept into the system was carried along by this huge tide. It was a Mad Hatter's Tea Party the last ten years under Bill Paley.

And that is not the only example, by any means. You can get severe misfunction in the high ranks of business. And, of course, if you're investing, it can make a hell of a lot of difference. If you take all the acquisitions that CBS made under Paley after the acquisition of the network itself, with all his dumb advisors—his investment bankers, management consultants, and so forth, who were getting paid very handsomely—it was absolutely terrible.

So life is an everlasting battle between those two forces—to get these advantages of scale on one side and a tendency to get a lot like the U.S. Agriculture Department on the other side—where they just sit around and so forth. I don't know exactly what they do. However, I do know that they do very little useful work.

On the subject of advantages of economies of scale, I find chain stores quite interesting. Just think about it. The concept of a chain store was a fascinating invention. You get this huge purchasing power—which means that you have lower merchandise costs. You get a whole bunch of little laboratories out there in which you can conduct experiments. And you get specialization.

If one little guy is trying to buy across twenty-seven different merchandise categories influenced by traveling salesmen, he's going to make a lot of dumb decisions. But if your buying is done in headquarters for a huge bunch of stores, you can get very bright people that know a lot about refrigerators and so forth to do the buying.

The reverse is demonstrated by the little store where one guy is doing all the buying. It's like the old story about the little store with salt all over its walls. And a stranger comes in and says to the store owner, "You must sell a lot of salt." And he replies, "No, I don't. But you should see the guy who sells me salt."

So there are huge purchasing advantages. And then there are the slick systems of forcing everyone to do what works. So a chain store can be a fantastic enterprise.

How does a guy in Bentonville, Arkansas, with no money, blow right by Sears, Roebuck? And he does it in his own lifetime—in fact, during his own late lifetime because he was already pretty old by the time he started out with one little store....

It's quite interesting to think about Wal-Mart starting from a single store in Arkansas—against Sears, Roebuck with its name, reputation and all of its billions. How does a guy in Bentonville, Arkansas, with no money, blow right by Sears, Roebuck? And he does it in his own lifetime—in fact, during his own late lifetime because he was already pretty old by the time he started out with one little store....

He played the chain store game harder and better than anyone else. Walton invented practically nothing. But he copied everything anybody else ever did

Wal-Mart

Founded in 1962 by Sam Walton with just one store in Rogers, Arkansas, Wal-Mart expanded to twenty-four stores in only five years. In 1970, Wal-Mart moved its distribution center and corporate headquarters to Bentonville, Arkansas, its current home. Growth continued throughout the United States and abroad to today's Wal-Mart, which has well over one million employees, better than $250 billion in revenues, and a market capitalization that exceeds $200 billion. The company is well-known for its slavish dedication to offering low prices to customers.

that was smart—and he did it with more fanaticism and better employee manipulation. So he just blew right by them all.

He also had a very interesting competitive strategy in the early days. He was like a prize-fighter who wanted a great record so he could be in the finals and make a big TV hit. So what did he do? He went out and fought forty-two palookas. Right? And the result was knockout, knockout, knockout—forty-two times.

Walton, being as shrewd as he was, basically broke other small town merchants in the early days. With his more efficient system, he might not have been able to tackle some titan head-on at the time. But with his better system, he could sure as hell destroy those small town merchants. And he went around doing it time after time after time. Then, as he got bigger, he started destroying the big boys.

Well, that was a very, very shrewd strategy.

You can say, "Is this a nice way to behave?" Well, capitalism is a pretty brutal place. But I personally think that the world is better for having Wal-Mart. I mean, you can idealize small town life. But I've spent a fair amount of time in small towns. And let me tell you—you shouldn't get too idealistic about all those businesses he destroyed.

Plus, a lot of people who work at Wal-Mart are very high-grade, bouncy people who are raising nice children. I have no feeling that an inferior culture destroyed a superior culture. I think that is nothing more than nostalgia and delusion. But, at any rate, it's an interesting model of how the scale of things and fanaticism combine to be very powerful.

And it's also an interesting model on the other side—how with all its great advantages, the disadvantages of bureaucracy did such terrible damage to Sears,

Juan Trippe and Pan Am

Juan Trippe (1899–1981) joined the Navy during World War I. Graduating from Yale in 1921, he sold bonds on Wall Street until launching Pan Am in 1927. Trippe developed routes and built the airline into an international travel provider. He did much to create demand for his industry, marketing "jet-set" glamour and making travel affordable for the common person.

Roebuck. Sears had layers and layers of people it didn't need. It was very bureaucratic. It was slow to think. And there was an established way of thinking. If you poked your head up with a new thought, the system kind of turned against you. It was everything in the way of a dysfunctional big bureaucracy that you would expect.

In all fairness, there was also much that was good about it. But it just wasn't as lean and mean and shrewd and effective as Sam Walton. And, in due time, all Sears' advantages of scale were not enough to prevent it from losing heavily to Wal-Mart and other similar retailers.

The net amount of money that's been made by the shareholders of airlines since Kitty Hawk is now a negative figure.

Here's a model that we've had trouble with. Maybe you'll be able to figure it out better. Many markets get down to two or three big competitors—or five or six. And in some of those markets, nobody makes any money to speak of. But in others, everybody does very well.

Over the years, we've tried to figure out why the competition in some markets gets sort of rational from the investor's point of view so that the shareholders do well, while in other markets there's destructive competition that destroys shareholder wealth.

If it's a pure commodity like airline seats, you can understand why no one makes any money. As we sit here, just think of what airlines have given to the world—safe travel, greater experience, time with your loved ones, you name it. Yet, the net amount of money that's been made by the shareholders of airlines since Kitty Hawk is now a negative figure—a substantial negative figure. Competition was so intense that, once it was unleashed by deregulation, it ravaged shareholder wealth in the airline business.

Kill Devil Hills was the site of the Wright brothers' first heavier-than-air flight in 1903—and, hence, the birthplace of aviation. In the 1930s, workers planted hearty grasses on the dune to prevent erosion. The Wright Brothers Memorial, located on the apex of the hill, is visible for miles in the otherwise barren landscape.

Kellogg

Dr. John Harvey Kellogg and his brother, William, were experimenting with new, "healthy" food items for patients at their Battle Creek Sanitarium in 1894 when they found that, by running boiled wheat dough through rollers and baking the result, they produced cereal flakes. William eventually began production of the new cereal product and, by 1906, was selling 2,900 cases per day. He continued to create new products and expanded the company into a breakfast food empire. Today, sales exceed $9 billion annually.

Yet, in other fields—like cereals, for example—almost all the big boys make out. If you're some kind of a medium-grade cereal maker, you might make fifteen percent on your capital. And if you're really good, you might make forty percent. But why are cereals so profitable—despite the fact that it looks to me like they're competing like crazy with promotions, coupons, and everything else? I don't fully understand it.

Obviously, there's a brand identity factor in cereals that doesn't exist in airlines. That must be the main factor that accounts for it.

And maybe the cereal makers, by and large, have learned to be less crazy about fighting for market share—because if you get even one person who's hell-bent on gaining market share.... For example, if I were Kellogg and I decided that I had to have sixty percent of the market, I think I could take most of the profit out of cereals. I'd ruin Kellogg in the process. But I think I could do it.

In some businesses, the participants behave like a demented Kellogg. In other businesses, they don't. Unfortunately, I do not have a perfect model for predicting how that's going to happen.

For example, if you look around at bottler markets, you'll find many markets where bottlers of Pepsi and Coke both make a lot of money and many others where they destroy most of the profitability of the two franchises. That must get down to the peculiarities of individual adjustment to market capitalism. I think you'd have to know the people involved to fully understand what was happening.

In microeconomics, of course, you've got the concept of patents, trademarks, exclusive franchises, and so forth. Patents are quite interesting. When I was young, I think more money went into patents than came out. Judges tended to throw them out—based on arguments about what was really invented and what relied on prior art. That isn't altogether clear.

But they changed that. They didn't change the laws. They just changed the administration—so that it all goes to one patent court. And that court is now very much more pro-patent. So I think people are now starting to make a lot of money out of owning patents.

Patent, Trademark, Exclusive Franchise

Patent: A grant made by a government conferring upon the creator of an invention the sole right to make, use, and sell that invention for a set period of time. An invention protected by such a grant.

Trademark: A name, symbol, or other device identifying a product, officially registered and legally restricted to the use of the owner or manufacturer. A distinctive characteristic by which a person or thing comes to be known.

Exclusive franchise: A right or license that is granted solely to an individual or group to market a company's goods or services in a particular territory under the company's trademark, trade name, or service mark and that often involves the use of rules and procedures designed by the company and services (as advertising) and facilities provided by the company in return for fees, royalties, or other compensation; also, a business granted such a right or license.

UNITED STATES PATENT-OFFICE DEPARTMENT, WASHINGTON, D. C.—[Photographed by A. Gardner, Washington, D. C.]

Trademarks, of course, have always made people a lot of money. A trademark system is a wonderful thing for a big operation if it's well known.

The exclusive franchise can also be wonderful. If there were only three television channels awarded in a big city and you owned one of them, there were only so many hours a day that you could be on. So you had a natural position in an oligopoly in the pre-cable days.

And if you get the franchise for the only food stand in an airport, you have a captive clientele, and you have a small monopoly of a sort.

The great lesson in microeconomics is to discriminate between when technology is going to help you and when it's going to kill you. And most people do not get this straight in their heads. But a fellow like Buffett does.

The great lesson in microeconomics is to discriminate between when technology is going to help you and when it's going to kill you.

For example, when we were in the textile business, which is a terrible commodity business, we were making low-end textiles—which are a real commodity product. And one day, the people came to Warren and said, "They've invented a new loom that we think will do twice as much work as our old ones." And Warren said, "Gee, I hope this doesn't work—because if it does, I'm going to close the mill." And he meant it.

When Technology is Going to Kill You:

In the *Terminator* series of science fiction films, Arnold Schwarzenegger portrays a chilling futuristic cyborg that kills without emotion.

What was he thinking? He was thinking, "It's a lousy business. We're earning substandard returns and keeping it open just to be nice to the elderly workers. But we're not going to put huge amounts of new capital into a lousy business."

And he knew that the huge productivity increases that would come from a better machine introduced into the production of a commodity product would all go to the benefit of the buyers of the textiles. Nothing was going to stick to our ribs as owners.

"They've invented a new loom that we think will do twice as much work as our old ones."

They don't do the second step of the analysis— which is to determine how much is going to stay home and how much is going to flow through to the customer.

That's such an obvious concept—that there are all kinds of wonderful new inventions that give you nothing as owners except the opportunity to spend a lot more money in a business that's still going to be lousy. The money still won't come to you. All of the advantages from great improvements are going to flow through to the customers.

Conversely, if you own the only newspaper in Oshkosh and they were to invent more efficient ways of composing the whole newspaper, then when you got rid of the old technology and got new, fancy computers and so forth, all of the savings would come right through to the bottom line.

In all cases, the people who sell the machinery—and, by and large, even the internal bureaucrats urging you to buy the equipment—show you projections with

NCR factory floor c. 1900

the amount you'll save at current prices with the new technology. However, they don't do the second step of the analysis—which is to determine how much is going to stay home and how much is just going to flow through to the customer. I've never seen a single projection incorporating that second step in my life. And I see them all the time. Rather, they always read: "This capital outlay will save you so much money that it will pay for itself in three years."

So you keep buying things that will pay for themselves in three years. And after twenty years of doing it, somehow you've earned a return of only about four percent per annum. That's the textile business.

And it isn't that the machines weren't better. It's just that the savings didn't go to you. The cost reductions came through all right. But the benefit of the cost reductions didn't go to the guy who bought the equipment. It's such a simple idea. It's so basic. And yet it's so often forgotten.

Then there's another model from microeconomics that I find very interesting. When technology moves as fast as it does in a civilization like ours, you get a phenomenon that I call competitive destruction. You know, you have the finest buggy whip factory, and, all of a sudden, in comes this little horseless carriage. And before too many years go by, your buggy whip business is dead. You either get into a different business or you're dead—you're destroyed. It happens again and again and again.

The cash register was one of the great contributions to civilization.

And when these new businesses come in, there are huge advantages for the early birds. And when you're an early bird, there's a model that I call "surfing"—when a surfer gets up and catches the wave and just stays there, he can go a long, long time. But if he gets off the wave, he becomes mired in shallows.

But people get long runs when they're right on the edge of the wave, whether it's Microsoft or Intel or all kinds of people, including National Cash Register in the early days.

The cash register was one of the great contributions to civilization. It's a wonderful story. Patterson was a small retail merchant who didn't make any money. One day, somebody sold him a crude cash register, which he put into his retail operation. And it instantly changed from losing money to earning a profit because it made it so much harder for the employees to steal.

But Patterson, having the kind of mind that he did, didn't think, "Oh, good for my retail business." He thought, "I'm going into the cash register business." And, of course, he created National Cash Register.

And he "surfed." He got the best distribution system, the biggest collection of patents, and the best of everything. He was a fanatic about everything important as the technology developed. I have in my files an early National Cash Register Company report in which Patterson described his methods and objectives. And a well-educated orangutan could see that buying into partnership with Patterson in those early days, given his notions about the cash register business, was a total one hundred percent cinch.

And, of course, that's exactly what an investor should be looking for. In a long life, you can expect to profit heavily from at least a few of those opportunities if you develop the wisdom and will to seize them. At any rate, "surfing" is a very powerful model.

However, Berkshire Hathaway, by and large, does not invest in these people that are "surfing" on complicated technology. After all, we're cranky and idiosyncratic— as you may have noticed.

National Cash Register Company

In 1884, John H. Patterson founded the National Cash Register Company (NCR), maker of the first mechanical cash registers. Two decades later, NCR introduced the first cash register powered by an electric motor. In the early 1950s, NCR branched into computer manufacturing for aviation and business applications. In the late 1990s, the firm shifted from a hardware-only company to a "full-solution" business automation provider.

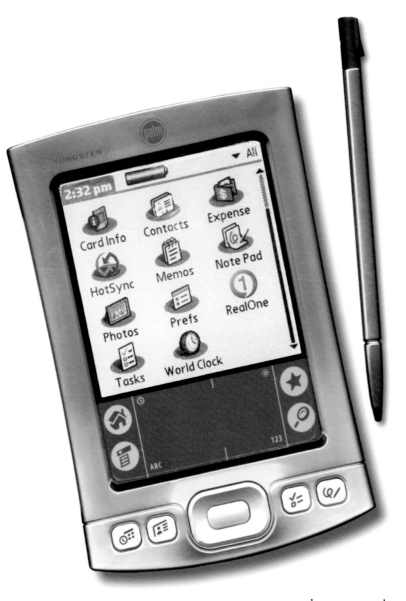

And Warren and I don't feel like we have any great advantage in the high-tech sector. In fact, we feel like we're at a big disadvantage in trying to understand the nature of technical developments in software, computer chips, or what have you. So we tend to avoid that stuff, based on our personal inadequacies.

Again, that is a very, very powerful idea. Every person is going to have a circle of competence. And it's going to be very hard to enlarge that circle. If I had to make my living as a musician.... I can't even think of a level low enough to describe where I would be sorted out to if music were the measuring standard of the civilization.

So you have to figure out what your own aptitudes are. If you play games where other people have the aptitudes and you don't, you're going to lose. And that's as close to certain as any prediction that you can make. You have to figure out where you've got an edge. And you've got to play within your own circle of competence.

Warren and I don't feel like we have any great advantage in the high-tech sector.

If you want to be the best tennis player in the world, you may start out trying and soon find out that it's hopeless—that other people blow right by you. However, if you want to become the best plumbing contractor in Bemidji, that is probably doable by two-thirds of you. It takes a will. It takes the intelligence. But after a while, you'd gradually know all about the plumbing business in Bemidji and master the art. That is an attainable objective, given enough discipline. And people who could never win a chess tournament or stand in center court in a respectable tennis tournament can rise quite high in life by slowly developing a circle of competence—which results partly from what they were born with and partly from what they slowly develop through work.

Paul and Babe, Bemidji, Minnesota. Paul Bunyan, of course, was the great lumberjack hero of storybook fame.

So some edges can be acquired. And the game of life to some extent for most of us is trying to be something like a good plumbing contractor in Bemidji. Very few of us are chosen to win the world's chess tournaments.

You have to figure out what your own aptitudes are. If you play games where other people have the aptitudes and you don't, you're going to lose.

Some of you may find opportunities "surfing" along in the new high-tech fields—the Intels, the Microsofts, and so on. The fact that we don't think we're very good at it and have pretty well stayed out of it doesn't mean that it's irrational for you to do it.

Well, so much for the basic microeconomic models, a little bit of psychology, a little bit of mathematics, helping create what I call the general substructure of worldly wisdom. Now, if you want to go on from carrots to dessert, I'll turn to stock picking—trying to draw on this general worldly wisdom as we go.

I don't want to get into emerging markets, bond arbitrage, and so forth. I'm talking about nothing but plain vanilla stock picking. That, believe me, is complicated enough. And I'm talking about common stock picking.

The first question is, "What is the nature of the stock market?" And that gets you directly to this efficient market theory that got to be the rage—a total rage—long after I graduated from law school.

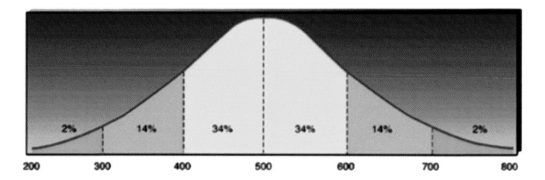

The iron rule of life is that only twenty percent of the people can be in the top fifth.

And it's rather interesting because one of the greatest economists of the world is a substantial shareholder in Berkshire Hathaway and has been from the very early days after Buffett was in control. His textbook always taught that the stock market was perfectly efficient and that nobody could beat it. But his own money went into Berkshire and made him wealthy. So, like Pascal in his famous wager, he hedged his bet.

Is the stock market so efficient that people can't beat it? Well, the efficient market theory is obviously roughly right—meaning that markets are quite efficient and it's quite hard for anybody to beat the market by significant margins as a stock picker by just being intelligent and working in a disciplined way.

Indeed, the average result has to be the average result. By definition, everybody can't beat the market. As I always say, the iron rule of life is that only twenty percent of the people can be in the top fifth. That's just the way it is. So the answer is that it's partly efficient and partly inefficient.

And, by the way, I have a name for people who went to the extreme efficient market theory—which is "bonkers." It was an intellectually consistent theory that enabled them to do pretty mathematics. So I understand its seductiveness to people with large mathematical gifts. It just had a difficulty in that the fundamental assumption did not tie properly to reality.

Again, to the man with a hammer, every problem looks like a nail. If you're good at manipulating higher mathematics in a consistent way, why not make an assumption that enables you to use your tool?

The model I like—to sort of simplify the notion of what goes on in a market for common stocks—is the pari-mutuel system at the race track. If you stop to think about it, a pari-mutuel system is a market. Everybody goes there and bets, and the odds change based on what's bet. That's what happens in the stock market.

Any damn fool can see that a horse carrying a light weight with a wonderful win rate and a good post position, etc., etc., is way more likely to win than a horse with a terrible record and extra weight and so on and so on. But if you look at the damn odds, the bad horse pays 100 to 1, whereas the good horse pays 3 to 2. Then, it's not clear which is statistically the best bet using the mathematics of Fermat and Pascal. The prices have changed in such a way that it's very hard to beat the system.

Thor's Hammer

Thor, an ancient Norse pagan deity, governed the atmosphere and environment. He was also the god of justice and law. Generally depicted as a well-built, red-bearded man with a fiery stare, Thor used a hammer that symbolized lightning, which, along with the thunderbolt, comprised his weapons against the enemies of heaven and earth. The hammer was also used in blessings, based on various important attributes—it could never be broken, it never missed its mark when thrown, it always returned to Thor's hand, and it could shrink in size so that Thor could conceal it in his shirt.

And then the track is taking seventeen percent off the top. So not only do you have to outwit all the other bettors, but you've got to outwit them by such a big margin that on average, you can afford to take seventeen percent of your gross bets off the top and give it to the house before the rest of your money can be put to work.

If you stop to think about it, a pari-mutuel system is a market. Everybody goes there and bets, and the odds change based on what's bet. That's what happens in the stock market.

Given those mathematics, is it possible to beat the horses using only one's intelligence? Intelligence should give some edge because lots of people who don't know anything go out and bet lucky numbers and so forth. Therefore, somebody who really thinks about nothing but horse performance and is shrewd and mathematical could have a very considerable edge, in the absence of the frictional cost caused by the house take.

Pari-mutuel System

A system of betting on races in which the winners divide the total amount bet, after deducting management expenses, in proportion to the sums they have wagered individually.

Unfortunately, what a shrewd horseplayer's edge does in most cases is to reduce his average loss over a season of betting from the seventeen percent that he would lose if he got the average result to maybe ten percent. However, there are actually a few people who can beat the game after paying the full seventeen percent.

I used to play poker, when I was young, with a guy who made a substantial living doing nothing but bet harness races. Now, harness racing is a relatively inefficient market. You don't have the depth of intelligence betting on harness races that you do on regular races. What my poker pal would do was to think about harness races as his main profession. And he would bet only occasionally when he saw some mispriced bet available. And by doing that, after paying the full handle to the house—which I presume was around seventeen percent—he made a substantial living.

You have to say that's rare. However, the market was not perfectly efficient. And if it weren't for that big seventeen percent handle, lots of people would regularly be beating lots of other people at the horse races. It's efficient, yes. But it's not perfectly efficient. And with enough shrewdness and fanaticism, some people will get better results than others.

The stock market is the same way—except that the house handle is so much lower. If you take transaction costs—the spread between the bid and the ask plus the commissions—and if you don't trade too actively, you're talking about fairly low transaction costs. So that, with enough fanaticism and enough discipline, some of the shrewd people are going to get way better results than average in the nature of things.

Gambling continues to be wildly popular throughout the world. Mah Jong is the preferred medium of gambling in much of Asia. The game resembles the card game of Rummy, and some people believe that playing cards were derived from Mah Jong tiles.

The one thing all those winning bettors in the whole history of people who've beaten the pari-mutuel system have is quite simple: they bet very seldom.

It is not a bit easy. And, of course, fifty percent will end up in the bottom half, and seventy percent will end up in the bottom seventy percent. But some people will have an advantage. And in a fairly low transaction cost operation, they will get better than average results in stock picking.

How do you get to be one of those who is a winner—in a relative sense—instead of a loser?

Here again, look at the pari-mutuel system. I had dinner last night by absolute accident with the president of Santa Anita. He says that there are two or three bettors who have a credit arrangement with the track, now that they have off-track betting, who are actually beating the house. The track is sending money out net after the full handle—a lot of it to Las Vegas, by the way—to people who are actually winning slightly, net, after paying the full handle. They're that shrewd about something with as much unpredictability as horse racing.

It's not given to human beings to have such talent that they can just know everything about everything all the time. But it is given to human beings who work hard at it—who look and sift the world for a mispriced bet—that they can occasionally find one.

And the wise ones bet heavily when the world offers them that opportunity. They bet big when they have the odds. And the rest of the time, they don't. It's just that simple.

Morning, Leaving for Work. Vincent Van Gogh. 1890. Oil on canvas. Hermitage, St. Petersburg, Russia.

The way to win is to work, work, work, work, and hope to have a few insights.

That is a very simple concept. And to me it's obviously right—based on experience not only from the pari-mutuel system, but everywhere else.

And yet, in investment management, practically nobody operates that way. We operate that way—I'm talking about Buffett and Munger. And we're not alone in the world. But a huge majority of people have some other crazy construct in their heads. And instead of waiting for a near cinch and loading up, they apparently ascribe to the theory that if they work a little harder or hire more business school students, they'll come to know everything about everything all the time. To me, that's totally insane.

How many insights do you need? Well, I'd argue that you don't need many in a lifetime. If you look at Berkshire Hathaway and all of its accumulated billions, the top ten insights account for most of it. And that's with a very brilliant man—Warren's a lot more able than I am and very disciplined—devoting his lifetime to it. I don't mean to say that he's only had ten insights. I'm just saying that most of the money came from ten insights.

So you can get very remarkable investment results if you think more like a winning pari-mutuel player. Just think of it as a heavy odds against game full of bullshit and craziness with an occasional mispriced something or other. And you're probably not going to be smart enough to find thousands in a lifetime. And when you get a few, you really load up. It's just that simple.

When Warren lectures at business schools, he says, "I could improve your ultimate financial welfare by giving you a ticket with only twenty slots in it so that you had twenty punches—representing all the investments that you got to make in a lifetime. And once you'd punched through the card, you couldn't make any more investments at all."

He says, "Under those rules, you'd really think carefully about what you did, and you'd be forced to load up on what you'd really thought about. So you'd do so much better."

Again, this is a concept that seems perfectly obvious to me. And to Warren, it seems perfectly obvious. But this is one of the very few business classes in the United States where anybody will be saying so. It just isn't the conventional wisdom.

I asked him, "My God, they're purple and green. Do fish really take these lures?" And he said, "Mister, I don't sell to fish."

To me, it's obvious that the winner has to bet very selectively. It's been obvious to me since very early in life. I don't know why it's not obvious to very many other people.

I think the reason why we got into such idiocy in investment management is best illustrated by a story that I tell about the guy who sold fishing tackle. I asked him, "My God, they're purple and green. Do fish really take these lures?" And he said, "Mister, I don't sell to fish."

Investment managers are in the position of that fishing tackle salesman. They're like the guy who was selling salt to the guy who already had too much

Federal Express

Frederick W. Smith was a Yale undergraduate student in 1965 when he wrote a term paper about the passenger route systems used by most airfreight companies. He saw the need for a system designed specifically for airfreight to accommodate time-sensitive shipments. In 1971, Smith bought controlling interest in Arkansas Aviation Sales. Smith quickly witnessed the difficulty in getting packages and other airfreight delivered within one to two days. He did the research necessary to create a more efficient distribution system. The company officially began operating in 1973 with fourteen small aircraft based at Memphis International Airport; eventually, company headquarters moved to Memphis as well. Unprofitable until July 1975, FedEx soon became the premier carrier of high-priority goods in the marketplace and the standard setter for the industry it established.

salt. And as long as the guy will buy salt, why, they'll sell salt. But that isn't what ordinarily works for the buyer of investment advice.

If you invested Berkshire Hathaway–style, it would be hard to get paid as an investment manager as well as they're currently paid—because you'd be holding a block of Wal-Mart and a block of Coca-Cola and a block of something else. You'd be sitting on your ass. And the client would be getting rich. And, after a while, the client would think, "Why am I paying this guy half-a-percent a year on my wonderful passive holdings?"

So what makes sense for the investor is different from what makes sense for the manager. And, as usual in human affairs, what determines the behavior are incentives for the decision maker.

As usual in human affairs, what determines the behavior are incentives for the decision maker, and "getting the incentives right" is a very, very important lesson.

From all business, my favorite case on incentives is Federal Express. The heart and soul of its system—which creates the integrity of the product—is having all its airplanes come to one place in the middle of the night and shift all the packages from plane to plane. If there are delays, the whole operation can't deliver a product full of integrity to Federal Express customers.

And it was always screwed up. They could never get it done on time. They tried everything—moral suasion, threats, you name it. And nothing worked.

Finally, somebody got the idea to pay all these people not so much an hour, but so much a shift—and when it's all done, they can all go home. Well, their problems cleared up overnight.

So getting the incentives right is a very, very important lesson. It was not obvious to Federal Express what the solution was. But maybe now, it will hereafter more often be obvious to you.

All right, we've now recognized that the market is efficient as a pari-mutuel system is efficient—with the favorite more likely than the long shot to do well in racing, but not necessarily give any betting advantage to those that bet on the favorite.

In the stock market, some railroad that's beset by better competitors and tough unions may be available at one-third of its book value. In contrast, IBM in its heyday might be selling at six times book value. So it's just like the pari-mutuel system. Any damn fool could plainly see that IBM had better business prospects than the railroad. But once you put the price into the formula, it wasn't so clear anymore what was going to work best for a buyer choosing between the stocks. So it's a lot like a pari-mutuel system. And, therefore, it gets very hard to beat.

What style should the investor use as a picker of common stocks in order to try to beat the market—in other words, to get an above average long-term result? A standard technique that appeals to a lot of people is called "sector rotation." You simply figure out when oils are going to outperform retailers, etc., etc., etc. You just kind of flit around being in the hot sector of the market making better choices than other people. And presumably, over a long period of time, you get ahead.

However, I know of no really rich sector rotator. Maybe some people can do it. I'm not saying they can't. All I know is that all the people I know who got rich—and I know a lot of them—did not do it that way.

The second basic approach is the one that Ben Graham used—much admired by Warren and me. As one factor, Graham had this concept of value to a private owner—what the whole enterprise would sell for if it were available. And that was calculable in many cases.

Then, if you could take the stock price and multiply it by the number of shares and get something that was one-third or less of sellout value, he would say

IBM's signature office product, the "Selectric" typewriter, used a replaceable, ball-shaped typing element rather than traditional-type bars or moveable carriages. The Selectric became a popular piece of office equipment because of its ease of use and availability, largely replacing standard electric typewriters, as above.

Benjamin Graham
(1894–1976)

Born in London, Benjamin Graham migrated with his family to America when he was very young. His father opened an importing business that quickly failed. Despite the challenges of poverty, Graham attended and graduated from Columbia University. He took a job as a chalker on Wall Street with Newburger, Henderson, and Loeb. His intelligence and capability were soon apparent, and by age twenty-five, he was a partner at the firm. The 1929 market crash almost wiped out Graham, but he learned valuable lessons about investing. In the 1930s, Graham published a series of books on investing that became classics. Among these impressive titles are *Security Analysis* and *The Intelligent Investor*. Graham introduced the concept of "intrinsic value" and the wisdom of buying stocks at a discount to that value.

that you've got a lot of edge going for you. Even with an elderly alcoholic running a stodgy business, this significant excess of real value per share working for you means that all kinds of good things can happen to you. You had a huge margin of safety—as he put it—by having this big excess value going for you.

But he was, by and large, operating when the world was in shell-shock from the 1930s—which was the worst contraction in the English-speaking world in about 600 years. Wheat in Liverpool, I believe, got down to something like a 600-year low, adjusted for inflation. People were so shell-shocked for a long time thereafter that Ben Graham could run his Geiger counter over this detritus from the collapse of the 1930s and find things selling below their working capital per share and so on.

And in those days, working capital actually belonged to the shareholders. If the employees were no longer useful, you just sacked them all, took the working capital, and stuck it in the owners' pockets. That was the way capitalism then worked.

Nowadays, of course, the accounting is not realistic—because the minute the business starts contracting, significant assets are not there. Under social norms and the new legal rules of the civilization, so much is owed to the employees, that the minute the enterprise goes into reverse, some of the assets on the balance sheet aren't there anymore.

Now, that might not be true if you run a little auto dealership yourself. You may be able to run it in a way that there's no health plan and this and that so that if the business gets lousy, you can take your working capital and go home. But IBM can't or at least didn't. Just look at what disappeared from its balance sheet when it decided that it had to change size both because the world had changed technologically and because its market position had deteriorated.

And in terms of blowing it, IBM is some example. Those were brilliant, disciplined people. But there was enough turmoil in technological change that IBM got bounced off the wave after "surfing" successfully for sixty years. And that was some collapse—an object lesson in the difficulties of technology and one of the reasons why Buffett and Munger don't like technology very much. We don't think we're any good at it, and strange things can happen.

At any rate, the trouble with what I call the classic Ben Graham concept is that gradually the world wised up, and those real obvious bargains disappeared. You could run your Geiger counter over the rubble, and it wouldn't click.

But such is the nature of people who have a hammer—to whom, as I mentioned, every problem looks like a nail—that the Ben Graham followers responded by changing the calibration on their Geiger counters. In effect, they started defining a bargain in a different way. And they kept changing the definition so that they could keep doing what they'd always done. And it still worked pretty well. So the Ben Graham intellectual system was a very good one.

Of course, the best part of it all was his concept of "Mr. Market." Instead of thinking the market was efficient, Graham treated it as a manic-depressive who comes by every day. And some days "Mr. Market" says, "I'll sell you some of my interest for way less than you think it's worth." And other days, he comes by and says, "I'll buy your interest at a price that's way higher than you think it's worth." And you get the option of deciding whether you want to buy more, sell part of what you already have, or do nothing at all.

To Graham, it was a blessing to be in business with a manic-depressive who gave you this series of options all the time. That was a very significant mental construct. And it's been very useful to Buffett, for instance, over his whole adult lifetime.

However, if we'd stayed with classic Graham the way Ben Graham did it, we would never have had the record we have. And that's because Graham wasn't trying to do what we did.

For example, Graham didn't want to ever talk to management. And his reason was that, like the best sort of professor aiming his teaching at a mass audience, he was trying to invent a system that anybody could use. And he didn't feel that

Perhaps the Soviets had this German proverb in mind when they selected the hammer for their revolutionary symbol:

**"One must either be the hammer...
or the anvil."**

the man in the street could run around and talk to management and learn things. He also had a concept that management would often couch the information very shrewdly to mislead. Therefore, it was very difficult. And that is still true, of course—human nature being what it is.

And so having started out as Grahamites—which, by the way, worked fine—we gradually got what I would call better insights. And we realized that some company that was selling at two or three times book value could still be a hell of a bargain because of momentums implicit in its position, sometimes combined with an unusual managerial skill plainly present in some individual or other, or some system or other.

And once we'd gotten over the hurdle of recognizing that a thing could be a bargain based on quantitative measures that would have horrified Graham, we started thinking about better businesses.

And, by the way, the bulk of the billions in Berkshire Hathaway has come from the better businesses. Much of the first $200 or $300 million came from scrambling around with our Geiger counter. But the great bulk of the money has come from the great businesses.

Most investment managers are in a game where the clients expect them to know a lot about a lot of things. We didn't have any clients who could fire us at Berkshire Hathaway.

And even some of the early money was made by being temporarily present in great businesses. Buffett Partnership, for example, owned American Express and Disney when they got pounded down.

[Most investment managers are] in a game where the clients expect them to know a lot about a lot of things. We didn't have any clients who could fire us at Berkshire Hathaway. So we didn't have to be governed by any such construct. And

Trump's signature message: "You're fired!"

Photo by Bill Davila/Reuters

we came to this notion of finding a mispriced bet and loading up when we were very confident that we were right. So we're way less diversified. And I think our system is miles better.

However, in all fairness, I don't think [a lot of money managers] could successfully sell their services if they used our system. But if you're investing for forty years in some pension fund, what difference does it make if the path from start to finish is a little more bumpy or a little different than everybody else's so long as it's all going to work out well in the end? So what if there's a little extra volatility.

In investment management today, everybody wants not only to win, but to have the path never diverge very much from a standard path except on the upside. Well, that is a very artificial, crazy construct. That's the equivalent in investment management to the custom of binding the feet of the Chinese women. It's the equivalent of what Nietzsche meant when he criticized the man who had a lame leg and was proud of it.

That is really hobbling yourself. Now, investment managers would say, "We have to be that way. That's how we're measured." And they may be right in terms of the way the business is now constructed. But from the viewpoint of a rational consumer, the whole system's "bonkers" and draws a lot of talented people into socially useless activity.

You're much more likely to do well if you start out to do something feasible instead of something that isn't feasible. Isn't that perfectly obvious?

And the Berkshire system is not "bonkers." It's so damned elementary that even bright people are going to have limited, really valuable insights in a very competitive world when they're fighting against other very bright, hardworking people.

And it makes sense to load up on the very few good insights you have instead of pretending to know everything about everything at all times. You're much more

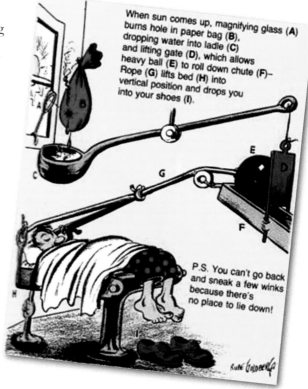

When sun comes up, magnifying glass (A) burns hole in paper bag (B), dropping water into ladle (C) and lifting gate (D), which allows heavy ball (E) to roll down chute (F)— Rope (G) lifts bed (H) into vertical position and drops you into your shoes (I).

P.S. You can't go back and sneak a few winks because there's no place to lie down!

Professor Lucifer Gorgonzola Butts, pushing the limits of feasibility in this classic Rube Goldberg "machine." Goldberg's invention cartoons were influenced by the "machine age" at the beginning of the century and by the complex new mechanisms invented to simplify life. Charlie, like so many Americans, recalls enjoying the wacky creations of Goldberg's imaginative mind.

likely to do well if you start out to do something feasible instead of something that isn't feasible. Isn't that perfectly obvious?

How many of you have fifty-six brilliant insights in which you have equal confidence? Raise your hands, please. How many of you have two or three insights that you have some confidence in? I rest my case.

I'd say that Berkshire Hathaway's system is adapting to the nature of the investment problem as it really is.

We've really made the money out of high-quality businesses. In some cases, we bought the whole business. And in some cases, we just bought a big block of stock. But when you analyze what happened, the big money's been made in the high-quality businesses. And most of the other people who've made a lot of money have done so in high-quality businesses.

Over the long term, it's hard for a stock to earn a much better return than the business which underlies it earns. If the business earns six percent on capital over forty years and you hold it for that forty years, you're not going to make much different than a six percent return—even if you originally buy it at a huge discount. Conversely, if a business earns eighteen percent on capital over twenty or thirty years, even if you pay an expensive looking price, you'll end up with one hell of a result.

So the trick is getting into better businesses. And that involves all of these advantages of scale that you could consider momentum effects.

How do you get into these great companies? One method is what I'd call the method of finding them small—get 'em when they're little. For example, buy Wal-Mart when Sam Walton first goes public and so forth. And a lot of people try to do just that. And it's a very beguiling idea. If I were a young man, I might actually go into it.

"It is not the strongest of the species that survives, nor the most intelligent, but the one most responsive to change."

—Charles Darwin

The Warbler Finch (*Certhidea olivacea*) is one of fourteen finch species Darwin discovered in the Galapagos Islands. In honor of his groundbreaking research, these species were given the name of Darwin's Finches.

But it doesn't work for Berkshire Hathaway anymore because we've got too much money. We can't find anything that fits our size parameter that way. Besides, we're set in our ways. But I regard finding them small as a perfectly intelligent approach for somebody to try with discipline. It's just not something that I've done.

Finding 'em big obviously is very hard because of the competition. So far, Berkshire's managed to do it. But can we continue to do it? What's the next Coca-Cola investment for us? Well, the answer to that is I don't know. I think it gets harder for us all the time.

And ideally—and we've done a lot of this—you get into a great business which also has a great manager because management matters. For example, it's made a hell of a difference to General Electric that Jack Welch came in instead of the guy who took over Westinghouse—one hell of a difference. So management matters, too.

And some of it is predictable. I do not think it takes a genius to understand that Jack Welch was a more insightful person and a better manager than his peers in other companies. Nor do I think it took tremendous genius to understand that Disney had basic momentums in place that are very powerful and that Eisner and Wells were very unusual managers.

So you do get an occasional opportunity to get into a wonderful business that's being run by a wonderful manager. And, of course, that's hog heaven day. If you don't load up when you get those opportunities, it's a big mistake.

Occasionally, you'll find a human being who's so talented that he can do things that ordinary skilled mortals can't. I would argue that Simon Marks—who was second generation in Marks & Spencer of England— was such a man. Patterson was such a man at National Cash Register. And Sam Walton was such a man.

These people do come along—and, in many cases, they're not all that hard to identify. If they've got a reasonable hand—with the

Simon Marks
(1888–1964)

Born in Leeds, England, to Polish immigrant parents, Simon Marks spent his formative years roaming around his father's retail store, Marks and Spencer. Following graduation from the rigorous local grammar school (the equivalent of high school today), Marks went into the family business. At age twenty-eight, he was appointed chairman and led the Marks and Spencer Company into many retailing innovations and considerable financial success. Outside of his company obligations, Marks worked passionately for the re-establishment of a Jewish state.

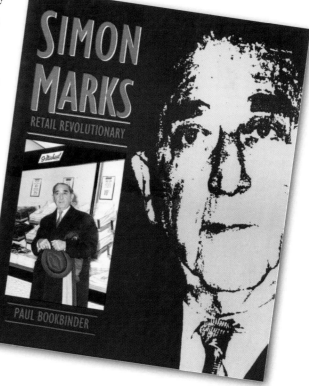

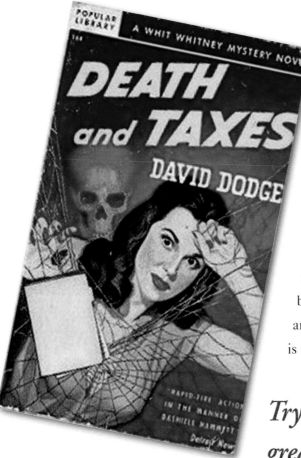

fanaticism and intelligence and so on that these people generally bring to the party—then management can matter much.

However, averaged out, betting on the quality of a business is better than betting on the quality of management. In other words, if you have to choose one, bet on the business momentum, not the brilliance of the manager.

But, very rarely, you find a manager who's so good that you're wise to follow him into what looks like a mediocre business.

Another very simple effect I very seldom see discussed either by investment managers or anybody else is the effect of taxes. If you're going to buy something that compounds for thirty years at fifteen percent per annum and you pay one thirty-five percent tax at the very end, the way that works out is that after taxes, you keep 13.3 percent per annum.

Trying to minimize taxes too much is one of the great standard causes of really dumb mistakes.

In contrast, if you bought the same investment but had to pay taxes every year of thirty-five percent out of the fifteen percent that you earned, then your return would be fifteen percent minus thirty-five percent of fifteen percent—or only 9.75 percent per year compounded. So the difference there is over 3.5 percent. And what 3.5 percent does to the numbers over long holding periods like thirty years is truly eye-opening. If you sit on your ass for long, long stretches in great companies, you can get a huge edge from nothing but the way income taxes work.

Even with a ten percent per annum investment, paying a thirty-five percent tax at the end gives you 8.3 percent after taxes as an annual compounded result after thirty years. In contrast, if you pay the thirty-five percent each year instead of at the end, your annual result goes down to 6.5 percent. So you add nearly two percent of after-tax return per annum if you only achieve an average return by historical standards from common stock investments in companies with low dividend payout ratios.

But in terms of business mistakes that I've seen over a long lifetime, I would say that trying to minimize taxes too much is one of the great standard causes of really dumb mistakes. I see terrible mistakes from people being overly motivated by tax considerations.

Warren and I personally don't drill oil wells. We pay our taxes. And we've done pretty well, so far. Anytime somebody offers you a tax shelter from here on in life, my advice would be don't buy it.

In fact, anytime anybody offers you anything with a big commission and a 200-page prospectus, don't buy it. Occasionally, you'll be wrong if you adopt "Munger's Rule." However, over a lifetime, you'll be a long way ahead—and you will miss a lot of unhappy experiences that might otherwise reduce your love for your fellow man.

There are huge advantages for an individual to get into a position where you make a few great investments and just sit on your ass: You're paying less to brokers. You're listening to less nonsense. And if it works, the governmental tax system gives you an extra one, two, or three percentage points per annum compounded.

And you think that most of you are going to get that much advantage by hiring investment counselors and paying them one percent to run around, incurring a lot of taxes on your behalf? Lots of luck.

Are there any dangers in this philosophy? Yes. Everything in life has dangers. Since it's so obvious that investing in great companies works, it gets horribly overdone from time to time. In the Nifty-Fifty days, everybody could tell which companies were the great ones. So they got up to fifty, sixty, and seventy times

"Warren and I personally don't drill oil wells. We pay our taxes. And we've done pretty well, so far. Anytime somebody offers you a tax shelter from here on in life, my advice would be don't buy it."

earnings. And just as IBM fell off the wave, other companies did, too. Thus, a large investment disaster resulted from too high prices. And you've got to be aware of that danger.

So there are risks. Nothing is automatic and easy. But if you can find some fairly priced great company and buy it and sit, that tends to work out very, very well indeed—especially for an individual.

Within the growth stock model, there's a sub-position: There are actually businesses that you will find a few times in a lifetime where any manager could raise the return enormously just by raising prices—and yet they haven't done it. So they have huge untapped pricing power that they're not using. That is the ultimate no-brainer.

That existed in Disney. It's such a unique experience to take your grandchild to Disneyland. You're not doing it that often. And there are lots of people in the country. And Disney found that it could raise those prices a lot, and the attendance stayed right up.

The successful Disney franchise includes not only theme parks and motion pictures, but also books, comics, and lucrative video sales.

So a lot of the great record of Eisner and Wells was utter brilliance but the rest came from just raising prices at Disneyland and Disneyworld and through video cassette sales of classic animated movies.

At Berkshire Hathaway, Warren and I raised the prices of See's Candy a little faster than others might have. And, of course, we invested in Coca-Cola—which had some untapped pricing power. And it also had brilliant management. So a Goizueta and Keough could do much more than raise prices. It was perfect.

You will get a few opportunities to profit from finding underpricing. There are actually people out there who don't price everything as high as the market will easily stand. And once you figure that out, it's like finding money in the street—if you have the courage of your convictions.

If you look at Berkshire's investments where a lot of the money's been made and you look for the models, you can see that we twice bought into two-newspaper towns which have since become one-newspaper towns. So we made a bet to some extent.

We faced a situation where you had both the top hand in a game that was clearly going to end up with one winner and a management with a lot of integrity and intelligence. It was a dream—an absolute, damn dream.

In one of those—the *Washington Post*—we bought it at about twenty percent of the value to a private owner. So we bought it on a Ben Graham–style basis—at one-fifth of obvious value—and, in addition, we faced a situation where you had both the top hand in a game that was clearly going to end up with one winner and a management with a lot of integrity and intelligence. That one was a real dream. They're very high class people—the Katharine Graham family. That's why it was a dream—an absolute, damn dream.

Of course, that came about back in '73–'74. And that was almost like 1932. That was probably a once-in-forty-years-type denouement in the markets. That investment's up about fifty times over our cost. If I were you, I wouldn't count on getting any investment in your lifetime quite as good as the *Washington Post* was in '73 and '74.

Let me mention another model. Of course, Gillette and Coke make fairly low-priced items and have a tremendous marketing advantage all over the world. And in Gillette's case, they keep "surfing" along new technology, which is fairly simple by the standards of microchips. But it's hard for competitors to do.

The Washington Post

In 1877, Stilson Hutchins launched *The Washington Post*. Three years later, the *Post* became the first daily newspaper in Washington to publish seven times a week. In 1946, Philip Graham became publisher; he moved up to president of the paper in 1959. The *Post* acquired *Newsweek Magazine* and established a joint news service with the *Los Angeles Times* in the early 1960s.

History of the Disposable Razor

King C. Gillette (1855-1932),
a traveling hardware salesman who
enjoyed improving the products he
sold, learned early that disposable items
made for big sales. In 1895, Gillette
had a revelation: if he could put a sharp
edge on a small square of sheet steel, he
could market an economical razor blade
that could be thrown away and replaced
when it grew dull. In 1901, Gillette and
William Emery Nickerson formed the
American Safety Razor Company (soon
thereafter renamed for Gillette himself).
For the first time, razor blades were sold
in multiple packages, with the razor
handle a one-time purchase. Production
began in 1903; Gillette won a patent for
his product the next year.

So they've been able to stay constantly near the edge of improvements in shaving. There are whole countries where Gillette has more than ninety percent of the shaving market.

GEICO is a very interesting model. It's another one of the one hundred or so models you ought to have in your head. I've had many friends in the sick-business-fix game over a long lifetime. And they practically all use the following formula—I call it the cancer surgery formula:

They look at this mess. And they figure out if there's anything sound left that can live on its own if they cut away everything else. And if they find anything sound, they just cut away everything else. Of course, if that doesn't work, they liquidate the business. But it frequently does work.

And GEICO had a perfectly magnificent business—submerged in a mess, but still working. Misled by success, GEICO had done some foolish things. They got to thinking that, because they were making a lot of money, they knew everything. And they suffered huge losses.

All they had to do was to cut out all the folly and go back to the perfectly wonderful business that was lying there. And when you think about it, that's a very simple model. And it's repeated over and over again.

And, in GEICO's case, think about all the money we passively made. It was a wonderful business combined with a bunch of foolishness that could easily be cut out. And people were coming in who were temperamentally and intellectually designed so they were going to cut it out. That is a model you want to look for.

And you may find one or two or three in a long lifetime that are very good. And you may find twenty or thirty that are good enough to be quite useful.

Finally, I'd like to once again talk about investment management. That is a funny business—because on a net basis, the whole investment management business together gives no value added to all buyers combined. That's the way it has to work.

On a net basis, the whole investment management business together gives no value added to all buyers combined. That's the way it has to work.

Of course, that isn't true of plumbing, and it isn't true of medicine. If you're going to make your careers in the investment management business, you face a very peculiar situation. And most investment managers handle it with psychological denial—just like a chiropractor. That is the standard method of handling the limitations of the investment management process. But if you want to live the best sort of life, I would urge each of you not to use the psychological denial mode.

I think a select few—a small percentage of the investment managers—can deliver value added. But I don't think brilliance alone is enough to do it. I think that you have to have a little of this discipline of calling your shots and loading up— if you want to maximize your chances of becoming one who provides above average real returns for clients over the long pull.

But I'm just talking about investment managers engaged in common stock picking. I am agnostic elsewhere. I think there may well be people who are so shrewd about currencies and this, that, and the other thing that they can achieve good long-term records operating on a pretty big scale in that way. But that doesn't happen to be my milieu. I'm talking about stock picking in American stocks.

I think it's hard to provide a lot of value added to the investment management client, but it's not impossible.

GEICO

Leo and Lillian Goodwin started the Government Employees Insurance Company (GEICO) during the depths of the Great Depression in 1936. Their strategy of direct marketing allowed the company to charge lower premiums while earning a profit. The company grew quickly, even though it focused at first primarily on federal employees and military officers. GEICO soon expanded its market to the general public. In 1951, Warren Buffett purchased his first shares of the company. He kept acquiring stock through the years until, in 1996, GEICO became a wholly owned subsidiary of Berkshire Hathaway.

Talk Two Revisited

As I reviewed Talk Two in 2005, I thought it would be improved by adding (1) an attempt to explain the extreme investment success of Harvard and Yale during the long bull market between the early 1990s and 2005, plus (2) a prediction about outcomes for the many pools of capital that are now trying to duplicate the past success of Harvard and Yale by copying their methods.

To me, it seems likely that, as Harvard and Yale de-emphasized conventional unleveraged holding of diversified U.S. common stocks, their investment success was boosted by factors including the three described below:

(1) By investing in LBO funds during a period when such funds were not so numerous and large as they now are, Harvard and Yale introduced leverage into their results from owning interests in U.S. businesses, thus boosting their outcome during the rising market. Moreover, the LBO structure gave them a way to make their leveraged business investments in a manner safer than is possible in a normal margin account, vulnerable to forced sales during panics. Good results followed even when net-after-cost results

from investments in LBO funds were no better than would have occurred through moderately leveraged investment in an index of U.S. stocks.

(2) In category after category, Harvard and Yale selected or directly employed investment managers who were way above average in ability, providing additional evidence that investment markets are not perfectly efficient and that some good investment results come from abnormal skill or other abnormal advantage. As one example, Harvard and Yale, by reason of their own prestige, were able to get into some of the most profitable high-tech venture-capital funds, not available to all other investors. These funds, using momentum provided by their own past success, had an opportunity advantage over less well established venture capital operations, in that the best entrepreneurs, quite logically, made early presentations to the best-regarded funds.

(3) Harvard and Yale wisely and opportunistically went into several then-non-traditional activities, like investing in distressed U.S. and foreign bonds and in leveraged "fixed income arbitrage," during a period when many good opportunities were available to skilled operators in the activities chosen.

However, I do not believe that the past investment methods (including asset allocations) of Harvard and Yale, slavishly imitated, will produce automatic good results for present- day users of those methods, including Harvard and Yale. Having helped establish a new convention in academic investment, Harvard and Yale will probably have to de-emphasize much of what they have formerly done if they are to achieve continuing investment distinction. Moreover, their growth in resources managed will make future success more difficult.

"Founded in 1636, Harvard is of course the oldest institution of higher learning in the United States. Their Latin motto translates simply as 'truth.' Not to be outdone, Yale University, founded some years later in 1701, went them one better by adding 'light' to the equation."

—Munger

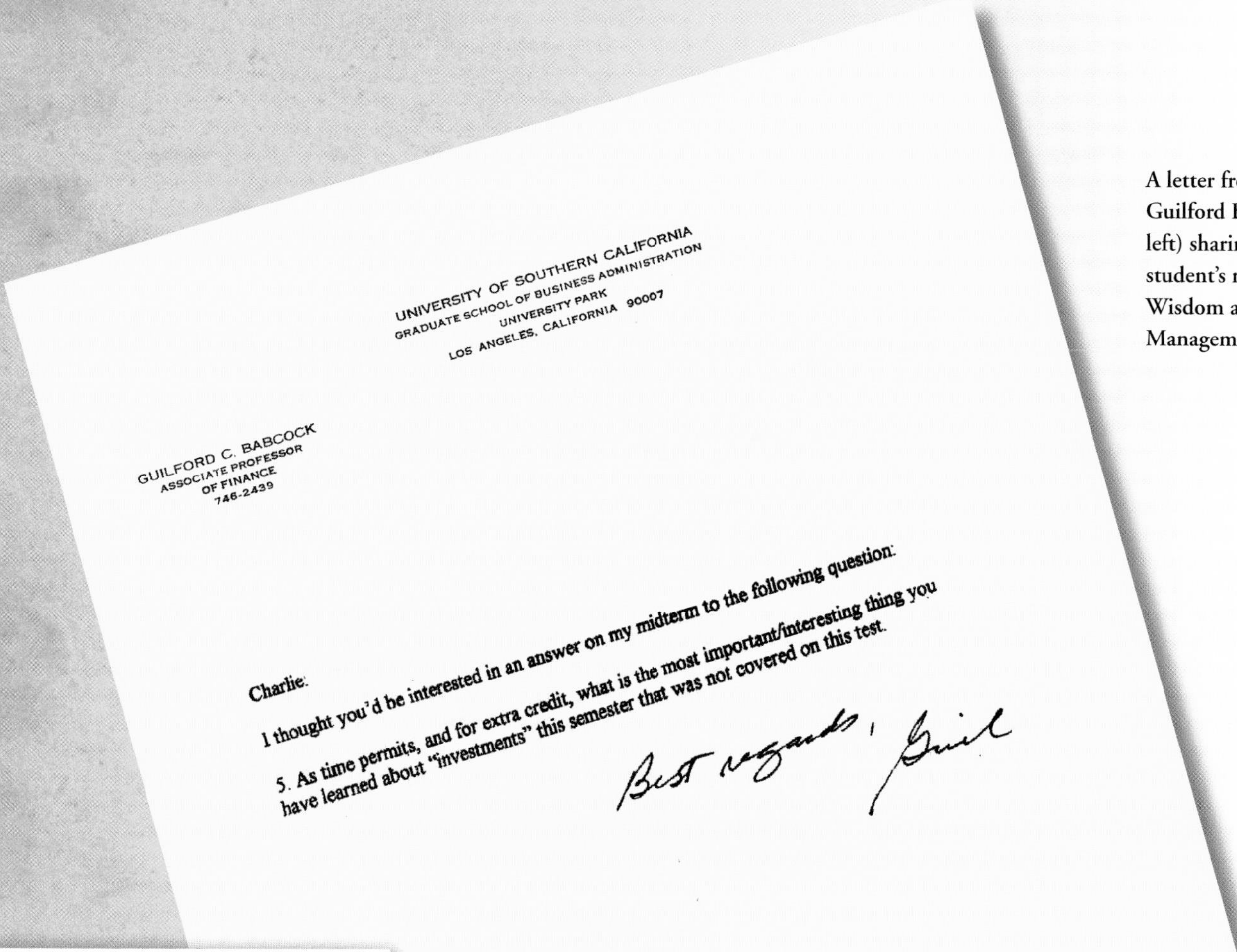

UNIVERSITY OF SOUTHERN CALIFORNIA
GRADUATE SCHOOL OF BUSINESS ADMINISTRATION
UNIVERSITY PARK
LOS ANGELES, CALIFORNIA 90007

GUILFORD C. BABCOCK
ASSOCIATE PROFESSOR
OF FINANCE
746-2439

Charlie:

I thought you'd be interested in an answer on my midterm to the following question:

5. As time permits, and for extra credit, what is the most important/interesting thing you have learned about "investments" this semester that was not covered on this test.

Best regards, Guil

A letter from USC finance professor Guilford Babcock (shown below and left) sharing with Charlie one of his student's reactions to the talk, "Worldly Wisdom as It Relates to Investment Management and Business."

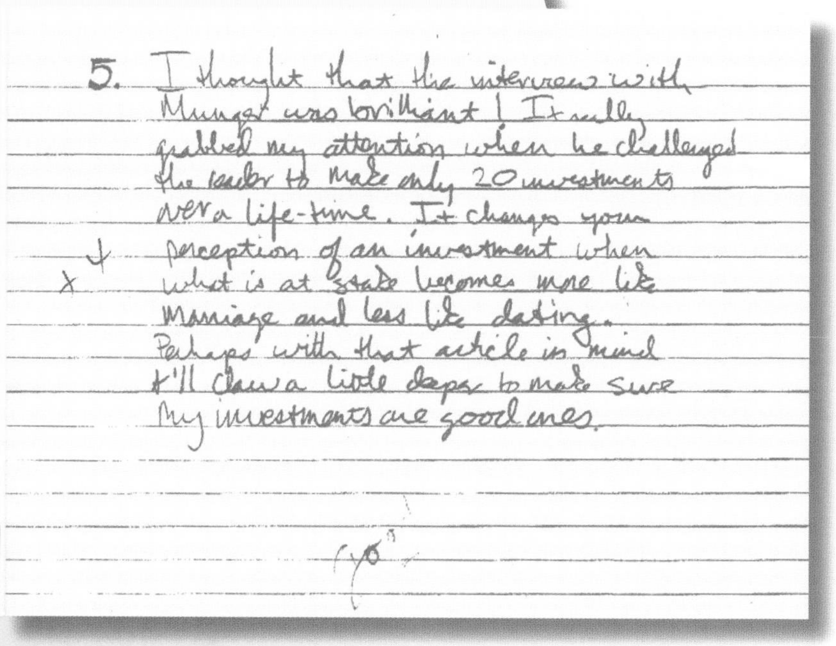

5. I thought that the interview with Munger was brilliant! It really grabbed my attention when he challenged the reader to make only 20 investments over a life-time. It changes your perception of an investment when what is at stake becomes more like marriage and less like dating. Perhaps with that article in mind I'll dig a little deeper to make sure my investments are good ones.

I Have Nothing to Add...

On occasion, Charlie will pose a challenging question to his audience, or receive one, and leave it unanswered. By so doing, he says, he encourages his listeners to "reach" for the answers themselves and, as a result, better learn and retain the information they discover. Charlie says his father routinely used this same technique with him, with results that still benefit him today.

In keeping with the promise of this book to present the wit and wisdom of Charlie Munger, we consider it a responsibility and duty to once and for all provide answers to some of the riddles and questions Charlie has long left us "reaching" for, but never quite grasping.

Here is a question occasioned by countless questions over the years at cocktail parties, etc.

Question: "All kinds of people ask me for some foolproof system for achieving financial security or saving for their retirement. I try to dodge those questions." [Editor: "But this time, Charlie, we're not going to let you dodge it."]

Answer: "Spend less than you make; always be saving something. Put it into a tax-deferred account. Over time, it will begin to amount to something. THIS IS SUCH A NO-BRAINER."

This talk was given in 1996 to the students of Professor William C. Lazier, who was the Nancy and Charles Munger professor of business at Stanford University Law School. This talk—published in *Outstanding Investor Digest* on December 29, 1997, and March 13, 1998—repeats many of the ideas and much of the language included in other talks. Your editor has abridged certain passages and added comments to maintain the logic and flow of the speech. Even with the abridgments, this talk includes many unique ideas as well as familiar ones expressed in novel ways.

A Lesson on Elementary, Worldly Wisdom, Revisited

Stanford Law School
April 19, 1996

Hoover Tower, Stanford University

What I'm going to try to do today is to extend the remarks I made two years ago at the U.S.C. Business School.... You were assigned a transcript of my U.S.C. talk. And there's nothing I said then that I wouldn't repeat today. But I want to amplify what I said then.

[It's] perfectly clear ... that if Warren Buffett had never learned anything new after graduating from the Columbia Business School, Berkshire would be a pale shadow of its present self. Warren would have gotten rich—because what he learned from Ben Graham at Columbia was enough to make anybody rich. But he wouldn't have the kind of enterprise Berkshire Hathaway is if he hadn't kept learning.

How do you get worldly wisdom? What system do you use to rise into the tiny top percentage of the world in terms of having sort of an elementary practical wisdom?

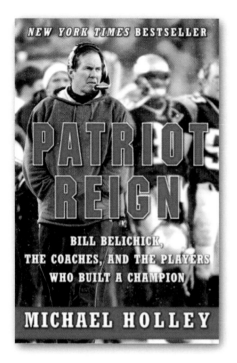

"The great leaders today are also the great teachers."

—Hall of Fame
quarterback Terry Bradshaw
on Bill Belichick, coach of
the New England Patriots,
winners of three Super Bowls
(and counting!)

I've long believed that a certain system—which almost any intelligent person can learn—works way better than the systems that most people use. As I said at the U.S.C. Business School, what you need is a latticework of mental models in your head. And you hang your actual experience and your vicarious experience (that you get from reading and so forth) on this latticework of powerful models. And, with that system, things gradually get to fit together in a way that enhances cognition.

[Charlie discusses several of the specific mental models elaborated in other talks.]

Your assigned reading for today included the latest annual letters from Jack Welch and Warren Buffett relating to General Electric and Berkshire Hathaway, respectively. Jack Welch has a Ph.D. in engineering. And Warren plainly could have gotten a Ph.D. in any field he wanted to pursue. And both gentlemen are inveterate teachers.

Worldly wisdom is quite academic when you get right down to it. Look at what General Electric has achieved—and, for that matter, what Berkshire Hathaway has achieved.

Of course, Warren had a professor/mentor—Ben Graham—for whom he had a great affection. Graham was so academic that when he graduated from Columbia, three different academic departments invited him into their Ph.D. programs and asked him to start teaching immediately as part of the Ph.D. program: [those three departments being] literature, Greek and Latin classics, and mathematics.

Graham had a very academic personality. I knew him. He was a lot like Adam Smith—very preoccupied, very brilliant. He even looked like an academic. And he was a good one. And Graham, without ever really trying to maximize the gaining of wealth, died rich—even though he was always generous and spent thirty years teaching at Columbia and authored or coauthored the best textbooks in his field.

So I would argue that academia has a lot to teach about worldly wisdom and that the best academic values really work.

Of course, when I urge a multidisciplinary approach—that you've got to have the main models from a broad array of disciplines and you've got to use them all—I'm really asking you to ignore jurisdictional boundaries.

And the world isn't organized that way. It discourages the jumping of jurisdictional boundaries. Big bureaucratic businesses discourage it. And, of course, academia itself discourages it. All I can say there is that, in that respect, academia is horribly wrong and dysfunctional.

And some of the worst dysfunctions in businesses come from the fact that they balkanize reality into little individual departments with territoriality and turf protection and so forth. So if you want to be a good thinker, you must develop a mind that can jump the jurisdictional boundaries.

You don't have to know it all. Just take in the best big ideas from all these disciplines. And it's not that hard to do.

I might try and demonstrate that point by [using the analogy of] the card game of contract bridge. Suppose you want to be good at declarer play in contract bridge. Well, you know the contract—you know what you have to achieve. And you can count up the sure winners you have by laying down your high cards and your invincible trumps.

Adam Smith
(1723–1790)

Adam Smith, born in a small village in Scotland, was an exceptional student and entered the University of Glasgow at age fourteen. He later attended Oxford, returned home to Glasgow, and began an academic career in logic and moral philosophy. His seminal work, *The Wealth of Nations*, remains the fountainhead of contemporary economic thought. Smith's explanation of how rational self-interest drives a free-market economy greatly influenced thinkers and economists in his own day and in the generations that followed. His work forms the basis of classical economics.

But if you're a trick or two short, how are you going to get the other needed tricks? Well, there are only six or so different, standard methods. You've got long suit establishment. You've got finesses. You've got throw-in plays. You've got crossruffs. You've got squeezes. And you've got various ways of misleading the defense into making errors. So it's a very limited number of models.

But if you only know one or two of those models, then you're going to be a horse's patoot in declarer play.

Furthermore, these things interact. Therefore, you have to know how the models interact. Otherwise, you can't play the hand right.

Similarly, I've told you to think forward and backward. Well, great declarers in bridge think, "How can I take the necessary winners?" But they think it through backwards, [too. They also think,] "What could possibly go wrong that could cause me to have too many losers? And both methods of thinking are useful. So [to win in] the game of life, get the needed models into your head and think it through forward and backward. What works in bridge will work in life.

That contract bridge is so out of vogue in your generation is a tragedy. China is way smarter than we are about bridge. They're teaching bridge in grade school now. And God knows the Chinese do well enough when introduced to capitalist civilization. If we compete with a bunch of people that really know how to play bridge when our people don't, it'll be just one more disadvantage we don't need.

Since your academic structure, by and large, doesn't encourage minds jumping jurisdictional boundaries, you're at a disadvantage because, in that one sense, even though academia's very useful to you, you've been mistaught.

My solution for you is one that I got at a very early age from the nursery: the story of the Little Red Hen. The punch line, of course, is, "'Then I'll do it myself,' said the Little Red Hen."

The *Little Red Hen* is a classic fable teaching the value of self-reliance in connection with important things. Charlie's advice on self-learning is reminiscent of Mark Twain's classic line, "I have never let my schooling interfere with my education."

"'Then I'll do it myself,' said the Little Red Hen."

So if your professors won't give you an appropriate multidisciplinary approach— if each wants to overuse his own models and underuse the important models in other disciplines—you can correct that folly yourself. Just because he's a horse's patoot, you don't have to be one, too. You can reach out and grasp the model that better solves the overall problem. All you have to do is know it and develop the right mental habits.

And it's kind of fun to sit there and outthink people who are way smarter than you are because you've trained yourself to be more objective and multidisciplinary....

Furthermore, there's a lot of money in it—as I can testify from my own personal experience.

Hershey Food Corporation

Raised in rural central Pennsylvania and possessed of little formal education, Milton S. Hershey (1857–1945) became one of America's wealthiest individuals. He started his own candy business, Lancaster Caramel Company, in 1876 and failed after only six years. Undaunted, he tried again and had great success. In 1893, he learned the art of chocolate making and started the Hershey Chocolate Company. As the company expanded into other food products, Hershey began to build the Pennsylvania town that bears his name. Hershey's utopian ideas and principles continue to influence the company and the town.

[In the unabridged edition Charlie presents a Coca-Cola business case study entitled, "Practical Thought About Practical Thought?" and discusses the importance of flavor.]

One of my favorite business stories comes from Hershey. They get their flavor because they make their cocoa butter in old stone grinders that they started with in the 1800s in Pennsylvania. And a little bit of the husk of the cocoa bean winds up in the chocolate. Therefore, they get that odd flavor that people like in Hershey's chocolate.

Hershey knew enough when they wanted to expand into Canada to know they shouldn't change their winning flavor.

Hershey knew enough when they wanted to expand into Canada to know they shouldn't change their winning flavor. Therefore, they copied their stone grinders. Well, it took them five years to duplicate their own flavor. As you can see, flavors can be quite tricky.

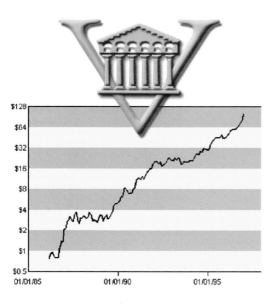

Value Line

Value Line's mission is "to help investors get the most accurate and independently created research information available, in any format they choose, and teach them how to use it to meet their financial objectives." In operation since 1931, Value Line has a solid reputation for reliability, objectivity, independence, and accuracy. Best known for the *Value Line Investment Survey*, the company publishes dozens of print and electronic research products.

Even today, there's a company called International Flavors and Fragrances. It's the only company I know that does something on which you can't get a copyright or a patent, but which nevertheless receives a permanent royalty. They manage to do that by helping companies develop flavors and aromas in their trademarked products—like shaving cream. The slight aroma of shaving cream is very important to consumption. So all of this stuff is terribly important.

[Continuing the Coca-Cola case study, Charlie explains how our understanding of graphic depictions of mathematical ideas are rooted in biology.]

My friend, Dr. Nat Myhrvold, who's the chief technology officer at Microsoft, is bothered by this. He's a Ph.D. physicist and knows a lot of math. And it disturbs him that biology could create a neural apparatus that could do automatic differential equations at fast speed—and, yet, everywhere he looks, people are total klutzes at dealing with ordinary probabilities and ordinary numbers.

By the way, I think Myhrvold's wrong to be amazed by that. The so-called fitness landscape of our ancestors forced them to know how to throw spears, run around, turn corners, and what have you long before they had to think correctly like Myhrvold. So I don't think he should be so surprised. However, the difference is so extreme that I can understand how he finds it incongruous.

Mankind invented a system to cope with the fact that we are so intrinsically lousy at manipulating numbers. It's called the graph.

At any rate, mankind invented a system to cope with the fact that we are so intrinsically lousy at manipulating numbers. It's called the graph. Oddly enough, it came out of the Middle Ages. And it's the only intellectual invention of the monks during the Middle Ages I know of that's worth a damn. The graph puts numbers in a form that looks like motion. So it's using some of this primitive neural stuff in your system in a way that helps you understand it. So the Value Line graphs are very useful.

The graph I've distributed is on log paper—which is based on the natural table of logarithms. And that's based on the elementary mathematics of compound interest—which is one of the most important models there is on earth. So there's a reason why that graph is in that form.

And if you draw a straight line through data points on a graph on log paper, it will tell you the rate at which compound interest is working for you. So these graphs are marvelously useful....

I don't use Value Line's predictions because our system works better for us than theirs—in fact, a lot better. But I can't imagine not having their graphs and their data. It's a marvelous, marvelous product....

[Charlie discusses the importance of trademarks to Coca-Cola's success and carries it over to a discussion of food products and Carnation.]

Now, when Carnation tried to make a deal for its trademark, there was this one guy who sold Carnation Fish. So help me God, that was his trade name. Don't ask me why. And every time they'd say, "We'll pay you $250,000," he'd say, "I want $400,000." And, then, four years later, they'd say, "We'll give you $1 million," and he'd say, "I want $2 million." And they just kept doing that all the way through. And they never did buy the trademark—at least, they hadn't bought it the last time I looked.

In the end, Carnation came to him sheepfacedly and said, "We'd like to put our quality control inspectors into your fish plants to make sure that your fish are perfect; and we'll pay all the costs"—which he quickly and smirkily allowed. So he got free quality control in his fish plants—courtesy of the Carnation Company.

This history shows the enormous incentive you create if you give a guy a trademark [he can protect]. And this incentive is very useful to the wider civilization. As you see, Carnation got so that it was protecting products that it didn't even own.

Carnation Company

In 1899, grocer E. A. Stuart founded the Pacific Coast Condensed Milk Company in the state of Washington based on the relatively new process of evaporation. Using a local tobacconist's store name, Carnation, he had a brand for his new milk product. Through attention to processes and clever marketing, Carnation became associated with its "Contented Cows" and high-quality milk products. In 1985, the company was acquired by Nestle.

That sort of outcome is very, very desirable [for society]. So there are some very fundamental microeconomic reasons why even communist countries should protect trademarks. They don't all do it, but there are very powerful reasons why they should. And, by and large, averaged out around the world, trademark protection's been pretty good.

[Charlie applies various mental models to Coca-Cola.]

However, if you don't have the basic models and the basic mental methods for dealing with the models, then all you can do is to sit there twiddling your thumbs as you look at the Value Line graph. But you don't have to twiddle your thumbs. You've got to learn one hundred models and a few mental tricks and keep doing it all of your life. It's not that hard.

And the beauty of it is that most people won't do it—partly because they've been miseducated. And I'm here trying to help you avoid some of the perils that might otherwise result from that miseducation.

OK. We've been through some of the general ideas in the search for worldly wisdom. And now I want to turn to something even more extreme and peculiar than the talk I've already given you. Of all the models that people ought to have in useful form and don't, perhaps the most important lie in the area of psychology....

I recently had an instructive experience: I just returned from Hong Kong. I have a pal there who's a headmaster of one of the leading schools. He gave me this book called *The Language Instinct,* written by Steven Pinker. Well, Pinker is a semanticist professor who rose in the shadow of Noam Chomsky—Linguistics Institute Professor at M.I.T.—who is probably the greatest semanticist who ever lived.

Steven Pinker
(b. 1954)

Born in Montreal, Steven Pinker earned a degree in experimental psychology at McGill University and then moved on to Harvard for his doctorate. He has taught at Harvard and MIT at various times and is currently the Johnstone Family Professor in the Department of Psychology at Harvard. Pinker is interested in language and the mind, including the field of visual cognition. That field encompasses the ability to imagine shapes and recognize faces and objects. He specializes in language development in children and has written many important papers and books on this and other topics.

And Pinker says that human language ability is not just learned—it's deeply buried, to a considerable extent, in the genome. It's not in the genome of the other animals, including the chimpanzee, to any really useful extent. It's a gift that came to humans. And Pinker proves his point pretty well.

Of course, Chomsky's already proven it. You have to be pretty ignorant not to realize that a good deal of language ability is right there in the human genome. And even though you have to work like hell to improve it through education, you start with a big leg up in your genes.

Pinker can't understand why Chomsky—who, again, is such a genius—takes the position that the jury's still out about why this ability is in the human genome. Pinker, in effect, says: "Like hell, the jury is still out! The language instinct got into humans in exactly the same way that everything else got there— through Darwinian natural selection."

> ## *"The language instinct got into humans in exactly the same way that everything else got there—through Darwinian natural selection."*

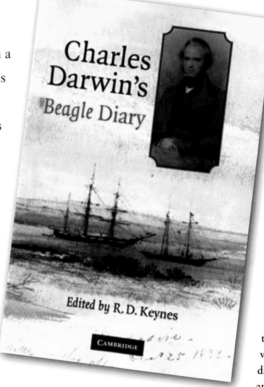

Young Charles Darwin was the unpaid "official naturalist" aboard the *H.M.S. Beagle* during its 1831–1836 around-the-world surveying voyage. The amazing differentiation of species among the Galapagos Islands off South America inspired Darwin to remark, "This appears to be one of those admirable provisions of Infinite Wisdom by which each created thing is adapted to the place for which it was intended."

Well, the junior professor is clearly right—and Chomsky's hesitation is a little daft.

But if the junior professor and I are right, how has a genius like Chomsky made an obvious misjudgment? The answer's quite clear to me—Chomsky is passionately ideological. He is an extreme egalitarian leftist who happens to be a genius. And he's so smart that he realized that if he concedes this particular Darwinian point, the implications threaten his leftist ideology. So he naturally has his conclusion affected by his ideological bias.

And that gets into another lesson in worldly wisdom: If ideology can screw up the head of Chomsky, imagine what it does to people like you and me.

Heavy ideology is one of the most extreme distorters of human cognition. Look at these Islamic fundamentalists who just gunned down a bunch of Greek tourists shouting, "God's work!"

Ideology does some strange things and distorts cognition terribly. If you get a lot of heavy ideology young—and then you start expressing it—you are really locking your brain into a very unfortunate pattern. And you are going to distort your general cognition.

> *If you get a lot of heavy ideology young—and then you start expressing it—you are really locking your brain into a very unfortunate pattern.*

"I wear the chains I forged in life," quoth Jacob Marley's ghost in Dickens' *A Christmas Carol.*

There's a very interesting history if you take Warren Buffett as an example of worldly wisdom: Warren adored his father—who was a wonderful man. But Warren's father was a very heavy ideologue (right wing, it happened to be), who hung around with other very heavy ideologues (right wing, naturally).

Warren observed this as a kid. And he decided that ideology was dangerous— and that he was going to stay a long way away from it. And he has throughout his whole life. That has enormously helped the accuracy of his cognition.

I learned the same lesson in a different way. My father hated ideology. Therefore, all I had to do was imitate my father and, thereby, stay on what I regard as the right path. People like Dornan on the right or Nader on the left have obviously gone a little daft. They're extreme examples of what ideology will do to you—particularly violently expressed ideology. Since it pounds ideas in better than it convinces out, it's a very dangerous thing to do.

Therefore, in a system of multiple models across multiple disciplines, I should add as an extra rule that you should be very wary of heavy ideology.

You can have heavy ideology in favor of accuracy, diligence, and objectivity. But a heavy ideology that makes you absolutely sure that the minimum wage should be raised or that it shouldn't—and it's kind of a holy construct where you know you're right—makes you a bit nuts.

This is a very complicated system. And life is one damn relatedness after another. It's all right to think that, on balance, you suspect that civilization is better if it lowers the minimum wage or raises it. Either position is OK. But being totally sure on issues like that with a strong, violent ideology, in my opinion, turns you into a lousy thinker. So beware of ideology-based mental misfunctions.

[Charlie laments how poorly the field of psychology deals with incentive-caused bias.]

About three centuries before the birth of Christ, Demosthenes said, "What a man wishes, that also will he believe."

Another reason that I mentioned Pinker, the semanticist who wrote the book that I told you about earlier, is that at the end of his book, he says (roughly), "I've read the psychology textbooks. And they're daft." He says, "This whole subject is misorganized and mistaught."

Well, I have far less in the way of qualifications than Pinker. In fact, I've never taken a single course in psychology. However, I've come to exactly the same conclusion—that the psychology texts, while they are wonderful in part, are also significantly daft.

In fact, just take simple psychological denial. About three centuries before the birth of Christ, Demosthenes said, "What a man wishes, that also will he believe." Well, Demosthenes was right.

Michael Faraday
(1791–1867)

Famous for his investigations of physics, chemistry, and electricity, Michael Faraday's wisdom includes:

"Nothing is too wonderful to be true."

"Work. Finish. Publish." (his advice to the young William Crookes, later a famous chemist and physicist in his own right)

"The five essential entrepreneurial skills for success are concentration, discrimination, organization, innovation, and communication."

"Why, sir, there is every possibility that you will soon be able to tax it!" (to Prime Minister William Gladstone, on the usefulness of electricity)

I had a family acquaintance whose much-loved son—who was brilliant and a star football player—flew off over the ocean and never came back. Well, his mother thought he was still alive. The mind will sometimes flip so that the wish becomes the belief. It will do so at various levels. Individuals vary in how much psychological denial they get. But miscognition from denial overwhelmingly pervades the reality that you're going to have to deal with. And yet, you won't find an adequate treatment of simple psychological denial in psychology texts.

So you can't learn psychology the way your professors teach it. You've got to learn everything they teach. But you've got to learn a lot more that they don't teach—because they don't handle their own subject correctly.

Psychology to me, as currently organized, is like electromagnetism after Faraday, but before Maxwell—a lot has been discovered, but no one mind has put it all together in proper form. And it should be done because it wouldn't be that hard to do—and it's enormously important.

Just open a psychology text, turn to the index, and look up envy. Well, envy made it into one or two or three of the Ten Commandments. Moses knew all about envy. The old Jews, when they were herding sheep, knew all about envy. It's just that psychology professors don't know about envy.

Books that thick are teaching a psychology course without envy?! And with no simple psychological denial?! And no incentive-caused bias?!

And psychological texts don't deal adequately with combinations of factors. I told you earlier to be aware of the lollapalooza effect when two or three or more forces are operating in the same direction.

Well, the single most publicized psychology experiment ever done is the Milgram experiment—where they asked people to apply what they had every reason to believe was heavy electrical torture on innocent fellow human beings. And they manipulated most of these decent volunteers into doing the torture.

So you can't learn psychology the way your professors teach it. You've got to learn everything they teach. But you've got to learn a lot more that they don't teach—because they don't handle their own subject correctly.

**Stanley Milgram
Experiments on Authority**

Stanley Milgram, born in 1933 in New York, grew up during World War II when Nazi atrocities became well known to the world. He earned a political science degree from Queens College and went on to Harvard for a Ph.D. in social relations. He took a faculty position at Yale, where he conducted a classic experiment that pitted the subject's moral beliefs against the demands of authority.

His experiment found that sixty-five percent of his subjects, ordinary residents of New Haven, were willing to give apparently harmful electric shocks to a pitifully protesting victim, simply because a scientific authority commanded them to, despite the fact that the victim did nothing to deserve punishment. Milgram's results have been used as partial explanation for the German atrocities of World War II.

Milgram performed the experiment right after Hitler had gotten a bunch of believing Lutherans, Catholics, and so forth to perform unholy acts they should have known were wrong. He was trying to find out how much authority could be used to manipulate high-grade people into doing things that were clearly and grossly wrong.

And he got a very dramatic effect. He managed to get high-grade people to do many awful things.

But for years, it was in the psychology books as a demonstration of authority—how authority could be used to persuade people to do awful things.

Of course, that's mere first-conclusion bias. That's not the complete and correct explanation. Authority is part of it. However, there were also quite a few other psychological principles, all operating in the same direction, that achieved that lollapalooza effect precisely because they acted in combination toward the same end.

People have gradually figured that out. And if you read the recent psychology texts at a place like Stanford, you'll see that they've now managed to get it about two-thirds right. However, here's the main experiment in all of psychology. And even at Stanford, they still leave out some of the important causes of Milgram's results.

How can smart people be so wrong? Well, the answer is that they don't do what I'm telling you to do—which is to take all the main models from psychology and use them as a checklist in reviewing outcomes in complex systems.

No pilot takes off without going through his checklist: A, B, C, D.... And no bridge player who needs two extra tricks plays a hand without going down his checklist and figuring out how to do it.

But these psychology professors think they're so smart that they don't need a checklist. But they aren't that smart. Almost nobody is. Or, maybe, nobody is.

No pilot takes off without going through his checklist: A, B, C, D.... But these psychology professors think they're so smart that they don't need a checklist.

If they used a checklist, they'd realize the Milgram experiment harnesses six psychological principles, at least—not three. All they'd have to do is to go down the checklist to see the ones that they missed.

Similarly, without this system of getting the main models and using them together in a multimodular way, you'll screw up time after time after time, too.

One reason psychology professors so screw up denial is that it's hard to do demonstrative experiments without conduct forbidden by ethics. To demonstrate how misery creates mental disfunction in people, think of what you'd have to do to your fellow human beings. And you'd have to do it without telling them about the injury to come. So, clearly, there are ethical reasons why it's practically impossible to do the experiments necessary to best lay out the ways human misery creates human mental misfunction.

Most professors solve this problem, in effect, by assuming, "If I can't demonstrate it with my experiments, then it doesn't exist." However, obviously, that's asinine. If something is very important but can't be perfectly and precisely demonstrated because of ethical constraints, you can't just treat it like it doesn't exist. You have to do the best you can with it—with such evidence as is available.

Pavlov himself spent the last ten years of his life torturing dogs. And he published. Thus, we have a vast amount of data about misery-caused mental misfunction in dogs—and its correction. Yet, it's in no introductory psychology book that you'll ever see.

I don't know whether they don't like the fact that Pavlov tortured dogs or whether B. F. Skinner, by overclaiming when he lapsed into his literary mode, made the drawing of implications from animal behavior into human behavior unpopular. However, for some crazy reason or other, the psychology books are grossly inadequate in dealing with misery-caused mental misfunction.

You may say, "What difference does all this psychological ignorance make?" Well, if I'm right, you need these models that are blanked out by this ignorance. And, furthermore, you need them in a form whereby, if there are twenty constructs,

Portrait of Ivan Pavlov, Mikhail Nesterov, 1935, The Tretyakov Gallery, Moscow

Ivan Pavlov
(1849–1936)

Ivan Pavlov was born in central Russia and attended seminary until age twenty-one, when he abandoned theology in favor of chemistry and physiology. Earning his M.D. in 1883, he excelled in physiology and surgical techniques. Later, he studied the secretory activity of digestion and ultimately formulated the laws of conditioned reflexes.

Pavlov's most famous experiment showed that dogs tend to salivate before food is actually delivered to their mouths. This result led him to a long series of experiments in which he manipulated the stimuli occurring before the presentation of food. He thereby established the basic laws for the establishment and extinction of what he called "conditional reflexes," later mistranslated from the original Russian as "conditioned reflexes." He was awarded the Nobel Prize in 1904 for his work on digestive secretions.

you have all twenty. In other words, you shouldn't be operating with ten. And you need to use them as a checklist. So you have to go back and put in your own head what I'd call the psychology of misjudgment in a form whereby you have all of the important models and you can use them.

And you especially need them when four or five forces from these models come together to operate in the same direction. In such cases, you often get lollapalooza effects—which can make you rich or they can kill you. So it's essential that you beware of lollapalooza effects.

There's only one right way to do it: You have to get the main doctrines together and use them as a checklist. And, to repeat for emphasis, you have to pay special attention to combinatorial effects that create lollapalooza consequences.

[Charlie discusses the lack of multidisciplinary teaching in the professions, especially how the field of psychology is virtually ignored in academia.]

You can also learn when you're playing the game of persuasion— for a reputable reason [I hope]—to combine these forces in a way that makes you more effective.

Let me give you an example of that—of wise psychology of yore. In Captain Cook's day, he took these long voyages. At the time, scurvy was the dread of the long voyage. And in scurvy, your living gums putrefy in your mouth—after which the disease gets unpleasant and kills you.

And being on a primitive sailing ship with a bunch of dying sailors is a very awkward business. So everybody was terribly interested in scurvy, but they didn't

The game of persuasion, the disreputable sort.

Elmer Gantry, a novel by Sinclair Lewis (1927) and later a film starring Burt Lancaster (1960), is a satiric depiction of a loud, overbearing huckster. Later he becomes a successful but greedy, shallow, and philandering minister to a large congregation.

know about vitamin C. Well, Captain Cook, being a smart man with a multiple-model kind of approach, noticed that Dutch ships had less scurvy than English ships on long voyages. So he said, "What are the Dutch doing that's different?"

And he noticed they had all these barrels of sauerkraut. So he thought, "I'm going on these long voyages. And it's very dangerous. Sauerkraut may help." So he laid in all this sauerkraut, which, incidentally, happens to contain a trace of vitamin C.

But English sailors were a tough, cranky, and dangerous bunch in that day. They hated "krauts." And they were used to their standard food and booze. So how do you get such English sailors to eat sauerkraut?

Well, Cook didn't want to tell 'em that he was doing it in the hope it would prevent scurvy—because they might mutiny and take over the ship if they thought that he was taking them on a voyage so long that scurvy was likely.

So here's what he did: Officers ate one place where the men could observe them. And for a long time, he served sauerkraut to the officers, but not to the men. And, then, finally, Captain Cook said, "Well, the men can have it one day a week."

In due course, he had the whole crew eating sauerkraut. I regard that as a very constructive use of elementary psychology. It may have saved God knows how many lives and caused God knows how much achievement. However, if you don't know the right techniques, you can't use them.

[Charlie discusses psychological effects in play in marketing of consumer items, such as Coca-Cola, Procter & Gamble products, Tupperware, etc.]

Captain James Cook
(1728–1779)

Born in Marton, England, James Cook developed an early fascination for the sea and taught himself cartography. He served in the Royal Navy, participating in the siege of Quebec City and showing a talent for surveying and cartography. He mapped much of the entrance to the Saint Lawrence River during the siege. Later, he mapped the coast of Newfoundland, which brought him to the attention of the Royal Society, sponsor of many of his great voyages. In addition to having first-class cartographic skills, Cook developed excellent seamanship and displayed great courage in exploring dangerous locations. His voyages are chronicled in books that were extremely popular in his day and remain so today.

Serpico
(1973)

Serpico was a popular film directed by Sidney Lumet, based on the book by journalist Peter Maas of a "true story." The plot concerns undercover police officer Frank Serpico who does his best arresting criminals of all types, but especially drug dealers, despite working in a corrupt police department. Serpico refuses to accept bribes and becomes sufficiently appalled at his shady colleagues that he testifies against them, thus placing his life in jeopardy. Set in the early 1970s, the film makes several references to "hippie" culture and thus appears somewhat dated to current viewers. Al Pacino appeared in the title role and earned an Academy Award nomination for his acting. The film was also nominated for a screenwriting Oscar.

Worldly wisdom is mostly very, very simple. And what I'm urging on you is not that hard to do if you have the will to plow through and do it. And the rewards are awesome—absolutely awesome.

But maybe you aren't interested in awesome rewards or avoiding a lot of misery or being more able to serve everything you love in life. And, if that's your attitude, then don't pay attention to what I've been trying to tell you—because you're already on the right track.

It can't be emphasized too much that issues of morality are deeply entwined with worldly wisdom considerations involving psychology. For example, take the issue of stealing. A very significant fraction of the people in the world will steal if (A) it's very easy to do and (B) there's practically no chance of being caught.

And once they start stealing, the consistency principle—which is a big part of human psychology—will soon combine with operant conditioning to make stealing habitual. So if you run a business where it's easy to steal because of your methods, you're working a great moral injury on the people who work for you.

> *It can't be emphasized too much that issues of morality are deeply entwined with worldly wisdom considerations involving psychology.*

Again, that's obvious. It's very, very important to create human systems that are hard to cheat. Otherwise, you're ruining your civilization because these big incentives will create incentive-caused bias and people will rationalize that bad behavior is OK.

Then, if somebody else does it, now you've got at least two psychological principles: incentive-caused bias plus social proof. Not only that, but you get Serpico effects: If enough people are profiting in a general social climate of doing wrong, then they'll turn on you and become dangerous enemies if you try and blow the whistle.

It's very dangerous to ignore these principles and let slop creep in. Powerful psychological forces are at work for evil.

How does this relate to the law business? Well, people graduate from places like Stanford Law School and go into the legislatures of our nation and, with the best of motives, pass laws that are easily used by people to cheat. Well, there could hardly be a worse thing you could do.

Let's say you have a desire to do public service. As a natural part of your planning, you think in reverse and ask, "What can I do to ruin our civilization?" That's easy. If what you want to do is to ruin your civilization, just go to the legislature and pass laws that create systems wherein people can easily cheat. It will work perfectly.

Take the workers' compensation system in California. Stress is real. And its misery can be real. So you want to compensate people for their stress in the workplace. It seems like a noble thing to do.

But the trouble with such a compensation practice is that it's practically impossible to delete huge cheating. And once you reward cheating, you get crooked lawyers, crooked doctors, crooked unions, etc., participating in referral schemes. You get a total miasma of disastrous behavior. And the behavior makes all the people doing it worse as they do it. So you were trying to help your civilization. But what you did was create enormous damage, net.

So it's much better to let some things go uncompensated—to let life be hard—than to create systems that are easy to cheat.

Let me give you an example: I have a friend who made an industrial product at a plant in Texas not far from the border. He was in a low-margin, tough business. He got massive fraud in the workers' compensation system—to the point that his premiums reached double-digit percentages of payroll. And it was not that dangerous to produce his product. It's not like he was a demolition contractor or something.

When the Incentives are Wrong: What a Pain!

Employee fraud in medical disability cases is often an outgrowth of hard-to-diagnose complaints such as ever-popular "back pain." But disability fraud extends as well to scams perpetrated by medical practitioners, including phantom treatments, double billing, unnecessary care, and unneeded tests. Charlie's point is that the system as designed invites cheating and that human beings are psychologically predisposed to commit fraud when available incentives overwhelm structural checks and balances. As he puts it, "If you want to change behaviors, you have to change motivations."

The importance of honesty was amplified by the Mormon Apostle Mark E. Petersen when he said:

"Honesty is a principle of salvation in the kingdom of God. Just as no man or woman can be saved without baptism, so no one can be saved without honesty."

So he pleaded with the union, "You've got to stop this. There's not enough money in making this product to cover all of this fraud."

But, by then, everyone's used to it. "It's extra income. It's extra money. Everybody does it. It can't be that wrong. Eminent lawyers, eminent doctors, eminent chiropractors—if there are any such things—are cheating."

And no one could tell them, "You can't do it anymore." Incidentally, that's Pavlovian mere association, too. When people get bad news, they hate the messenger. Therefore, it was very hard for the union representative to tell all of these people that the easy money was about to stop. That is not the way to advance as a union representative.

So my friend closed his plant and moved the work to Utah among a community of believing Mormons.

So my friend closed his plant and moved the work to Utah among a community of believing Mormons. Well, the Mormons aren't into workers' compensation fraud—at least they aren't in my friend's plant. And guess what his workers' compensation expense is today? It's two percent of payroll [—down from double-digits.]

This sort of tragedy is caused by letting the slop run. You must stop slop early. It's very hard to stop slop and moral failure if you let it run for a while.

[Charlie describes his notion of "deprival super-reaction syndrome" as it relates to gambling and the New Coke debacle of the mid-1980s.]

Of course, as I said before, there is one big consideration that needs huge and special attention as part of any use of techniques deliberately harnessing elementary psychological forces: And that is that once you know how to do it, there are real moral limits regarding how much you should do it. Not all of what you know how to do should you use to manipulate people.

Also, if you're willing to transcend the moral limits and the person you're trying to manipulate realizes what you're doing because he also understands the psychology, he'll hate you. There is wonderfully persuasive evidence of this effect taken from labor relations— some in Israel. So not only are there moral objections, but there are also practical objections—big ones in some cases....

What makes investment hard, as I said at U.S.C., is that it's easy to see that some companies have better businesses than others. But the price of the stock goes up so high that, all of a sudden, the question of which stock is the best to buy gets quite difficult.

Q: How do you incorporate psychology in your investment decisions? I think it would be more than just picking products that will appeal to everybody like Coke. After all, there are a lot of smart people out there who obviously think just the way that you showed us today. So are you looking for failure in the thinking of other investors when you go about picking successful companies?

What makes investment hard, as I said at U.S.C., is that it's easy to see that some companies have better businesses than others. But the price of the stock goes up so high that, all of a sudden, the question of which stock is the best to buy gets quite difficult.

The University of Southern California, boasting recent back-to-back national football championships, was founded in 1880 and is the oldest private research university in the West. There are 16,500 undergraduate and 15,500 graduate and professional students attending the university.

We've never eliminated the difficulty of that problem. And ninety-eight percent of the time, our attitude toward the market is ... [that] we're agnostics. We don't know. Is GM valued properly vis-à-vis Ford? We don't know.

We're always looking for something where we think we have an insight which gives us a big statistical advantage. And sometimes it comes from psychology, but often it comes from something else. And we only find a few—maybe one or two a year. We have no system for having automatic good judgment on all investment decisions that can be made. Ours is a totally different system.

We just look for no-brainer decisions. As Buffett and I say over and over again, we don't leap seven-foot fences. Instead, we look for one-foot fences with big rewards on the other side. So we've succeeded by making the world easy for ourselves, not by solving hard problems.

Q: Based on statistical analysis and insight?

Well, certainly when we do make a decision, we think that we have an insight advantage. And it's true that some of the insight is statistical in nature. However, again, we find only a few of those.

We just look for no-brainer decisions. As Buffett and I say over and over again, we don't leap seven-foot fences.

It doesn't help us merely for favorable odds to exist. They have to be in a place where we can recognize them. So it takes a mispriced opportunity that we're smart enough to recognize. And that combination doesn't occur often.

But it doesn't have to. If you wait for the big opportunity and have the courage and vigor to grasp it firmly when it arrives, how many do you need? For example, take the top ten business investments Berkshire Hathaway's ever made. We would be very rich if we'd never done anything else—in two lifetimes.

So, once again, we don't have any system for giving you perfect investment judgment on all subjects at all times. That would be ridiculous. I'm just trying to give you a method you can use to sift reality to obtain an occasional opportunity for rational reaction.

If you take that method into something as competitive as common stock picking, you're competing with many brilliant people. So, even with our method, we only get a few opportunities. Fortunately, that happens to be enough.

Q: Have you been successful in creating an atmosphere where people below you can do the same things you're talking about doing yourself? For example, you talked about the tendency towards commitment and consistency….

Mostly about the terrible mistakes it causes you to make.

Q: How have you created an atmosphere comfortable [enough] for people to abandon that tendency and admit that they've made a mistake?

For example, someone here earlier this year from Intel talked about problems that occurred with their Pentium chip. One of the most difficult things for them to do was to realize they'd been going about it the wrong way and turn course. And it's very difficult to do that in a complex structure. How do you foster that?

Intel and its ilk create a coherent culture where teams solve difficult problems on the cutting edge of science. That's radically different from Berkshire Hathaway. Berkshire is a holding company. We've decentralized all the power except for natural headquarters-type capital allocation.

By and large, we've chosen people we admire enormously to have the power beneath us. It's easy for us to get along with them on average because we love and admire them. And they create the culture for whatever invention and reality recognition is going on in their businesses. And included in that reality recognition is the recognition that previous conclusions were incorrect.

But we're a totally different kind of company. It's not at all clear to me that Warren or I would be that good at doing what Andy Grove does. We don't have

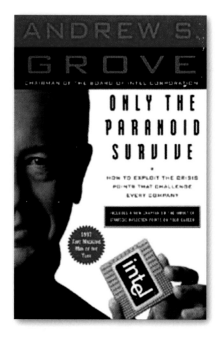

Andy Grove
(b. 1936)

Born András Grós in Budapest, Hungary, Grove earned a bachelor's degree in chemical engineering from the City College of New York and a Ph.D. from the University of California, Berkeley. He worked at Fairchild Semiconductor before becoming the fourth employee at the nascent Intel Corporation. He became Intel's president in 1979, its CEO in 1987, and its chairman and CEO in 1997. Author of several academic and mass-trade books, his 1996 work, *Only the Paranoid Survive,* was hugely popular. Grove continues to work at Intel as a senior advisor. This book is on Charlie's recommended book list.

special competence in that field. We are fairly good at relating to brilliant people we love. But we have defects. For example, some regard me as absent-minded and opinionated. I might be a mess at Intel.

However, both Warren and I are very good at changing our prior conclusions. We work at developing that facility because, without it, disaster often comes.

Q: Would you talk a little bit about your seeming predilection away from investing in high technology stocks—on your own part and the part of Berkshire Hathaway. One of the things I've found eye-opening and a little surprising is how the difficulties of running a low-tech business and those of running a high-tech business aren't all that different.

They're all hard. But why should it be easy to get rich? In a competitive world, shouldn't it be impossible for there to be an easy way for everybody to get rich? Of course, they're all hard.

And, yes—a low-tech business can be plenty hard. Just try to open a restaurant and make it succeed.

The reason we're not in high-tech businesses is that we have a special lack of aptitude in that area. And, yes—a low-tech business can be plenty hard. Just try to open a restaurant and make it succeed.

Q: You seem to be suggesting that there's special aptitude required in high-tech businesses—that they're harder. But aren't they equally difficult?

The advantage of low-tech stuff for us is that we think we understand it fairly well. The other stuff we don't. And we'd rather deal with what we understand.

Why should we want to play a competitive game in a field where we have no advantage—maybe a disadvantage—instead of in a field where we have a clear advantage?

Catching Up with George McGovern

Q: Someone mentioned to me that you tried to open up a bed-and-breakfast, and you ran into a lot of rules and regulations that made being a small businessman difficult.

A: I had a 140-room hotel in Stamford, Connecticut, for about three years, and it just didn't work. You know, the hotel business may be the most difficult place in the world to make a living unless you happen to own the Waldorf-Astoria. It was not a success.

I got sued a couple times by people who had accidents, one out in the parking lot of the hotel and one leaving the restaurant. I saw all the difficulties—record-keeping, keeping track of the tax applications, paying the help. It gave me a new appreciation for the problems of small businesses.

Saturday, 24 July 2004, Interview 2004© by Bill Steigerwald and the *Pittsburgh Tribune-Review*

Each of you will have to figure out where your talents lie. And you'll have to use your advantages. But if you try to succeed in what you're worst at, you're going to have a very lousy career. I can almost guarantee it. To do otherwise, you'd have to buy a winning lottery ticket or get very lucky somewhere else.

Q: Warren Buffett has said that the investment Berkshire made in an airline was a good example of what not to do. What chain of thinking led to that wrong decision?

We were not buying stock in USAir on the theory that the common shareholders were certain to prosper—because the history of the airline business in terms of taking care of shareholders has been terrible. It was a preferred stock with a mandatory redemption. In effect, we were loaning money to USAir, and we had this equity kicker.

We weren't guessing whether it would be a great place for the shareholders. We were guessing whether it would remain prosperous enough to pay off a credit instrument—carrying a fixed dividend and a mandatory redemption. And we guessed that the business would not get so bad that we'd have a credit threat for which we were not being adequately compensated by the high rate we were getting. As it happened, USAir went right to the brink of going broke. It was hanging by a thread for several months. It's since come back. And we'll probably get all our money back plus the whole coupon. But it was a mistake. [Editor's note: Berkshire did indeed come out whole on its USAir investment.}

US Airways, like United Airlines and several other, smaller carriers, recently joined a long list of airlines that have sought bankruptcy protection. Other notables on the list (historically) include Continental, Eastern, and Pan Am.

Give wings to your heart.

US Airways has teamed up with CVOA to offer the lowest possible priced air-villa packages to Puerto Rico and most of the glorious Caribbean island chain, Aruba, and the Bahamas.

US AIRWAYS

The history of the airline business in terms of taking care of share-holders has been terrible.

I don't want you to think we have any way of learning or behaving so you won't make a lot of mistakes. I'm just saying that you can learn to make fewer mistakes than other people—and how to fix your mistakes faster when you do make them.

But there's no way that you can live an adequate life without [making] many mistakes.

In fact, one trick in life is to get so you can handle mistakes. Failure to handle psychological denial is a common way for people to go broke. You've made an enormous commitment to something. You've poured effort and money in. And the more you put in, the more that the whole consistency principle makes you think, "Now it has to work. If I put in just a little more, then it'll work."

The Card Players, Theodor Rombouts, Oil on canvas, Residenzgalerie, Salzburg

Part of what you must learn is how to handle mistakes and new facts that change the odds. Life, in part, is like a poker game, wherein you have to learn to quit sometimes when holding a much-loved hand.

And deprival super-reaction syndrome also comes in: You're going to lose the whole thing if you don't put in a little more. People go broke that way—because they can't stop, rethink, and say, "I can afford to write this one off and live to fight again. I don't have to pursue this thing as an obsession—in a way that will break me."

Q: Could you talk about the thoughts that went into your decision to swap your Capital Cities stock for Disney rather than taking cash. In the media, it was reported that you mentioned thinking about taking the cash.

Disney's a perfectly marvelous company, but it's also very high-priced. Part of what it does is to make ordinary movies—which is not a business that attracts me at all. However, part of what Disney has is better than a great gold mine. My grandchildren—I mean, those videocassettes…

Disney is an amazing example of autocatalysis…. They had all those movies in the can. They owned the copyright. And just as Coke could prosper when refrigeration came, when the videocassette was invented, Disney didn't have to invent anything or do anything except take the thing out of the can and stick it on the cassette.

Disney is an amazing example of autocatalysis…. They had all those movies in the can. They owned the copyright. And just as Coke could prosper when refrigeration came, when the videocassette was invented, Disney didn't have to invent anything or do anything except take the thing out of the can and stick it on the cassette. And every parent and grandparent wanted his descendents to sit around and watch that stuff at home on videocassette. So Disney got this enormous tail wind from life. And it was billions of dollars worth of tail wind.

Obviously, that's a marvelous model if you can find it. You don't have to invent anything. All you have to do is to sit there while the world carries you forward….

Frank Wells
(1932–1994)

President of the Disney Company until his untimely death in 1994, Wells was greatly respected. For thirty years he carried a scrap of paper in his wallet that read, "Humility is the essence of life."

Disney's done a lot of new things right. Don't misunderstand me. But a lot of what happened to Disney was like what a friend of mine said about an ignorant fraternity brother of his who succeeded in life: "He was a duck sitting on a pond. And they raised the level of the pond."

Eisner and Wells were brilliant in how they ran Disney. But the huge tail wind from videocassette sales on all of the old stuff that was there when they came in, that was just an automatic break for the new management.

To be fair, they have been brilliant about creating new stuff—like *Pocahontas* and *The Lion King*—to catch the same tailwind. But by the time it's done, *The Lion King* alone is going to do plural billions. And, by the way, when I say "when it's done," I mean fifty years from now or something. But plural billions—from one movie?

Q: Could you talk about why you left the law?

I had a huge family. Nancy and I supported eight children…. And I didn't realize that the law was going to get as prosperous as it suddenly got. The big money came into law shortly after I left it. By 1962, I was mostly out. And I was totally out by 1965. So that was a long time ago.

Also, I preferred making the decisions and gambling my own money. I usually thought I knew better than the client anyway. So why should I have to do it his way? So partly, it was having an opinionated personality. And partly, it was a desire to get resources permitting independence.

Also, the bulk of my clients were terrific. But there were one or two I didn't enjoy. Plus, I like the independence of a capitalist. And I'd always had sort of a gambling personality. I like figuring things out and making bets. So I simply did what came naturally.

Q: Do you ever gamble Las Vegas–style?

I won't bet $100 against house odds between now and the grave. I don't do that. Why should I? I will gamble recreationally with my pals. And I'll occasionally play a much better bridge player, like Bob Hamman, who might be the best card player in the world. But I know I'm paying for the fun of playing with him. That's recreational.

As for gambling with simple mechanical house odds against me, why in the world would I ever want to do that—particularly given how I detest the manipulative culture of legalized gambling. So I don't like legalized gambling.

In 1931 the Nevada legislature approved a legalized gambling bill authored by Phil Tobin, a northern Nevada rancher. Tobin had never visited Las Vegas and said he had no interest in gambling. His legislation was designed "to raise needed taxes for public schools." The same rationale has been used to promote state lotteries.

And I'm not comfortable in Las Vegas, even though it does now include a higher percentage of wholesome family recreation. I don't like to be with many of the types who hang around card parlors and so forth.

On the other hand, I do like the manly art of wagering, so to speak. And I like light social gambling among friends. But I do not like the professional gambling milieu.

**Important Books
by Benjamin Graham**

Security Analysis (1934)

The Interpretation of Financial Statements (1937)

World Commodities and World Currency (1944)

The Intelligent Investor (1949)

Benjamin Graham: The Memoirs of the Dean of Wall Street (1996, posthumous)

Q: Could you say something about how the mutual fund and money management business has changed since you got into it—and the growth of capital markets?

Actually, I didn't really get into it. I had a little private partnership for fourteen years—up until a little over twenty years ago. However, I never had enough money from other people to amount to a hill of beans—at least by current investment-management standards. So I've never really been part of the mutual fund business.

But the money management business has been one of the great growth businesses in the recent history of the United States. It's created many affluent professionals and multimillionaires. It's been a perfect gold mine for people who got in it early. The growth of pension funds, the value of American corporations, and the world's wealth have created a fabulous profession for many and carried lots of them up to affluence.

And we deal with them in a variety of ways. However, we haven't been part of it for many years. We've basically invested our own money for a long, long time.

Q: Do you expect this [bull] run to continue?

Well, I'd be amazed if the capitalized value of all American business weren't considerably higher twenty-five years from now. And if people continue to trade with one another and shuffle these pieces of paper around, then money management may continue to be a marvelous business for the managers. But except for what might be called our own money, we're really not in it.

Q: I was interested in the evolution of your investment strategy from when you first began—using the Ben Graham model—to the Berkshire Hathaway model. Would you recommend that model to a beginning investor—i.e., dumping most of it or all of it into one opportunity we think is a great one and leaving it there for decades? Or is that strategy really for a more mature investor?

Each person has to play the game given his own marginal utility considerations and in a way that takes into account his own psychology. If losses are going to make you miserable—and some losses are inevitable—you might be wise to utilize a very conservative pattern of investment and saving all your life. So you have to adapt your strategy to your own nature and your own talents. I don't think there's a one-size-fits-all investment strategy that I can give you.

Mine works for me. But, in part, that's because I'm good at taking losses. I can take 'em psychologically. And, besides, I have very few. The combination works fine.

Q: You and Buffett have said that Berkshire's stock is overvalued and you wouldn't recommend buying it.

We didn't say [we thought it was overvalued]. We just said that we wouldn't buy it or recommend that our friends buy it at the prices then prevailing. But that just related to Berkshire's intrinsic value as it was at that time.

Q: If I had the money, I would buy it—because you've been saying that your returns will go down for twenty years….

Well, I hope that your optimism is justified. But I do not change my opinion. After all, today, we're in uncharted territory. I sometimes tell my friends, "I'm doing the best I can. But I've never grown old before. I'm doing it for the first time. And I'm not sure that I'll do it right."

I sometimes tell my friends, "I'm doing the best I can. But I've never grown old before. I'm doing it for the first time. And I'm not sure that I'll do it right."

Warren and I have never been in this kind of territory—with high valuations and a huge amount of capital. We've never done it before. So we're learning.

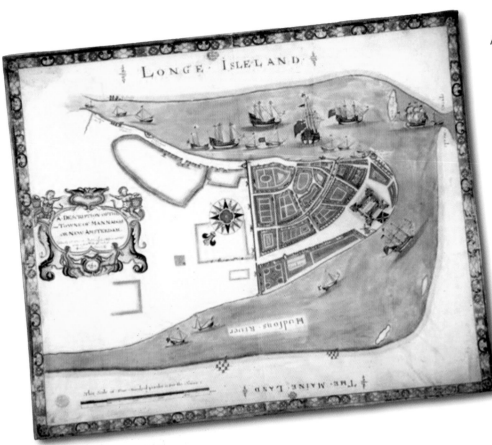

The wealth of the world will compound at no such rate.

Oh, I don't think that we share that with him. Graham, great, great though he was as a man, had a screw loose as he tried to predict outcomes for the stock market as a whole. In contrast, Warren and I are almost always agnostic about the market.

The Limits to Compounding

The $24 real estate investment by the Dutch to buy the island of Manhattan would today, by some estimates, be roughly equivalent to $3 trillion.

Over 378 years, that's about a seven percent annual compound rate of return.

On the other hand, we have said that common stocks generally have generated returns of ten to eleven percent after inflation for many years and that those returns can't continue for a very long period. And they can't. It's simply impossible. The wealth of the world will compound at no such rate. Whatever experience Stanford has had in its portfolio for the last fifteen years, its future experience is virtually certain to be worse. It may still be okay. But it's been a hog heaven period for investors over the last fifteen years. Bonanza effects of such scale can't last forever.

Q: Berkshire's annual report got a lot of press for being pessimistic and for expressing concern about the shrinking pool of opportunities as the company gets bigger and bigger. Where does that leave you ten years from now?

We've said over and over that our future rate of compounding our shareholders' wealth is going to go down compared to our past—and that our size will be an anchor dragging on performance. And we've said over and over again that this is not an opinion, but a promise.

However, let's suppose that we were able to compound our present book value at fifteen percent per annum from this point. That would not be so bad and would work out okay for our long-term shareholder. I'm just saying that we could afford to slow down some, as we surely will, and still do okay for the long-term shareholder.

By the way, I'm not promising that we will compound our present book value at fifteen percent per annum.

Q: You talked about how important it was not to have an extreme ideology. What responsibility, if any, do you think the business and legal communities have for helping inner-city areas, spreading the wealth and so on?

I'm all for fixing social problems. I'm all for being generous to the less fortunate.

Good Samaritan

Good Samaritan Hospital of Los Angeles, founded in 1885, is a world-class academic medical center affiliated with the University of Southern California Keck School of Medicine. Performing about 4,200 surgeries and receiving 25,400 emergency room visits annually, it is organized as a not-for-profit corporation. Good Samaritan's longtime chairman of the board is Charles T. Munger.

I'm all for fixing social problems. I'm all for being generous to the less fortunate. And I'm all for doing things where, based on a slight preponderance of the evidence, you guess that it's likely to do more good than harm.

What I'm against is being very confident and feeling that you know, for sure, that your particular intervention will do more good than harm, given that you're dealing with highly complex systems wherein everything is interacting with everything else.

Q: So [what you're saying is to] just make sure that what you're doing [is doing more good]....

You can't make sure. That's my point....

On the other hand, I did recently reverse [the conclusions of] two sets of engineers. How did I have enough confidence in such a complicated field to do that? Well, you might think, "Oh, this guy is just an egomaniac who's made some money and thinks he knows everything."

Well, I may be an egomaniac, but I don't think I know everything. But I saw huge reasons in the circumstances for bias in each set of engineers as each recommended a course of action very advantageous to itself. And what each was saying was so consonant with a natural bias that it made me distrust it. Also, perhaps I knew enough engineering to know that [what they were saying] didn't make sense.

Finally, I found a third engineer who recommended a solution I approved. And, thereafter, the second engineer came to me and said, "Charlie, why didn't I think of that?"—which is to his credit. It was a much better solution, both safer and cheaper.

You must have the confidence to override people with more credentials than you whose cognition is impaired by incentive-caused bias or some similar psychological force that is obviously present. But there are also cases where you have to recognize that you have no wisdom to add—and that your best course is to trust some expert.

In effect, you've got to know what you know and what you don't know. What could possibly be more useful in life than that?

Q: You discussed Coke's mistake. Do you have any thoughts about where Apple went wrong?"

Let me give you a very good answer—one I'm copying from Jack Welch, the CEO of General Electric. He has a Ph.D. in engineering. He's a star businessman. He's a marvelous guy. And recently, in Warren's presence, someone asked him, "Jack, what did Apple do wrong?"

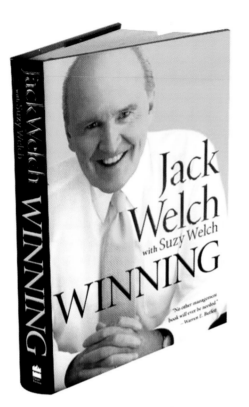

Jack Welch
(b. 1935)

Born John Francis Welch Jr. in Massachusetts, Welch earned a Ph.D. in chemical engineering before joining General Electric in 1960. He worked his way up the corporate ladder, becoming chairman and CEO in 1980. During his twenty years of leadership at GE, Welch increased the value of the company from $13 billion to several hundred billion dollars.

His answer? "I don't have any special competence that would enable me to answer that question." And I'll give you the very same answer. That's not a field in which I'm capable of giving you any special insight.

On the other hand, in copying Jack Welch, I am trying to teach you something. When you don't know and you don't have any special competence, don't be afraid to say so.

There's another type of person I compare to an example from biology: When a bee finds nectar, it comes back and does a little dance that tells the rest of the hive, as a matter of genetic programming, which direction to go and how far. So about forty or fifty years ago, some clever scientist stuck the nectar straight up. Well, the nectar's never straight up in the ordinary life of a bee. The nectar's out. So the bee finds the nectar and returns to the hive. But it doesn't have the genetic programming to do a dance that says straight up. So what does it do?

Well, if it were like Jack Welch, it would just sit there. But what it actually does is to dance this incoherent dance that gums things up. And a lot of people are like that bee. They attempt to answer a question like that. And that is a huge mistake. Nobody expects you to know everything about everything.

I try to get rid of people who always confidently answer questions about which they don't have any real knowledge. To me, they're like the bee dancing its incoherent dance. They're just screwing up the hive.

Q: As someone who's been in legal practice and business, how did you incorporate, or did you incorporate, these models into your legal practice? And how did it work? I suspect many of us have seen law firms that don't appear to adhere to these kinds of models.

Well, the models are there. But just as there are perverse incentives in academia, there are perverse incentives in law firms. In fact, in some respects, at the law firms, it's much worse.

Here's another model from law practice: When I was very young, my father practiced law. One of his best friends, Grant McFayden—Omaha's Pioneer Ford dealer—was a client. He was a perfectly marvelous man—a self-made Irishman

Apple Computer

With the 1976 release of the Apple 1 by Steven Jobs and Stephen Wozniak, Apple Computer was born. Through a series of improvements and innovations, Apple built a reputation for quality and the user-friendliest computers on the market. In the early 1990s, Apple began to lose its market share to Intel- and Windows-based computers. Despite what many observers maintained was superior technology and performance, Apple came close to irrelevance because of the marketing heft behind the Windows-based products. In the late 1990s, Apple's iMac and PowerBook products began an impressive resurgence. The recent introduction of the iPod personal audio device has greatly enhanced Apple's position in the market.

who'd run away uneducated from a farm as a youth because his father beat him. So he made his own way in the world. And he was a brilliant man of enormous charm and integrity—just a wonderful, wonderful man.

In contrast, my father had another client who was a blowhard, overreaching, unfair, pompous, difficult man. And I must have been fourteen years old or thereabouts when I asked, "Dad, why do you do so much work for Mr. X—this overreaching blowhard—instead of working more for wonderful men like Grant McFayden?"

My father said, "Grant McFayden treats his employees right, his customers right, and his problems right. And if he gets involved with a psychotic, he quickly walks over to where the psychotic is and works out an exit as fast as he can. Therefore, Grant McFayden doesn't have enough remunerative law business to keep you in Coca-Cola. But Mr. X is a walking minefield of wonderful legal business."

W. C. Fields as *The Bank Dick* (1940): a quintessential, unreasonable blowhard.

As you go through life, sell your services once in a while to an unreasonable blowhard if that's what you must do to feed your family. But run your own life like Grant McFayden. That was a great lesson.

This case demonstrates one of the troubles with practicing law. To a considerable extent, you're going to be dealing with grossly defective people. They create an enormous amount of the remunerative law business. And even when your own client is a paragon of virtue, you'll often be dealing with gross defectives on the other side or even on the bench. That's partly what drove me out of the profession.

The rest was my own greed, but my success in serving greed partly allowed me to make easier the process of being honorable and sensible. Like Ben Franklin observed, "It's hard for an empty sack to stand upright."

I'd argue that my father's model when I asked him about the two clients was totally correct didaction. He taught me the right lesson. The lesson? As you go through life, sell your services once in a while to an unreasonable blowhard if that's what you must do to feed your family. But run your own life like Grant McFayden. That was a great lesson.

And he taught it in a very clever way—because instead of just pounding it in, he told it to me in a way that required a slight mental reach. And I had to make the reach myself in order to get the idea that I should behave like Grant McFayden. And because I had to reach for it, he figured I'd hold it better. And, indeed, I've held it all the way through until today—through all of these decades. That's a very clever teaching method.

There, again, we're talking about elementary psychology. It's elementary literature. Good literature makes the reader reach a little for understanding. Then, it works better. You hold it better. It's the commitment and consistency tendency. If you've reached for it, the idea's pounded in better.

Good literature makes the reader reach a little for understanding. If you've reached for it, the idea's pounded in better.

As a lawyer or executive, you'll want to teach somebody what my father taught me or maybe you'll want to teach them something else. And you can use lessons like this. Isn't that a great way to teach a child? My father used indirection on purpose. And look at how powerfully it worked—like Captain Cook's wise use of psychology. I've been trying to imitate Grant McFayden ever since—for all my life. I may have had a few lapses. But at least I've been trying.

Good Literature

Irving Stone
(1903–1989)

An American writer known for his biographical novels of famous historical personalities and events, Irving Stone produced important works that included *Lust for Life*, based on the life of Vincent van Gogh (1934), *The Agony and the Ecstasy*, based on the life of Michelangelo (1961), and *Origin*, based on the life of Charles Darwin (1980). *Men to Match My Mountains* (1956) is an often spellbinding account about the bold pioneers who opened the Far West and California during the 1840s.

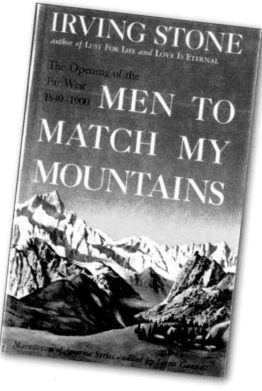

Henry Emerson
Editor and Publisher
Outstanding Investor Digest

Henry Emerson has spent eighteen
years interacting with some of the
world's greatest money managers—
including both Warren Buffett and
Charlie Munger. His indispensable
newsletter is designed to "bring our
subscribers the most valuable material
that we can—the calendar be damned."
Emerson's publication is a must-read for
investors of every stripe.

Q: At the end of your article in OID, *you
mentioned that only a select few investment
managers actually add value. Since you're
speaking to an audience of future lawyers,
what would you encourage us to do in order to
be able to add value in our profession?*

To the extent you become a person
who thinks correctly, you can add great
value. To the extent you've learned
it so well that you have enough
confidence to intervene where it takes
a little courage, you can add great
value. And to the extent that you
can prevent or stop some asininity
that would otherwise destroy your firm, your client, or
something that you care about, you can add great value.

And there are constructive tricks you can use. For example, one reason why my
old classmate, Joe Flom of Skadden Arps, has been such a successful lawyer is that
he's very good at dreaming up little, vivid examples that serve to pound the point
home in a way that really works. It's enormously helpful when you're serving clients
or otherwise trying to persuade someone in a good cause to come up with a little
humorous example.

The ability to do that is a knack. So you could argue that the Joe Floms of the
world are almost born with a gift. But he's honed the gift. And to one degree or
another, all of you were born with the gift. And you can hone it, too.

Occasionally, you get into borderline stuff. For instance, suppose you've got
a client who really wants to commit tax fraud. If he doesn't push the tax law way
beyond the line, he can't stand it. He can't shave in the morning if he thinks there's
been any cheating he could get by with that he hasn't done. And there are people
like that. They just feel they aren't living aggressively enough.

You can approach that situation in either of two ways: (A) You can say, "I just won't work for him," and duck it. Or, (B) you can say, "Well, the circumstances of my life require that I work for him. And what I'm doing for him doesn't involve my cheating. Therefore, I'll do it."

And if you see he wants to do something really stupid, it probably won't work to tell him, "What you're doing is bad. I have better morals than you."

That offends him. You're young. He's old. Therefore, instead of being persuaded, he's more likely to react with, "Who in the hell are you to establish the moral code of the whole world?"

But, instead, you can say to him, "You can't do that without three other people beneath you knowing about it. Therefore, you're making yourself subject to blackmail. You're risking your reputation. You're risking your family, your money, etc."

That is likely to work. And you're telling him something that's true. Do you want to spend a lot of time working for people where you have to use methods like that to get them to behave well? I think the answer is no. But if you're hooked with it, appealing to his interest is likely to work better as a matter of human persuasion than appealing to anything else. That, again, is a powerful psychological principle with deep biological roots.

I saw that psychological principle totally blown at Salomon. Salomon's general counsel knew that the CEO, Gutfreund, should have promptly told the federal authorities all about Salomon's trading improprieties in which Gutfreund didn't participate and which he hadn't caused. And the general counsel urged Gutfreund to do it. He told Gutfreund, in effect, "You're probably not legally required to do that, but it's the right thing to do. You really should."

But it didn't work. The task was easy to put off—because it was unpleasant. So that's what Gutfreund did—he put it off.

And the general counsel had very little constituency within Salomon except for the CEO. If the CEO went down, the general counsel was going down with him. Therefore, his whole career was on the line. So to save his career, he needed to talk

John Gutfreund at Salomon Brothers

John Gutfreund, chairman and CEO of Salomon Brothers, paid a high price for inaction when he was put on notice of company misdeeds. In 1991, a Salomon trader made an illegal $3.2 billion bid for U.S. treasury securities. Although the transaction was reported to top management only days later, Gutfreund did not take the warning seriously and failed to report it for more than three months. Gutfreund knew as soon as the matter came out in the press that his delay in reporting had torpedoed his thirty-eight-year career with Salomon. He called in one of Salomon's outside directors, Warren Buffett, to save the company and restore its reputation. Buffett handled the complicated project masterfully, and the firm survived and prospered; it was later sold for $9 billion to Travelers.

the dilatory CEO into doing the right thing.

It would've been child's play to get that job done right. All the general counsel had to do was to tell his boss, "John, this situation could ruin your life. You could lose your wealth. You could lose your reputation." And it would have worked. CEOs don't like the idea of being ruined, disgraced, and fired.

March 3, 2004, New York, New York: Former WorldCom CEO Bernard Ebbers in handcuffs on his way to court for his arraignment after surrendering at FBI Headquarters in 26 Federal Plaza. Ebbers was charged with nine counts of conspiracy to commit securities fraud and making false statements to the SEC in connection with the collapse of WorldCom. He was found guilty in March of 2005 and, as of this writing, is headed to prison, perhaps for life.

Photo by Allan Tannenbaum / Polaris

CEOs don't like the idea of being ruined, disgraced, and fired.

And the ex–general counsel of Salomon is brilliant and generous—and he had the right idea. However, he lost his job because he didn't apply a little elementary psychology. He failed to recognize that what works best in most cases is to appeal to a man's interest.

But you don't have to get similarly lousy results when you face similar situations. Just remember what happened to Gutfreund and his general counsel. The right lessons are easily learned if you'll work at it. And if you do learn them, you can be especially useful at crucial moments when others fail. And to the extent that you do become wise, diligent, objective, and, especially able to persuade in a good cause, then you're adding value.

Q: Would you discuss how the threat of litigation—shareholder lawsuits and so forth—and legal complexity in general have affected decision-making in big business?

Well, every big business screams about its legal costs, screams about the amount of regulation, screams about the complexity of its life, screams about the plaintiffs' bar—particularly the class action plaintiffs' bar. So there's an absolute catechism on that where you could just copy the screams from one corporation to another and you'd hardly have to change a word.

But what causes the screams has, so far, been a godsend for the law firms. The big law firms have had a long updraft. And they now tend to kind of cluck like an undertaker in a plague. An undertaker, of course, would look very unseemly if he were jumping up and down and playing his fiddle during the plague. So law firm partners say, "Oh, isn't it sad—all this complexity, all this litigation, all this unfairness."

> *An undertaker, of course, would look very unseemly if he were jumping up and down and playing his fiddle during the plague.*

But, really, they're somewhat schizophrenic on the subject because it's been very good for [them]. Some recent California initiatives created some interesting conduct. Part of the defense bar lobbied quietly against certain propositions and, effectively, against their clients because they didn't want their clients to catch 'em in the process. And the reason that they did so was because it became harder for plaintiffs to bring cases.

If you make a living fighting overreaching and it keeps your children in school and somebody proposes a system that eliminates it—well, that's an adult experience and an adult choice that you have to make.

Officer Daniel Rodriguez, the so-called "singing cop," singing at the 2002 Winter Olympics [AP photo]. Officer Rodriguez was a great comfort to New Yorkers and America at large in the aftermath of the 9-11 tragedy.

So big corporations adapt. They have more litigation. They have to have a bigger legal department. They scream about what they don't like. But they adapt.

Q: But hasn't that legal complexity consumed a lot more of companies' resources over the last few decades?

The answer is yes. There's hardly a corporation in America that isn't spending more on lawsuits and on compliance with various regulations than it was twenty years ago. And, yes, some of the new regulation is stupid and foolish. And some was damn well necessary. And it will ever be thus, albeit with some ebb and flow.

Q: But have you seen or experienced any change in decision making at corporations in their being less likely to take on riskier investments for fear of failure or liability?

The only place I saw—with another friend, not Warren [Buffett]—[was where] I was part owner of the biggest shareholder in a company that invented a better policeman's helmet. It was made of Kevlar or something of that sort. And they brought it to us and wanted us to [manufacture] it.

As a matter of ideology, we're very pro-police. I believe civilization needs a police force—although I don't believe in policemen creating too many widows and orphans unnecessarily either. But we like the idea of a better policeman's helmet.

However, we took one look at it and said to the people who invented it, "We're a rich corporation. We can't afford to make a better policeman's helmet. That's just

"As a matter of ideology, we're very pro-police."

how the civilization works. All risks considered, it can't work for us. But we want the civilization to have these."

"So we don't maximize what we sell it for it. Get somebody else to make it. Transfer the technology or whatever to somebody who can do it. But we're not going to."

Thus, we didn't try to disadvantage policemen [by keeping them from] getting new helmets, but we decided not to manufacture helmets ourselves.

There are businesses—given the way the civilization has developed—where being the only deep pocket around is bad business. In high school football, for example, a paraplegic or quadriplegic will inevitably be created occasionally. And who with deep pockets can the injured person best sue other than the helmet manufacturer? Then everyone feels sorry, the injuries are horrible, and the case is dangerous for the manufacturer....

I think big, rich corporations are seldom wise to make football helmets in the kind of a civilization we're in. And maybe it should be harder to successfully sue helmet makers.

I think big, rich corporations are seldom wise to make football helmets in the kind of a civilization we're in.

I know two different doctors—each of whom had a sound marriage. And when the malpractice premiums got high enough, they divorced their wives and transferred most of their property to their wives. And they continued to practice—only without malpractice insurance.

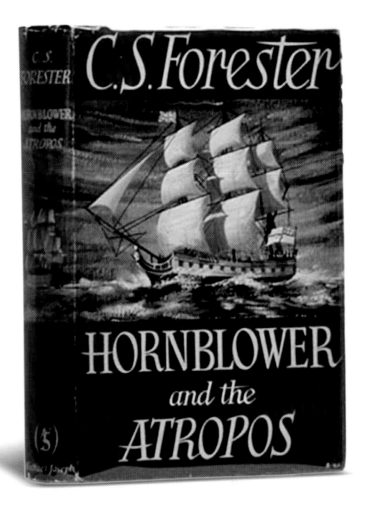

**British Blockade
of the French Coast
(1803–1814)**

Winter in the Bay of Biscay brings ferocious gales, vicious tides, mountainous seas, and bitter discomfort for ships' crews. As chronicled by C. S. Forester in his *Hornblower* series, the consequences for any ship's captain who might allow his ship to go aground while on blockade duty were severe. Regardless of the circumstances, the officer faced almost certain court-martial and the severest of punishments, even including death. Not surprisingly, only one ship of the line was lost in all those years, and she ran on an uncharted rock.

They were angry at the civilization. They needed to adapt. And they trusted their wives. So that was that. And they've not carried any malpractice insurance since.

People adapt to a changing litigation climate. They have various ways of doing it. That's how it's always been and how it's always going to be.

> *I like the Navy system.... If a captain... turns his ship over to a competent first mate in tough conditions and he takes the ship aground...the captain's naval career is over.*

What I personally hate most are systems that make fraud easy. Probably way more than half of all the chiropractic income in California comes from pure fraud. For example, I have a friend who had a little fender bender—an auto accident—in a tough neighborhood. And he got two chiropractors' cards and one lawyer's card before he'd even left the intersection. They're in the business of manufacturing claims that necks hurt.

In California, I believe the Rand statistics showed that we have twice as many personal injuries per accident as in many other states. And we aren't getting twice as much real injury per accident. So the other half of that is fraud. People just get so that they think everybody does it, and it's all right to do. I think it's terrible to let that stuff creep in.

If I were running the civilization, compensation for stress in workers' comp would be zero—not because there's no work-caused stress, but because I think the net social damage of allowing stress to be compensated at all is worse than what would happen if a few people that had real work-caused stress injuries went uncompensated.

I like the Navy system. If you're a captain in the Navy and you've been up for twenty-four hours straight and have to go to sleep and you turn the ship over to a competent first mate in tough conditions and he takes the ship aground—clearly through no fault of yours—they don't court-martial you, but your naval career is over.

You can say, "That's too tough. That's not law school. That's not due process." Well, the Navy model is better in its context than would be the law school model. The Navy model really forces people to pay attention when conditions are tough—because they know that there's no excuse.

Napoleon said he liked luckier generals—he wasn't into supporting losers. Well, the Navy likes luckier captains.

It doesn't matter why your ship goes aground, your career is over. Nobody's interested in your fault. It's just a rule that we happen to have—for the good of all, all effects considered.

I like some rules like that. I think that the civilization works better with some of these no-fault rules. But that stuff tends to be anathema around law schools. "It's not due process. You're not really searching for justice."

Well, I am searching for justice when I argue for the Navy rule—for the justice of fewer ships going aground. Considering the net benefit, I don't care if

Napoleon Bonaparte, Emperor of France, acquired control of most of western and central Europe by conquest or alliance until his defeat at the Battle of the Nations near Leipzig in 1813. He later staged a comeback known as the Hundred Days, before being defeated at the Battle of Waterloo in 1815. This painting, *Bonaparte Crossing the Alps at Grand-Saint-Bernard*, by Jacques-Louis David is in the collection of the Chateaux de Malmaison et Bois-Preau, Rueil-Malmaison, France

one captain has some unfairness in his life. After all, it's not like he's being court-martialed. He just has to look for a new line of work. And he keeps vested pension rights and so on. So it's not like it's the end of the world.

So I like things like that. However, I'm in a minority.

Q: I'd like to hear you talk a little bit more about judgment. In your talk, you said we should read the psychology textbooks and take the fifteen or sixteen principles that are best of the ones that make sense....

The ones that are obviously important and obviously right. That's correct.... And then you stick in the ones that are obviously important and not in the books—and you've got a system.

Q: Right. My problem seems to be the prior step, which is determining which ones are obviously right. And that seems to me to be the more essential question to ask.

Sheep, blissfully uncomplicated and certainly with all the answers they will ever need in life, block a country road in the Yorkshire Dales in England.

Well, if you're like me, it's kind of fun for it to be a little complicated. If you want it totally easy and laid out, maybe you should join some cult that claims to provide all the answers.

No, no. You overestimate the difficulty. Do you have difficulty understanding that people are heavily influenced by what other people think and what other people do—and that some of that happens on a subconscious level?

Q: No, I don't. I understand that.

Well, you can go right through the principles. And, one after another, they're like that. It's not that hard....

Do you have any difficulty with the idea that operant conditioning works—that people will repeat what worked for them the last time?

Q: It just seems to me like there's a lot of other things out there, as well, that also make a lot of sense. The system would quickly get too complicated, I imagine—as a result of too much cross-talk.

Well, if you're like me, it's kind of fun for it to be a little complicated. If you want it totally easy and totally laid out, maybe you should join some cult that claims to provide all the answers. I don't think that's a good way to go. I think you'll just have to endure the world—as complicated as it is. Einstein has a marvelous statement on that: "Everything should be made as simple as possible, but no more simple."

I'm afraid that's the way it is. If there are twenty factors and they interact some, you'll just have to learn to handle it—because that's the way the world is. But you won't find it that hard if you go at it Darwin-like, step by step with curious persistence. You'll be amazed at how good you can get.

Q: You've given us about three of the models that you use. I wondered where you found the other ones. And, second, do you have an easier way for us to find them than going through a psychology textbook? I'm not averse to doing that, but it takes longer.

There are a relatively small number of disciplines and a relatively small number of truly big ideas. And it's a lot of fun to figure it out. Plus, if you figure it out and do the outlining yourself, the ideas will stick better than if you memorize 'em using somebody else's cram list.

Even better, the fun never stops. I was miseducated horribly. And I hadn't bothered to pick up what's called modern Darwinism. I do a lot of miscellaneous reading, too. But I just missed it. And in the last year, I suddenly realized I was a total damned fool and hadn't picked it up properly. So I went back. And with the aid of Dawkins—Oxford's great biologist—and others, I picked it up.

Modern Darwinism or Modern Darwinian Synthesis

The terms, "modern Darwinism" and "modern Darwinian synthesis" describe work of the late 1930s and 1940s which blended the discoveries of geneticists and natural historians to determine how changes in genes could account for evolution of bio-diversity.

"Well, it was an absolute circus for me in my seventies to get the modern Darwinian synthesis in my head. It's so awesomely beautiful and so awesomely right [that the organism acts, and has evolved, to further the interests of its genes]. And it's so simple once you get it."

Were Charlie to teach a Remedial Worldly Wisdom course for law students, it would no doubt include his "Fundamental four-discipline combination of math, physics, chemistry, and engineering," as well as accounting, history, psychology, philosophy, statistics, biology, and economics. It might, in fact, last somewhat longer than "three weeks or a month."

Well, it was an absolute circus for me in my seventies to get the modern Darwinian synthesis in my head. It's so awesomely beautiful and so awesomely right. And it's so simple once you get it. So one beauty of my approach is that the fun never stops. I suppose that it does stop eventually when you're drooling in the convalescent home at the end. But, at least, it lasts a long time.

If I were czar of a law school—although, of course, no law school will permit a czar (they don't even want the dean to have much power)—I'd create a course that I'd call "Remedial Worldly Wisdom" that would, among other useful things, include a fair amount of properly taught psychology. And it might last three weeks or a month....

I think you could create a course that was so interesting— with pithy examples and powerful examples and powerful principles—that it would be a total circus. And I think that it would make the whole law school experience work better.

People raise their eyebrows at that idea. "People don't do that kind of thing." They may not like the derision that's implicit in the title: "Remedial Worldly Wisdom." But the title would be my way of announcing, "Everybody ought to know this." And, if you call it remedial, isn't that what you're saying? "This is really basic and everybody has to know it."

Such a course would be a perfect circus. The examples are so legion. I don't see why people don't do it. They may not do it mostly because they don't want to. But also, maybe they don't know how. And maybe they don't know what it is.

But the whole law school experience would be much more fun if the really basic ideas were integrated and pounded in with good examples for a month or so before you got into conventional law school material. I think the whole system of education would work better. But nobody has any interest in doing it.

And when law schools do reach out beyond traditional material, they often do it in what looks to me like a pretty dumb way. If you think psychology is badly taught in America, you should look at corporate finance. Modern portfolio theory? It's demented! It's truly amazing.

I don't know how these things happen. Hard science and engineering tend to be pretty reliably done. But the minute you get outside of those areas, a certain amount of inanity seems to creep into academia—even [in] academia involving people with very high I.Q.'s.

But, boy, what a school would be like that pounded a lot of the silliness out. But the right way to pound it out is not to have some seventy-plus-year-old capitalist come in and tell seniors, "Here's a little remedial worldly wisdom." This is not the way to do it.

Many of the legal doctrines are tied to other doctrines. They're joined at the hip. And, yet, they teach you those legal doctrines without pointing out how they're tied to the other important doctrines. That's insanity— absolute insanity.

On the other hand, a month at the start of law school that really pounded in the basic doctrines…. Many of the legal doctrines are tied to other doctrines. They're joined at the hip. And, yet, they teach you those legal doctrines without pointing out how they're tied to the other important doctrines?! That's insanity—absolute insanity.

Why do we have a rule that judges shouldn't talk about legal issues that aren't before them? In my day, they taught us the rule, but not in a way giving reasons tied to the guts of undergraduate courses. It's crazy that people don't have those reasons. The human mind is not constructed so that it works well without having reasons. You've got to hang reality on a theoretical structure with reasons. That's the way it hangs together in usable form so that you're an effective thinker.

And to teach doctrines—either with no reasons or with poorly explained reasons?! That's wrong!

Another reason why I like the idea of having a course on remedial worldly wisdom is that it would force more sense on the professors. It would be awkward for them to teach something that was contravened by lessons that were obviously correct and emphasized in a course named "Remedial Worldly Wisdom." Professors doing so would really have to justify themselves.

Is that a totally crazy idea? It may be crazy to expect it to be done. However, if somebody had done it, would you have found it useful?

I'm always asked this question: "Spoon-feed me what you know." And, of course, what they're often saying is, "Teach me now to get rich with soft white hands faster. And not only let me get rich faster, but teach me faster, too."

Q: I think it would be a wonderful thing to have. Unfortunately, when it's created, we won't be here anymore. You're proposing that this would be good to teach people in a course form so it would be accessible to them. Is there any way that it could be more accessible to us—other than having to...

I get requests for pointers to easy learning all the time. And I'm trying to provide a little easy learning today. But one talk like this is not the right way to do it. The right way to do it would be in a book.

I hope what I'm saying will help you be more effective and better human beings. And if you don't get rich, that won't bother me. But I'm always asked this question: "Spoon-feed me what you know." And, of course, what they're often saying is, "Teach me now to get rich with soft white hands faster. And not only let me get rich faster, but teach me faster, too."

I don't have much interest in writing a book myself. Plus it would be a lot of work for somebody like me to try and do it in my seventies. And I have plenty else to do in life. So I'm not going to do it. But it's a screaming opportunity for somebody. And I'd provide funds to support the writing of an appropriate book if I found someone with the wisdom and the will to do the job right.

Let me turn to some of the probable reasons for present bad education. Part of the trouble is caused by the balkanization of academia. For instance, psychology is most powerful when combined with doctrines from other academic departments. But if your psychology professor doesn't know the other doctrines, then he isn't capable of doing the necessary integration.

And how would anyone get to be a psychology professor in the first place if he were good with nonpsychology doctrines and constantly worked nonpsychology doctrines into his material? Such a would-be professor would usually offend his peers and superiors.

There have been some fabulous psychology professors in the history of the world. Cialdini of Arizona State was very useful to me, as was B. F. Skinner—for his experimental results, if divorced from his monomania and utopianism. But averaged

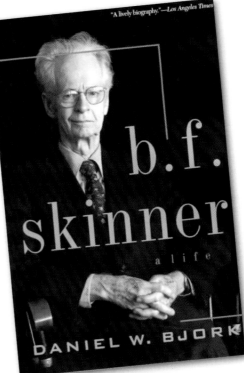

"A lively biography."—*Los Angeles Times*

B. F. Skinner
(1904–1990)

Born Burrhus Frederic Skinner in Pennsylvania to an attorney father and a strong and intelligent mother, B. F. Skinner enjoyed school and did well enough to get to college. Following graduation, he wrote newspaper articles on labor problems and lived in Greenwich Village. Tiring of a bohemian lifestyle, he decided to return to Harvard, where he earned a Ph.D. in psychology. Skinner's great contributions to psychology are his experiments in operant conditioning and behaviorism. Operant conditioning can be summarized as follows: "A behavior is followed by a consequence, and the nature of the consequence modifies the organism's tendency to repeat the behavior in the future."

**Yerkes Observatory
University of Chicago**

The University of Chicago was founded in 1890 by the American Baptist Education Society and John D. Rockefeller. The University, which Rockefeller once described as, "the best investment I ever made," now has an enrollment of over 4,000 undergraduates and 9,000 graduate, professional and other students. It boasts more than seventy Nobel Prize winners among its faculty members, students and researchers.

out, I don't believe that psychology professors in America are people whose alternative career paths were in the toughest part of physics. And that may be one of the reasons why they don't get it quite right.

The schools of education, even at eminent universities, are pervaded by psychology. And they're almost an intellectual disgrace. It's not unheard of for academic departments—even at great institutions—to be quite deficient in important ways. And including a lot of material labeled as psychological is no cure-all.

And given academic inertia, all academic deficiencies are very hard to fix. Do you know how they tried to fix psychology at the University of Chicago? Having tenured professors who were terrible, the president there actually abolished the entire psychology department.

And Chicago, in due course, will probably bring back a new and different psychology department. Indeed, by now, it probably has. Perhaps conditions are now better. And I must admit that I admire a college president who will do something like that.

I do not wish to imply in my criticism that the imperfections of academic psychology teaching are all attributable to some kind of human fault common only to such departments. Instead, the causes of many of the imperfections lie deep in the nature of things—in irritating peculiarities that can't be removed from psychology.

Let me demonstrate by a "thought experiment" involving a couple of questions: Are there not many fields that need a synthesizing super-mind like that of James Clerk Maxwell, but are destined never to attract one? And is academic psychology, by its nature, one of the most unfortunate of all the would-be attractors of super-minds? I think the answers are yes and yes.

One can see this by considering the case of any of the few members of each generation who can, as fast as fingers can move, accurately work through the problem sets in thermodynamics, electromagnetism, and physical chemistry. Such a person will be begged by some of the most eminent people alive to enter the upper reaches of hard science.

Will such a super-gifted person instead choose academic psychology wherein lie very awkward realities: (A) that the tendencies demonstrated by social psychology paradoxically grow weaker as more people learn them, and, (B) that clinical (patient-treating) psychology has to deal with the awkward reality that happiness, physiologically measured, is often improved by believing things that are not true? The answer, I think, is plainly no. The super-mind will be repelled by academic psychology much as Nobel laureate physicist Max Planck was repelled by economics, wherein he saw problems that wouldn't yield to his methods.

Q: We talk a lot about trade-offs between the quality of our life and our professional commitments. Is there time for a professional life, learning about these models, and doing whatever else interests you? Do you find time to do fun things besides learning?

I've always taken a fair amount of time to do what I really wanted to do—some of which was merely to fish or play bridge or play golf.

Each of us must figure out his or her own lifestyle. You may want to work seventy hours a week for ten years to make partner at Cravath and thereby obtain the obligation to do more of the same. Or you may say, "I'm not willing to pay that price." Either way, it's a totally personal decision that you have to make by your own lights.

But, whatever you decide, I think it's a huge mistake not to absorb elementary worldly wisdom if you're capable of doing it because it makes you better able to serve others, it makes you better able to serve yourself, and it makes life more fun. So if you have an aptitude for doing it, I think you'd be crazy not to. Your life will be enriched—not only financially, but in a host of other ways—if you do.

Max Planck
(1858–1947)

Max Planck, a German physicist—shown here with Albert Einstein—is known for his work on thermodynamics and radiation. His wisdom includes:

"Science cannot solve the ultimate mystery of nature. And that is because, in the last analysis, we ourselves are a part of the mystery that we are trying to solve."

"Scientific discovery and scientific knowledge have been achieved only by those who have gone in pursuit of it without any practical purpose whatsoever in view."

"A new scientific truth does not triumph by convincing its opponents and making them see the light, but rather because its opponents eventually die, and a new generation grows up that is familiar with it."

"It is not the possession of truth, but the success which attends the seeking after it, that enriches the seeker and brings happiness to him."

Now this has been a very peculiar talk for some businessman to come in and give at a law school—some guy who's never taken a course in psychology telling you that all of the psychology textbooks are wrong. This is very eccentric. But all I can tell you is that I'm sincere.

There's a lot of simple stuff that many of you are quite capable of learning. And your lives will work way better, too, if you do. Plus, learning it is a lot of fun. So I urge you to learn it.

An Obligation to Teach

"Both Warren and I, in the makeup of our personalities and in our ethical systems, believe being an effective teacher is a high calling. My occasional speeches and my allowing this book to go forward and Warren's writing of those annual reports and his occasional speeches and his contact with business school students—it's all part of a teaching obligation. Properly done, if teaching isn't the highest calling of man, it is near it.

"We think it is such a high calling that we subject people to it all the time who don't have the slightest intention of ever learning anything from it. Very few people have taught with more rejection than we have and yet maintained as much enthusiasm."

—Munger

Q: Are you, in effect, fulfilling your responsibility to share the wisdom that you've acquired over the years?

Sure. Look at Berkshire Hathaway. I call it the ultimate didactic enterprise. Warren's never going to spend any money. He's going to give it all back to society. He's just building a platform so people will listen to his notions. Needless to say, they're very good notions. And the platform's not so bad either. But you could argue that Warren and I are academics in our own way.

Q: Most of what you've said is very compelling. And your quest for knowledge and, therefore, command of the human condition and money are all laudable goals.

I'm not sure the quest for money is so laudable.

Q: Well, then—understandable.

That I'll take. I don't sneer, incidentally, at making sales calls or proofreading bond indentures. If you need the money, it's fun earning it. And if you have to try a bunch of cases in the course of your career, you'll learn something doing that. You ought to do something to earn money. Many activities are dignified by the fact that you earn money.

Q: I understand your skepticism about overly ideological people. But is there an ideological component to what you do? Is there something that you're irrationally passionate about?

Yeah, I'm passionate about wisdom. I'm passionate about accuracy and some kinds of curiosity. Perhaps I have some streak of generosity in my nature and a desire to serve values that transcend my brief life. But maybe I'm just here to show off. Who knows?

I believe in the discipline of mastering the best that other people have ever figured out. I don't believe in just sitting down and trying to dream it all up yourself. Nobody's that smart….

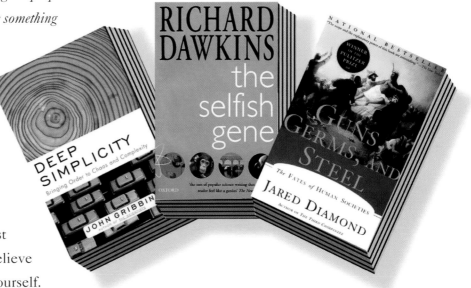

"The best that is known and taught in the world— nothing less can satisfy a teacher worthy of the name."

—Sir William Osler

Talk Three Revisited

When I gave Talk Three in 1996, I argued that intense political animosity should generally be avoided because it causes much mental malfunction, even in brilliant brains. Since then, political animosity has increased greatly, both on the left and right, with sad effects on the ability of people to recognize reality, exactly as I would have expected.

Naturally, I don't like this result. The grain of my emotional nature is to respond as Archimedes might respond if he complained now to God: "How could you put in those dark ages after I published my formulas?" Or as Mark Twain once complained: "These are sad days in literature. Homer is dead. Shakespeare is dead. And I myself am not feeling at all well."

Fortunately, I am still able to refrain from complaint in the mode of Mark Twain. After all, I never had more than a shred of illusion that any views of mine would much change the world. Instead, I always knew that aiming low was the best path for me and so I merely sought (1) to learn from my betters a few practical mental tricks that would help me avoid some of the worst miscognitions common in my age cohort, and (2) to pass on my mental tricks only to a few people who could easily learn from me because they already almost knew my tricks. Having pretty well accomplished these very limited objectives, I see no reason to complain now about the un-wisdom of the world. Instead, what works best for me in coping with all disappointment is what I call the Jewish method: humor.

As I revisit Talk Three in October of 2005, I still like its emphasis on the desirability of making human systems as cheating-proof as is practicable, even if this leaves some human misery unfixed.

And I fondly recall Talk Three's emphasis on both the life-handling lessons I learned from my father's friend, Grant McFayden, and one teaching method I learned from my father. I owe a lot to these long-dead predecessors, and if you like *Poor Charlie's Almanack*, so do you.

"The man who doesn't read good books has no advantage over the man who can't read them."

—Mark Twain

In the run-up to publishing the first edition of *Poor Charlie's Almanack*, Charlie remarked that one of the most important talks in our list, "The Psychology of Human Misjudgment," could use "a little revising" to bring it in line with his most current views on the subject. Little did we know, Charlie's "little" revision would amount to a full-scale rewrite, with loads of new material, and a "stop-the-press" completion schedule. The talk features Charlie's original concept of "behavioral finance," which has now burgeoned into its own academic field of study. As attendee Donald Hall recalls, "Charlie was espousing his well-reasoned views on behavioral finance before the term was even coined."

Charlie also addresses the importance of recognizing patterns to determine how humans behave, both rationally and irrationally. He shares with us his checklist of twenty-five standard causes of human misjudgment, which contains observations that are ingenious, counterintuitive, and important—values Charlie treasures in the work of other great thinkers throughout history. He also emphasizes the "lollapalooza" power of psychological misjudgments in combination.

Here then, written exclusively for *Poor Charlie's Almanack*, is Charlie's magnum opus on why we behave the way we do. We wish you success in the application of these ideas in your own personal and business endeavors.

The Psychology of Human Misjudgment

Selections from three of Charlie's talks, combined into one talk never made, after revisions by Charlie in 2005 that included considerable new material.

The three talks were:

(1) The Bray Lecture at the Caltech Faculty Club, February 2, 1992;

(2) Talk under the Sponsorship of the Cambridge Center for Behavioral Studies at the Harvard Faculty Club, October 6, 1994; and

(3) Talk under the Sponsorship of the Cambridge Center for Behavioral Studies at the Boston Harbor Hotel, April 24, 1995.

The extensive revision by Charlie in 2005, made from memory unassisted by any research, occurred because Charlie thought he could do better at age eighty-one than he did more than ten years earlier when he (1) knew less and was more harried by a crowded life and (2) was speaking from rough notes instead of revising transcripts.

PREFACE

When I read transcripts of my psychology talks given about fifteen years ago, I realized that I could now create a more logical but much longer "talk," including most of what I had earlier said.

But I immediately saw four big disadvantages.

First, the longer "talk," because it was written out with more logical completeness, would be more boring and confusing to many people than any earlier talk. This would happen because I would use idiosyncratic definitions of psychological tendencies in a manner reminiscent of both psychology textbooks and Euclid. And who reads textbooks for fun or revisits Euclid?

Second, because my formal psychological knowledge came only from skimming three psychology textbooks about fifteen years ago, I know virtually nothing about any academic psychology later developed. Yet, in a longer talk containing guesses, I would be criticizing much academic psychology. This sort of intrusion into a professional territory by an amateur would be sure to be resented by professors who would rejoice in finding my errors and might be prompted to respond to my published criticism by providing theirs. Why should I care about new criticism? Well, who likes new hostility from articulate critics with an information advantage?

Third, a longer version of my ideas would surely draw some disapproval from people formerly disposed to like me. Not only would there be stylistic and substantive objections, but also there would be perceptions of arrogance in an old man who displayed much disregard for conventional wisdom while "popping-off" on a subject in which he had never taken a course. My old Harvard Law classmate, Ed Rothschild, always called such a popping-off "the shoe button complex," named for the condition of a family friend who spoke in oracular style on all subjects after becoming dominant in the shoe button business.

Fourth, I might make a fool of myself.

Despite these four very considerable objections, I decided to publish the much-expanded version. Thus, after many decades in which I have succeeded mostly by restricting action to jobs and methods in which I was unlikely to fail, I have now chosen a course of action in which (1) I have no significant personal benefit to gain, (2) I will surely give some pain to family members and friends, and (3) I may make myself ridiculous. Why am I doing this?

One reason may be that my nature makes me incline toward diagnosing and talking about errors in conventional wisdom. And despite years of being smoothed out by the hard knocks that were inevitable for one with my attitude, I don't believe life ever knocked all the boy's brashness out of the man.

A second reason for my decision is my approval of the attitude of Diogenes when he asked: "Of what use is a philosopher who never offends anybody?"

My third and final reason is the strongest. I have fallen in love with my way of laying out psychology because it has been so useful for me. And so, before I die, I want to imitate to some extent the bequest practices of three characters: the protagonist in John Bunyan's *Pilgrim's Progress*, Benjamin Franklin, and my first employer, Ernest Buffett. Bunyan's character, the knight wonderfully named "Old Valiant for Truth," makes the only practical bequest available to him when he says at the end of his life: "My sword I leave to him who can wear it." And like this man, I don't mind if I have misappraised my sword, provided I have tried

to see it correctly, or that many will not wish to try it, or that some who try to wield it may find it serves them not. Ben Franklin, to my great benefit, left behind his autobiography, his *Almanacks*, and much else. And Ernest Buffett did the best he could in the same mode when he left behind "How to Run a Grocery Store and a Few Things I Have Learned about Fishing." Whether or not this last contribution to the genre was the best, I will not say. But I will report that I have now known four generations of Ernest Buffett's descendants and that the results have encouraged my imitation of the founder.

The Psychology of Human Misjudgment

I have long been very interested in standard thinking errors.

However, I was educated in an era wherein the contributions of non-patient-treating psychology to an understanding of misjudgment met little approval from members of the mainstream elite. Instead, interest in psychology was pretty well confined to a group of professors who talked and published mostly for themselves, with much natural detriment from isolation and groupthink.

And so, right after my time at Caltech and Harvard Law School, I possessed a vast ignorance of psychology. Those institutions failed to require

knowledge of the subject. And, of course, they couldn't integrate psychology with their other subject matter when they didn't know psychology. Also, like the Nietzsche character who was proud of his lame leg, the institutions were proud of their willful avoidance of "fuzzy" psychology and "fuzzy" psychology professors.

I shared this ignorant mindset for a considerable time. And so did a lot of other people. What are we to think, for instance, of the Caltech course catalogue that for years listed just one psychology professor, self-described as a "Professor of Psychoanalytical Studies," who taught both "Abnormal Psychology" and "Psychoanalysis in Literature"?

Soon after leaving Harvard, I began a long struggle to get rid of the most dysfunctional part of my psychological ignorance. Today, I will describe my long struggle for elementary wisdom and a brief summary of my ending notions. After that, I will give examples, many quite vivid and interesting to me, of both psychology at work and antidotes to psychology-based dysfunction. Then, I will end by asking and answering some general questions raised by what I have said. This will be a long talk.

When I started law practice, I had respect for the power of genetic evolution and appreciation of man's many evolution-based resemblances to less cognitively-gifted animals and insects. I was aware that man was a "social animal," greatly and automatically influenced by behavior he observed in men around him. I also knew that man lived, like barnyard animals and monkeys, in limited-size dominance hierarchies, wherein he tended to respect authority and to like and cooperate with his own hierarchy members while displaying considerable distrust and dislike for competing men not in his own hierarchy.

But this generalized, evolution-based theory structure was inadequate to enable me to cope properly with the cognition I encountered. I was soon surrounded by much extreme irrationality, displayed in patterns and subpatterns. So surrounded, I could see that I was not going to cope as well as I wished with life unless I could acquire a better theory-structure on which to hang my observations and experiences. By then, my craving for more theory had a long history. Partly, I had always loved theory as an aid in puzzle solving and as a means of satisfying my monkey-like curiosity. And, partly, I had found that theory-structure was a superpower in helping one get what one wanted, as I had early discovered in school wherein I had excelled without labor, guided by theory, while many others, without mastery of theory, failed despite monstrous effort. Better theory, I thought, had always worked for me and, if now available, could make me acquire capital and independence faster and better assist everything I loved. And so I slowly developed my own system of psychology, more or less in the self-help style of Ben Franklin and with the determination displayed in the refrain of the nursery story: "'Then I'll do it myself,' said the little red hen."

I was greatly helped in my quest by two turns of mind. First, I had long looked for insight by inversion in the intense manner counseled by the great algebraist, Jacobi: "Invert, always invert." I sought good judgment mostly by collecting instances of bad judgment, then pondering ways to avoid such outcomes. Second, I became so avid a collector of instances of bad judgment that I paid no attention to boundaries between professional territories. After all, why should I search for some tiny, unimportant, hard-to-find new stupidity in my own field when some large, important, easy-to-find stupidity was just over the fence in the other fellow's professional territory? Besides, I could already see that real-world problems didn't neatly lie within territorial boundaries. They jumped right across. And I was dubious of any approach that, when two things were inextricably intertwined and interconnected, would try and think about one thing but not the other. I was afraid, if I tried any such restricted approach, that I would end up, in the immortal words of John L. Lewis, "with no brain at all, just a neck that had haired over."

Pure curiosity, somewhat later, made me wonder how and why destructive cults were often able, over a single long weekend, to turn many tolerably normal people into brainwashed zombies and thereafter keep them in that state indefinitely. I resolved that I would eventually find a good answer to this cult question if I could do so by general reading and much musing.

I also got curious about social insects. It fascinated me that both the fertile female honeybee and the fertile female harvester ant could multiply their quite different normal life expectancies by exactly twenty by engaging in one gangbang in the sky. The extreme success of the ants also fascinated me—how a few behavioral algorithms caused such extreme evolutionary success grounded in extremes of cooperation within the breeding colony and, almost always, extremes of lethal hostility toward ants outside the breeding colony, even ants of the same species.

Motivated as I was, by midlife I should probably have turned to psychology textbooks, but I didn't, displaying my share of the outcome predicted by the German folk saying: "We are too soon old and too late smart." However, as I later found out, I may have been lucky to avoid for so long the academic psychology that was then laid out in most textbooks. These would not then have guided me well with respect to cults and were often written as if the authors were collecting psychology experiments as a boy collects butterflies—with a passion for more butterflies and more contact with fellow collectors and little craving for synthesis in what is already possessed. When I finally got to the psychology texts, I was reminded of the observation of Jacob Viner, the great economist, that many an academic is like the truffle hound, an animal so trained and bred for one narrow purpose that it is no good at anything else. I was also appalled by hundreds of pages of extremely nonscientific musing about comparative weights of nature and nurture in human outcomes. And I found that introductory psychology texts, by and large, didn't deal appropriately with a fundamental issue: Psychological tendencies tend to be both numerous and inseparably intertwined, now and forever, as they interplay in life. Yet the complex parsing out of effects from intertwined tendencies was usually avoided by the writers of the elementary texts. Possibly the authors did not wish, through complexity, to repel entry of new devotees to their discipline. And, possibly, the cause of their inadequacy was the one given by Samuel Johnson in response to a woman who inquired as to what accounted for his dictionary's misdefinition of the word "pastern." "Pure ignorance," Johnson replied. And, finally, the text writers showed little interest in describing standard antidotes to standard psychology-driven folly, and they thus avoided most discussion of exactly what most interested me.

But academic psychology has some very important merits alongside its defects. I learned this eventually, in the course of general reading, from a book, *Influence*, aimed at a popular audience, by a distinguished psychology professor, Robert Cialdini, at Arizona State, a very big university. Cialdini had made himself into a super-tenured "Regents' Professor" at a very young age by devising, describing, and explaining a vast group of clever experiments in which man manipulated man to his detriment, with all of this made possible by man's intrinsic thinking flaws.

I immediately sent copies of Cialdini's book to all my children. I also gave Cialdini a share of Berkshire stock [Class A] to thank him for what he had done for me and the public. Incidentally, the sale by Cialdini of hundreds of thousands of copies of a book about social psychology was a huge feat, considering that Cialdini didn't claim that he was going to improve your sex life or make you any money.

Part of Cialdini's large book-buying audience came because, like me, it wanted to learn how to become less often tricked by salesmen and circumstances. However, as an outcome not sought by Cialdini, who is a profoundly ethical man, a huge number of his books were bought by salesmen who wanted to learn how to become more effective in misleading customers. Please remember this perverse outcome when my discussion comes to incentive-caused bias as a consequence of the superpower of incentives.

With the push given by Cialdini's book, I soon skimmed through three much used textbooks covering introductory psychology. I also pondered considerably while craving synthesis and taking into account all my previous training and experience. The result was Munger's partial summary of the non-patient-treating, non-nature vs. nurture-weighing parts of nondevelopmental psychology. This material was stolen from its various discoverers (most of whose names I did not even try to learn), often with new descriptions and titles selected to fit Munger's notion of what makes recall easy for Munger, then revised to make Munger's use easy as he seeks to avoid errors.

I will start my summary with a general observation that helps explain what follows. This observation is grounded in what we know about social insects. The limitations inherent in evolution's development of the nervous-system cells that control behavior are beautifully demonstrated by these insects, which often have a mere 100,000 or so cells in their entire nervous systems, compared to man's multiple billions of cells in his brain alone.

Each ant, like each human, is composed of a living physical structure plus behavioral algorithms in its nerve cells. In the ant's case, the behavioral algorithms are few in number and almost entirely genetic in origin. The ant learns a little behavior from experiences, but mostly it merely responds to ten or so stimuli with a few simple responses programmed into its nervous system by its genes.

Naturally, the simple ant behavior system has extreme limitations because of its limited nerve-system repertoire. For instance, one type of ant, when it smells a pheromone given off by a dead ant's body in the hive, immediately responds by cooperating with other ants in carrying the dead body out of the hive. And Harvard's great E.O. Wilson performed one of the best psychology experiments ever done when he painted dead-ant pheromone on a live ant. Quite naturally, the other ants dragged this useful live ant out of the hive even though it kicked and otherwise protested throughout the entire process. Such is the brain of the ant. It has a simple program of responses that generally work out all right, but which are imprudently used by rote in many cases.

Another type of ant demonstrates that the limited brain of ants can be misled by circumstances as well as by clever manipulation from other creatures. The brain of this ant contains a simple behavioral program that directs the ant, when walking, to follow the ant ahead. And when these ants stumble into walking in a big circle, they sometimes walk round and round until they perish.

It seems obvious, to me at least, that the human brain must often operate counterproductively just like the ant's, from unavoidable oversimplicity in its mental process, albeit usually in trying to solve problems more difficult than those faced by ants that don't have to design airplanes.

The perception system of man clearly demonstrates just such an unfortunate outcome. Man is easily fooled, either by the cleverly thought out manipulation of man, by circumstances occurring by accident, or by very effective manipulation practices that man has stumbled into during "practice evolution" and kept in place because they work so well. One such outcome is caused by a quantum effect in human perception. If stimulus is kept below a certain level, it does not get through. And, for this reason, a magician was able to make the Statue of Liberty disappear after a certain amount of magician lingo expressed in the dark. The audience was not aware that it was sitting on a platform that was rotating so slowly, below man's sensory threshold, that no one could feel the acceleration implicit in the considerable rotation. When a surrounding curtain was then opened in the place on the platform where the Statue had earlier appeared, it seemed to have disappeared.

And even when perception does get through to man's brain, it is often misweighted, because what is registered in perception is in shockingness of apparent contrast, not the standard scientific units that make possible science and good engineering.

A magician demonstrates this sort of contrast-based error in your nervous system when he removes your wristwatch without your feeling it. As he does this, he applies pressure of touch on your wrist that you would sense if it was the only pressure of touch you were experiencing. But he has concurrently applied other intense pressure of touch on your body, but not on your wrist, "swamping" the wrist pressure by creating a high-contrast touch pressure elsewhere. This high contrast takes the wrist pressure below perception.

Some psychology professors like to demonstrate the inadequacy of contrast-based perception by having students put one hand in a bucket of hot water and one hand in a bucket of cold water. They are then suddenly asked to remove both hands and place them in a single bucket of room-temperature water. Now, with both hands in the same water, one hand feels as if it has just been put in cold water and the other hand feels as if it has just been placed in hot water. When one thus sees perception so easily fooled by mere contrast, where a simple temperature gauge would make no error, and realizes that cognition mimics perception in being misled by mere contrast, he is well on the way toward understanding, not only how magicians fool one, but also how life will fool one. This can occur, through deliberate human manipulation or otherwise, if one doesn't take certain precautions

against often-wrong effects from generally useful tendencies in his perception and cognition.

Man's—often wrong but generally useful—psychological tendencies are quite numerous and quite different. The natural consequence of this profusion of tendencies is the grand general principle of social psychology: cognition is ordinarily situation-dependent so that different situations often cause different conclusions, even when the same person is thinking in the same general subject area.

With this introductory instruction from ants, magicians, and the grand general principle of social psychology, I will next simply number and list psychology-based tendencies that, while generally useful, often mislead. Discussion of errors from each tendency will come later, together with description of some antidotes to errors, followed by some general discussion. Here are the tendencies:

One:	Reward and Punishment Superresponse Tendency
Two:	Liking/Loving Tendency
Three:	Disliking/Hating Tendency
Four:	Doubt-Avoidance Tendency
Five:	Inconsistency-Avoidance Tendency
Six:	Curiosity Tendency

Seven:	Kantian Fairness Tendency
Eight:	Envy/Jealousy Tendency
Nine:	Reciprocation Tendency
Ten:	Influence-from-Mere-Association Tendency
Eleven:	Simple, Pain-Avoiding Psychological Denial
Twelve:	Excessive Self-Regard Tendency
Thirteen:	Overoptimism Tendency
Fourteen:	Deprival-Superreaction Tendency
Fifteen:	Social-Proof Tendency
Sixteen:	Contrast-Misreaction Tendency
Seventeen:	Stress-Influence Tendency
Eighteen:	Availability-Misweighing Tendency
Nineteen:	Use-It-or-Lose-It Tendency
Twenty:	Drug-Misinfluence Tendency
Twenty-One:	Senescence-Misinfluence Tendency
Twenty-Two:	Authority-Misinfluence Tendency

Twenty-Three:	Twaddle Tendency
Twenty-Four:	Reason-Respecting Tendency
Twenty-Five:	Lollapalooza Tendency—The Tendency to Get Extreme Consequences from Confluences of Psychological Tendencies Acting in Favor of a Particular Outcome

One:
Reward and Punishment Superresponse Tendency

I place this tendency first in my discussion because almost everyone thinks he fully recognizes how important incentives and disincentives are in changing cognition and behavior. But this is not often so. For instance, I think I've been in the top five percent of my age cohort almost all my adult life in understanding the power of incentives, and yet I've always underestimated that power. Never a year passes but I get some surprise that pushes a little further my appreciation of incentive superpower.

One of my favorite cases about the power of incentives is the Federal Express case. The integrity of the Federal Express system requires that all packages be shifted rapidly among airplanes in one central airport each night. And the system has no integrity for the customers if the night work shift can't accomplish its assignment fast. And Federal Express had one hell of a time getting the night shift to do the right thing. They tried moral suasion. They tried everything in the world without luck. And, finally, somebody got the happy thought that it was foolish to pay the night shift by the hour when what the employer wanted was not maximized billable hours of employee service but fault-free, rapid performance of a particular task. Maybe, this person thought, if they paid the employees per shift and let all night shift employees go home when all the planes were loaded, the system would work better. And, lo and behold, that solution worked.

Early in the history of Xerox, Joe Wilson, who was then in the government, had a similar experience. He had to go back to Xerox because he couldn't understand why its new machine was selling so poorly in relation to its older and inferior machine. When he got back to Xerox, he found out that the commission arrangement with the salesmen gave a large and perverse incentive to push the inferior machine on customers, who deserved a better result.

And then there is the case of Mark Twain's cat that, after a bad experience with a hot stove, never again sat on a hot stove, or a cold stove either.

We should also heed the general lesson implicit in the injunction of Ben Franklin in *Poor Richard's Almanack*: "If you would persuade, appeal to interest and not to reason." This maxim is a wise guide to a great and simple precaution in life: Never, ever, think about something else when you should be thinking about the power of incentives. I once saw a very smart house counsel for a major investment bank lose his job, with no moral fault, because he ignored the lesson in this maxim of Franklin. This counsel failed to persuade his client because he told him his moral duty, as correctly conceived by the counsel, without also telling the client in vivid terms that he was very likely to be clobbered to smithereens if he didn't behave as his counsel recommended. As a result, both client and counsel lost their careers.

We should also remember how a foolish and willful ignorance of the superpower of rewards caused Soviet communists to get their final result as described by one employee: "They pretend to pay us and we pretend to work." Perhaps the most important rule in management is "Get the incentives right."

But there is some limit to a desirable emphasis on incentive superpower. One case of excess emphasis happened at Harvard, where B. F. Skinner, a psychology professor, finally made himself ridiculous. At one time, Skinner may have been the best-known psychology professor in the world. He partly deserved his peak reputation because his early experiments using rats and pigeons were ingenious, and his results were both counterintuitive and important. With incentives, he could cause more behavior change, culminating in conditioned reflexes in his rats and pigeons, than he could in any other way. He made obvious the extreme stupidity, in dealing with children or employees, of rewarding behavior one didn't want more of. Using food rewards, he even caused strong superstitions, predesigned by himself, in his pigeons. He demonstrated again and again a great recurring, generalized behavioral algorithm in nature: "Repeat behavior that works." He also demonstrated that prompt rewards worked much

better than delayed rewards in changing and maintaining behavior. And, once his rats and pigeons had conditioned reflexes, caused by food rewards, he found what withdrawal pattern of rewards kept the reflexive behavior longest in place: random distribution. With this result, Skinner thought he had pretty well explained man's misgambling compulsion whereunder he often foolishly proceeds to ruin. But, as we shall later see when we discuss other psychological tendencies that contribute to misgambling compulsion, he was only partly right. Later, Skinner lost most of his personal reputation (a) by overclaiming for incentive superpower to the point of thinking he could create a human utopia with it and (b) by displaying hardly any recognition of the power of the rest of psychology. He thus behaved like one of Jacob Viner's truffle hounds as he tried to explain everything with incentive effects. Nonetheless, Skinner was right in his main idea: Incentives are superpowers. The outcome of his basic experiments will always remain in high repute in the annals of experimental science. And his method of monomaniacal reliance on rewards, for many decades after his death, did more good than anything else in improving autistic children.

When I was at Harvard Law School, the professors sometimes talked about an overfocused, Skinner-like professor at Yale Law School. They used to say: "Poor old Eddie Blanchard, he thinks declaratory judgments will cure cancer." Well, that's the way Skinner got with his very extreme emphasis on incentive superpower. I always call the "Johnny-one-note" turn of mind that eventually so diminished Skinner's reputation the man-with-a-hammer tendency, after the folk saying: "To a man with only a hammer every problem looks pretty much like a nail." Man-with-a-hammer tendency does not exempt smart people like Blanchard and Skinner. And it won't exempt you if you don't watch out. I will return to man-with-a-hammer tendency at various times in this talk because, fortunately, there are effective antidotes that reduce the ravages of what pretty much ruined the personal reputation of the brilliant Skinner.

One of the most important consequences of incentive superpower is what I call "incentive-caused bias." A man has an acculturated nature making him a pretty decent fellow, and yet, driven both consciously and subconsciously by incentives, he drifts into immoral behavior in order to get what he wants, a result he facilitates by rationalizing his bad behavior, like the salesmen at Xerox who harmed customers in order to maximize their sales commissions.

Here, my early education involved a surgeon who over the years sent bushel baskets full of normal gall bladders down to the pathology lab in the leading hospital in Lincoln, Nebraska, my grandfather's town. And, with that permissive quality control for which community hospitals are famous, many years after this surgeon should've been removed from the medical staff, he was. One

of the doctors who participated in the removal was a family friend, and I asked him: "Did this surgeon think, 'Here's a way for me to exercise my talents'—this guy was very skilled technically—'and make a high living by doing a few maimings and murders every year in the course of routine fraud?'" And my friend answered: "Hell no, Charlie. He thought that the gall bladder was the source of all medical evil, and, if you really loved your patients, you couldn't get that organ out rapidly enough."

Now that's an extreme case, but in lesser strength, the cognitive drift of that surgeon is present in every profession and in every human being. And it causes perfectly terrible behavior. Consider the presentations of brokers selling commercial real estate and businesses. I've never seen one that I thought was even within hailing distance of objective truth. In my long life, I have never seen a management consultant's report that didn't end with the same advice: "This problem needs more management consulting services." Widespread incentive-caused bias requires that one should often distrust, or take with a grain of salt, the advice of one's professional advisor, even if he is an engineer. The general antidotes here are: (1) especially fear professional advice when it is especially good for the advisor; (2) learn and use the basic elements of your advisor's trade as you deal with your advisor; and (3) double check, disbelieve, or replace much of what you're told, to the degree that seems appropriate after objective thought.

The power of incentives to cause rationalized, terrible behavior is also demonstrated by Defense Department procurement history. After the Defense Department had much truly awful experience with misbehaving contractors motivated under contracts paying on a cost-plus-a-percentage-of-cost basis, the reaction of our republic was to make it a crime for a contracting officer in the Defense Department to sign such a contract, and not only a crime, but a felony.

And, by the way, although the government was right to create this new felony, much of the way the rest of the world is run, including the operation of many law firms and a lot of other firms, is still under what is, in essence, a cost-plus-a-percentage-of-cost reward system. And human nature, bedeviled by incentive-caused bias, causes a lot of ghastly abuse under these standard incentive patterns of the world. And many of the people who are behaving terribly you would be glad to have married into your family, compared to what you're otherwise likely to get.

Now there are huge implications from the fact that the human mind is put together this way. One implication is that people who create things like cash registers, which make dishonest behavior hard to accomplish, are some of the effective saints of our civilization because, as Skinner so well knew, bad behavior is intensely habit-forming when it is rewarded. And so the cash register was a great moral instrument when it was created. And, by

the way, Patterson, the great evangelist of the cash register, knew that from his own experience. He had a little store, and his employees were stealing him blind, so that he never made any money. Then people sold him a couple of cash registers, and his store went to profit immediately. He promptly closed the store and went into the cash register business, creating what became the mighty National Cash Register Company, one of the glories of its time. "Repeat behavior that works" is a behavioral guide that really succeeded for Patterson, after he applied one added twist. And so did high moral cognition. An eccentric, inveterate do-gooder (except when destroying competitors, all of which he regarded as would-be patent thieves), Patterson, like Carnegie, pretty well gave away all his money to charity before he died, always pointing out that "shrouds have no pockets." So great was the contribution of Patterson's cash register to civilization, and so effectively did he improve the cash register and spread its use, that in the end, he probably deserved the epitaph chosen for the Roman poet Horace: "I did not completely die."

The strong tendency of employees to rationalize bad conduct in order to get rewards requires many antidotes in addition to the good cash control promoted by Patterson. Perhaps the most important of these antidotes is use of sound accounting theory and practice. This was seldom better demonstrated than at Westinghouse, which had a subsidiary that made loans having no connection to the rest of Westinghouse's businesses. The officers of Westinghouse, perhaps influenced by envy of General Electric, wanted to expand profits from loans to outsiders. Under Westinghouse's accounting practice, provisions for future credit losses on these loans depended largely on the past credit experience of its lending subsidiary, which mainly made loans unlikely to cause massive losses.

Now there are two special classes of loans that naturally cause much trouble for lenders. The first is ninety-five percent-of-value construction loans to any kind of real estate developer, and the second is any kind of construction loan on a hotel. So, naturally, if one was willing to loan approximately ninety-five percent of the real cost to a developer constructing a hotel, the loan would bear a much-higher-than-normal interest rate because the credit-loss danger would be much higher than normal. So, sound accounting for Westinghouse in making a big, new mass of ninety-five percent-of-value construction loans to hotel developers would have been to report almost no profit, or even a loss, on each loan until, years later, the loan became clearly worth par. But Westinghouse instead plunged into big-time construction lending on hotels, using accounting that made its lending officers look good because it showed extremely high starting income from loans that were very inferior to the loans from which the company had suffered small credit losses in the past. This terrible accounting was allowed by both international and outside accountants for Westing-

house as they displayed the conduct predicted by the refrain: "Whose bread I eat, his song I sing."

The result was billions of dollars of losses. Who was at fault? The guy from the refrigerator division, or some similar division, who as lending officer was suddenly in charge of loans to hotel developers? Or the accountants and other senior people who tolerated a nearly insane incentive structure, almost sure to trigger incentive-caused bias in a lending officer? My answer puts most blame on the accountants and other senior people who created the accounting system. These people became the equivalent of an armored car cash-carrying service that suddenly decided to dispense with vehicles and have unarmed midgets hand-carry its customers' cash through slums in open bushel baskets.

I wish I could tell you that this sort of thing no longer happens, but this is not so. After Westinghouse blew up, General Electric's Kidder Peabody subsidiary put a silly computer program in place that allowed a bond trader to show immense fictional profits. And after that, much accounting became even worse, perhaps reaching its nadir at Enron.

And so incentive-caused bias is a huge, important thing, with highly important antidotes, like the cash register and a sound accounting system. But when I came years ago to the psychology texts, I found that, while they were about one thousand pages long, there was little therein that dealt with incentive-caused bias and no mention of Patterson or sound accounting systems. Somehow incentive-caused bias and its antidotes pretty well escaped the standard survey courses in psychology, even though incentive-caused bias had long been displayed prominently in much of the world's great literature, and antidotes to it had long existed in standard business routines. In the end, I concluded that when something was obvious in life but not easily demonstrable in certain kinds of easy-to-do, repeatable academic experiments, the truffle hounds of psychology very often missed it.

In some cases, other disciplines showed more interest in psychological tendencies than did psychology, at least as explicated in psychology textbooks. For instance, economists, speaking from the employer's point of view, have long had a name for the natural results of incentive-caused bias: "agency cost." As the name implies, the economists have typically known that, just as grain is always lost to rats, employers always lose to employees who improperly think of themselves first. Employer-installed antidotes include tough internal audit systems and severe public punishment for identi-fied miscreants, as well as misbehavior-preventing routines and such machines as cash registers. From the employee's point of view, incentive-caused bias quite naturally causes opposing abuse from the employer: the sweatshop, the unsafe work place, etc. And these bad results for employees have antidotes not only in pressure from unions but

also in government action, such as wage and hour laws, work-place-safety rules, measures fostering unionization, and workers' compensation systems. Given the opposing psychology-induced strains that naturally occur in employment because of incentive-caused bias on both sides of the relation-ship, it is no wonder the Chinese are so much into Yin and Yang.

The inevitable ubiquity of incentive-caused bias has vast, generalized consequences. For instance, a sales force living only on commissions will be much harder to keep moral than one under less pressure from the compensation arrangement. On the other hand, a purely commissioned sales force may well be more efficient per dollar spent. Therefore, difficult decisions involving trade-offs are common in creating compensation arrangements in the sales function.

The extreme success of free-market capitalism as an economic system owes much to its preven-tion of many of bad effects from incentive-caused bias. Most capitalist owners in a vast web of free-market economic activity are selected for ability by surviving in a brutal competition with other owners and have a strong incentive to prevent all waste in operations within their ownership. After all, they live on the difference between their competitive prices and their overall costs and their businesses will perish if costs exceed sales. Replace such owners by salaried employees of the state and you will normally get a substantial reduction in overall efficiency as each employee who replaces an owner is subject to incentive-caused bias as he determines what service he will give in exchange for his salary and how much he will yield to peer pressure from many fellow employees who do not desire his creation of any strong performance model.

Another generalized consequence of incentive-caused bias is that man tends to "game" all human systems, often displaying great ingenuity in wrongly serving himself at the expense of others. Anti-gaming features, therefore, constitute a huge and necessary part of almost all system design. Also needed in system design is an admonition: Dread, and avoid as much you can, rewarding people for what can be easily faked. Yet our legislators and judges, usually including many lawyers educated in eminent universities, often ignore this injunction. And society consequently pays a huge price in the deterioration of behavior and efficiency, as well as the incurrence of unfair costs and wealth transfers. If education were improved, with psychological reality becoming better taught and assimilated, better system design might well come out of our legislatures and courts.

Of course, money is now the main reward that drives habits. A monkey can be trained to seek and work for an intrinsically worthless token, as if it were a banana, if the token is routinely exchangeable for a banana. So it is also with humans working for money—only more so, because human money is exchangeable for many desired things in addition to food, and one ordinarily gains status from either holding or spending it. Moreover, a rich person will often, through habit, work or connive energetically for more money long after he has almost no real need for more. Averaged out, money is a mainspring of modern civilization, having little precedent in the behavior of nonhuman animals. Money rewards are also intertwined with other forms of reward. For instance, some people use money to buy status and others use status to get money, while still others sort of do both things at the same time.

Although money is the main driver among rewards, it is not the only reward that works. People also change their behavior and cognition for sex, friendship, companionship, advancement in status, and other nonmonetary items.

"Granny's Rule" provides another example of reward superpower, so extreme in its effects that it must be mentioned here. You can successfully manipulate your own behavior with this rule, even if you are using as rewards items that you already possess! Indeed, consultant Ph. D. psychologists often urge business organizations to improve their reward systems by teaching executives to use "Granny's Rule" to govern their own daily behavior. Granny's Rule, to be specific, is the requirement that children eat their carrots before they get dessert. And the business version requires that executives force themselves daily to first do their unpleasant and necessary tasks before rewarding themselves by proceeding to their pleasant tasks. Given reward superpower, this practice is wise and sound. Moreover, the rule can also be used in the nonbusiness part of life. The emphasis on daily use of this practice is not accidental. The consultants well know, after the teaching of Skinner, that prompt rewards work best.

Punishments, of course, also strongly influence behavior and cognition, although not so flexibly and wonderfully as rewards. For instance, illegal price fixing was fairly common in America when it was customarily punished by modest fines. Then, after a few prominent business executives were removed from their eminent positions and sent to federal prisons, price-fixing behavior was greatly reduced.

Military and naval organizations have very often been extreme in using punishment to change behavior, probably because they needed to cause extreme behavior. Around the time of Caesar, there was a European tribe that, when the assembly horn blew, always killed the last warrior to reach his assigned place, and no one enjoyed fighting this tribe. And George Washington hanged farm-boy deserters forty feet high as an example to others who might contemplate desertion.

Two:
Liking/Loving Tendency

A newly hatched baby goose is programmed, through the economy of its genetic program, to "love" and follow the first creature that is nice to it, which is almost always its mother. But, if the mother goose is not present right after the hatching, and a man is there instead, the gosling will "love" and follow the man, who becomes a sort of substitute mother.

Somewhat similarly, a newly arrived human is "born to like and love" under the normal and abnormal triggering outcomes for its kind. Perhaps the strongest inborn tendency to love—ready to be triggered—is that of the human mother for its child. On the other hand, the similar "child-loving" behavior of a mouse can be eliminated by the deletion of a single gene, which suggests there is some sort of triggering gene in a mother mouse as well as in a gosling.

Each child, like a gosling, will almost surely come to like and love, not only as driven by its sexual nature, but also in social groups not limited to its genetic or adoptive "family." Current extremes of romantic love almost surely did not occur in man's remote past. Our early human ancestors were surely more like apes triggered into mating in a pretty mundane fashion.

And what will a man naturally come to like and love, apart from his parent, spouse and child? Well, he will like and love being liked and loved. And so many a courtship competition will be won by a person displaying exceptional devotion, and man will generally strive, lifelong, for the affection and approval of many people not related to him.

One very practical consequence of Liking/ Loving Tendency is that it acts as a conditioning device that makes the liker or lover tend (1) to ignore faults of, and comply with wishes of, the object of his affection, (2) to favor people, products, and actions merely associated with the object of his affection (as we shall see when we get to "Influence-from-Mere-Association Tendency," and (3) to distort other facts to facilitate love.

The phenomenon of liking and loving causing admiration also works in reverse. Admiration also causes or intensifies liking or love. With this "feedback mode" in place, the consequences are often extreme, sometimes even causing deliberate self-destruction to help what is loved.

Liking or loving, intertwined with admiration in a feedback mode, often has vast practical consequences in areas far removed from sexual attachments. For instance, a man who is so constructed that he loves admirable persons and ideas with a special intensity has a huge advantage in life. This blessing came to both Buffett and myself in large measure, sometimes from the same persons and ideas. One common, beneficial example for us both was Warren's uncle, Fred Buffett, who cheerfully did the endless grocery-store work that Warren and I ended up admiring from a safe distance. Even now, after I have known so many other people, I doubt if it is possible to be a nicer man than Fred Buffett was, and he changed me for the better.

There are large social policy implications in the amazingly good consequences that ordinarily come from people likely to trigger extremes of love and admiration boosting each other in a feedback mode. For instance, it is obviously desirable to attract a lot of lovable, admirable people into the teaching profession.

Three:
Disliking/Hating Tendency

In a pattern obverse to Liking/Loving Tendency, the newly arrived human is also "born to dislike and hate" as triggered by normal and abnormal triggering forces in its life. It is the same with most apes and monkeys.

As a result, the long history of man contains almost continuous war. For instance, most American Indian tribes warred incessantly, and some tribes would occasionally bring captives home to women so that all could join in the fun of torturing captives to death. Even with the spread of religion, and the advent of advanced civilization, much modern war remains pretty savage. But we also get what we observe in present-day Switzerland and the United States, wherein the clever political arrangements of man "channel" the hatreds and dislikings of individuals and groups into nonlethal patterns including elections.

But the dislikings and hatreds never go away completely. Born into man, these driving tendencies remain strong. Thus, we get maxims like the one from England: "Politics is the art of marshalling hatreds." And we also get the extreme popularity of very negative political advertising in the United States.

At the family level, we often see one sibling hate his other siblings and litigate with them endlessly if he can afford it. Indeed, a wag named Buffett has repeatedly explained to me that "a major difference between rich and poor people is that the rich people can spend their lives suing their relatives." My father's law practice in Omaha was full of such intrafamily hatreds. And when I got to the Harvard Law School and its professors taught me "property law" with no mention of sibling rivalry in the family business, I appraised the School as a pretty unrealistic place that wore "blinders" like the milk-wagon horses of yore. My current guess is that sibling rivalry has not yet made it into property law as taught at Harvard.

Disliking/Hating Tendency also acts as a conditioning device that makes the disliker/hater tend to (1) ignore virtues in the object of dislike, (2) dislike people, products, and actions merely associated with the object of his dislike, and (3) distort other facts to facilitate hatred.

Distortion of that kind is often so extreme that miscognition is shockingly large. When the World Trade Center was destroyed, many Pakistanis immediately concluded that the Hindus did it, while many Muslims concluded that the Jews did it. Such factual distortions often make mediation between opponents locked in hatred either difficult or impossible. Mediations between Israelis and Palestinians are difficult because facts in one side's history overlap very little with facts from the other side's.

Four:
Doubt-Avoidance Tendency

The brain of man is programmed with a tendency to quickly remove doubt by reaching some decision.

It is easy to see how evolution would make animals, over the eons, drift toward such quick elimination of doubt. After all, the one thing that is surely counterproductive for a prey animal that is threatened by a predator is to take a long time in deciding what to do. And so man's Doubt-Avoidance Tendency is quite consistent with the history of his ancient, nonhuman ancestors.

So pronounced is the tendency in man to quickly remove doubt by reaching some decision that behavior to counter the tendency is required from judges and jurors. Here, delay before decision making is forced. And one is required to so comport himself, prior to conclusion time, so that he is wearing a "mask" of objectivity. And the "mask" works to help real objectivity along, as we shall see when we next consider man's Inconsistency-Avoidance Tendency.

Of course, once one has recognized that man has a strong Doubt-Avoidance Tendency, it is logical to believe that at least some leaps of religious faith are greatly boosted by this tendency. Even if one is satisfied that his own faith comes from revelation, one still must account for the inconsistent faiths of others. And man's Doubt-Avoidance Tendency is almost surely a big part of the answer.

What triggers Doubt-Avoidance Tendency? Well, an unthreatened man, thinking of nothing in particular, is not being prompted to remove doubt through rushing to some decision. As we shall see later when we get to Social-Proof Tendency and Stress-Influence Tendency, what usually triggers Doubt-Avoidance Tendency is some combination of (1) puzzlement and (2) stress. And both of these factors naturally occur in facing religious issues.

Thus, the natural state of most men is in some form of religion. And this is what we observe.

Five:
Inconsistency-Avoidance Tendency

The brain of man conserves programming space by being reluctant to change, which is a form of inconsistency avoidance. We see this in all human habits, constructive and destructive. Few people can list a lot of bad habits that they have eliminated, and some people cannot identify even one of these. Instead, practically everyone has a great many bad habits he has long maintained despite their being known as bad. Given this situation, it is not too much in many cases to appraise early-formed habits as destiny. When Marley's miserable ghost says, "I wear the chains I forged in life," he is talking about chains of habit that were too light to be felt before they became too strong to be broken.

The rare life that is wisely lived has in it many good habits maintained and many bad habits avoided or cured. And the great rule that helps here is again from Franklin's *Poor Richard's Almanack*: "An ounce of prevention is worth a pound of cure." What Franklin is here indicating, in part, is that Inconsistency-Avoidance Tendency makes it much easier to prevent a habit than to change it.

Also tending to be maintained in place by the anti-change tendency of the brain are one's previous conclusions, human loyalties, reputational identity, commitments, accepted role in a civilization, etc. It is not entirely clear why evolution would program into man's brain an anti-change mode alongside his tendency to quickly remove doubt. My guess is the anti-change mode was significantly caused by a combination of the following factors:

(1) It facilitated faster decisions when speed of decision was an important contribution to the survival of nonhuman ancestors that were prey.

(2) It facilitated the survival advantage that our ancestors gained by cooperating in groups, which would have been more difficult to do if everyone was always changing responses.

(3) It was the best form of solution that evolution could get to in the limited number of generations between the start of literacy and today's complex modern life.

It is easy to see that a quickly reached conclusion, triggered by Doubt-Avoidance Tendency, when combined with a tendency to resist any change in that conclusion, will naturally cause a lot of errors in cognition for modern man. And so it observably works out. We all deal much with others whom we correctly diagnose as imprisoned in poor conclusions that are maintained by mental habits they formed early and will carry to their graves.

So great is the bad-decision problem caused by Inconsistency-Avoidance Tendency that our courts have adopted important strategies against it. For instance, before making decisions, judges and juries are required to hear long and skillful presentations of evidence and argument from the side they will not naturally favor, given their ideas in place. And this helps prevent considerable bad thinking from "first conclusion bias." Similarly, other modern decision makers will often force groups to consider skillful counterarguments before making decisions.

And proper education is one long exercise in augmentation of high cognition so that our wisdom becomes strong enough to destroy wrong thinking maintained by resistance to change. As Lord Keynes pointed out about his exalted intellectual group at one of the greatest universities in the world, it was not the intrinsic difficulty of new ideas that prevented their acceptance. Instead, the new ideas were not accepted because they were inconsistent with old ideas in place. What Keynes was reporting is that the human mind works a lot like the human egg. When one sperm gets into a human egg, there's an automatic shut-off device that bars any other sperm from getting in. The human mind tends strongly toward the same sort of result.

And so, people tend to accumulate large mental holdings of fixed conclusions and attitudes that are not often reexamined or changed, even though there is plenty of good evidence that they are wrong.

Moreover, this doesn't just happen in social science departments, like the one that once thought Freud should serve as the only choice as a psychology teacher for Caltech. Holding to old errors even happens, although with less frequency and severity, in hard science departments. We have no less an authority for this than Max Planck, Nobel laureate, finder of "Planck's constant." Planck is famous not only for his science but also for saying that even in physics the radically new ideas are seldom really accepted by the old guard. Instead, said Planck, the progress is made by a new generation that comes along, less brain-blocked by its previous conclusions. Indeed, precisely this sort of brain-blocking happened to a degree in Einstein. At his peak, Einstein was a great destroyer of his own ideas, but an older Einstein never accepted the full implications of quantum mechanics.

One of the most successful users of an antidote to first conclusion bias was Charles Darwin. He trained himself, early, to intensively consider any evidence tending to disconfirm any hypothesis of his, more so if he thought his hypothesis was a particularly good one. The opposite of what Darwin did is now called confirmation bias, a term of opprobrium. Darwin's practice came from his acute recognition of man's natural cognitive faults arising from Inconsistency-Avoidance Tendency. He provides a great example of psychological insight correctly used to advance some of the finest mental work ever done.

Inconsistency-Avoidance Tendency has many good effects in civilization. For instance, rather than act inconsistently with public commitments, new or old public identities, etc., most people are more loyal in their roles in life as priests, physicians, citizens, soldiers, spouses, teachers, employees, etc.

One corollary of Inconsistency-Avoidance Tendency is that a person making big sacrifices in the course of assuming a new identity will intensify his devotion to the new identity. After all, it would be quite inconsistent behavior to make a large sacrifice for something that was no good. And thus civilization has invented many tough and solemn initiation ceremonies, often public in nature, that intensify new commitments made.

Tough initiation ceremonies can intensify bad contact as well as good. The loyalty of the new, "made-man" mafia member, or of the military officer making the required "blood oath" of loyalty to Hitler, was boosted through the triggering of Inconsistency-Avoidance Tendency.

Moreover, the tendency will often make man a "patsy" of manipulative "compliance-practitioners," who gain advantage from triggering his subconscious Inconsistency-Avoidance Tendency. Few people demonstrated this process better than Ben Franklin. As he was rising from obscurity in Philadelphia and wanted the approval of some important man, Franklin would often maneuver that man into doing Franklin some unimportant favor, like lending Franklin a book. Thereafter, the man would admire and trust Franklin more because a nonadmired and nontrusted Franklin would be inconsistent with the appraisal implicit in lending Franklin the book.

During the Korean War, this technique of Franklin's was the most important feature of the Chinese brainwashing system that was used on enemy prisoners. Small step by small step, the technique often worked better than torture in altering prisoner cognition in favor of Chinese captors.

The practice of Franklin, whereunder he got approval from someone by maneuvering him into treating Franklin favorably, works viciously well in reverse. When one is maneuvered into deliberately hurting some other person, one will tend to disapprove or even hate that person. This effect, from Inconsistency-Avoidance Tendency, accounts for the insight implicit in the saying: "A man never forgets where he has buried the hatchet." The effect accounts for much prisoner abuse by guards, increasing their dislike and hatred for prisoners that exists as a consequence of the guards' reciprocation of hostility from prisoners who are treated like animals. Given the psychology-based hostility natural in prisons between guards and prisoners, an intense, continuous effort should be made (1) to prevent prisoner abuse from starting and (2) to stop it instantly when it starts because it will grow by feeding on itself, like a cluster of infectious disease. More psychological acuity on this subject, aided by more insightful teaching, would probably improve the overall effectiveness of the U.S. Army.

So strong is Inconsistency-Avoidance Tendency that it will often prevail after one has merely pretended to have some identity, habit, or conclusion. Thus, for a while, many an actor sort of believes he is Hamlet, Prince of Denmark. And many a hypocrite is improved by his pretensions of virtue. And many a judge and juror, while pretending objectivity, is gaining objectivity. And many a trial lawyer or other advocate comes to believe what he formerly only pretended to believe.

While Inconsistency-Avoidance Tendency, with its "status quo bias," immensely harms sound education, it also causes much benefit. For instance, a near-ultimate inconsistency would be to teach something to others that one did not believe true. And so, in clinical medical education, the learner is forced to "see one, do one, and then teach one," with the teaching pounding the learning into the teacher. Of course, the power of teaching to influence the cognition of the teacher is not always a benefit to society. When such power flows into political and cult evangelism, there are often bad consequences.

For instance, modern education often does much damage when young students are taught dubious political notions and then enthusiastically push these notions on the rest of us. The pushing seldom convinces others. But as students pound into their mental habits what they are pushing out, the students are often permanently damaged. Educational institutions that create a climate where much of this goes on are, I think, irresponsible. It is important not to thus put one's brain in chains before one has come anywhere near his full potentiality as a rational person.

Six:
Curiosity Tendency

There is a lot of innate curiosity in mammals, but its nonhuman version is highest among apes and monkeys. Man's curiosity, in turn, is much stronger than that of his simian relatives. In advanced human civilization, culture greatly increases the effectiveness of curiosity in advancing knowledge. For instance, Athens (including its colony, Alexandria) developed much math and science out of pure curiosity while the Romans made almost no contribution to either math or science. They instead concentrated their attention on the "practical" engineering of mines, roads, aqueducts, etc. Curiosity, enhanced by the best of modern education (which is by definition a minority part in many places), much helps man to prevent or reduce bad consequences arising from other psychological tendencies. The curious are also provided with much fun and wisdom long after formal education has ended.

Seven:
Kantian Fairness Tendency

Kant was famous for his "categorical imperative," a sort of a "golden rule" that required humans to follow those behavior patterns that, if followed by all others, would make the surrounding human system work best for everybody. And it is not too much to say that modern acculturated man displays, and expects from others, a lot of fairness as thus defined by Kant.

In a small community having a one-way bridge or tunnel for autos, it is the norm in the United States to see a lot of reciprocal courtesy, despite the absence of signs or signals. And many freeway drivers, including myself, will often let other drivers come in front of them, in lane changes or the like, because that is the courtesy they desire when roles are reversed. Moreover, there is, in modern human culture, a lot of courteous lining up by strangers so that all are served on a "first-come-first-served" basis.

Also, strangers often voluntarily share equally in unexpected, unearned good and bad fortune. And, as an obverse consequence of such "fair-sharing" conduct, much reactive hostility occurs when fair-sharing is expected yet not provided.

It is interesting how the world's slavery was pretty well abolished during the last three centuries after being tolerated for a great many previous centuries during which it coexisted with the world's major religions. My guess is that Kantian Fairness Tendency was a major contributor to this result.

Eight:
Envy/Jealousy Tendency

A member of a species designed through evolutionary process to want often-scarce food is going to be driven strongly toward getting food when it first sees food. And this is going to occur often and tend to create some conflict when the food is seen in the possession of another member of the same species. This is probably the evolutionary origin of the envy/jealousy Tendency that lies so deep in human nature.

Sibling jealousy is clearly very strong and usually greater in children than adults. It is often stronger than jealousy directed at strangers. Kantian Fairness Tendency probably contributes to this result.

Envy/jealousy is extreme in myth, religion, and literature wherein, in account after account, it triggers hatred and injury. It was regarded as so pernicious by the Jews of the civilization that preceded Christ that it was forbidden, by phrase after phrase, in the laws of Moses. You were even warned by the Prophet not to covet your neighbor's donkey.

And envy/jealousy is also extreme in modern life. For instance, university communities often go bananas when some university employee in money management, or some professor in surgery, gets annual compensation in multiples of the standard professorial salary. And in modern investment banks, law firms, etc., the envy/jealousy effects are usually more extreme than they are in university faculties. Many big law firms, fearing disorder from envy/jealousy, have long treated all senior partners alike in compensation, no matter how different their contributions to firm welfare. As I have shared the observation of life with Warren Buffett over decades, I have heard him wisely say on several occasions: "It is not greed that drives the world, but envy."

And, because this is roughly right, one would expect a vast coverage of envy/jealousy in psychology textbooks. But no such vast coverage existed when I read my three textbooks. Indeed, the very words "envy" and "jealousy" were often absent from indexes.

Nondiscussion of envy/jealousy is not a phenomenon confined to psychology texts. When did any of you last engage in any large group discussion of some issue wherein adult envy/jealousy was identified as the cause of someone's argument? There seems to be a general taboo against any such claim. If so, what accounts for the taboo?

My guess is that people widely and generally sense that labeling some position as driven by envy/jealousy will be regarded as extremely insulting to the position taker, possibly more so when the diagnosis is correct than when it is wrong. And if calling a position "envy-driven" is perceived as the equivalent of describing its holder as a childish mental basket case, then it is quite understandable how a general taboo has arisen.

But should this general taboo extend to psychology texts when it creates such a large gap in the correct, psychological explanation of what is widespread and important? My answer is no.

Nine:
Reciprocation Tendency

The automatic tendency of humans to reciprocate both favors and disfavors has long been noticed as extreme, as it is in apes, monkeys, dogs, and many less cognitively gifted animals. The tendency clearly facilitates group cooperation for the benefit of members. In this respect, it mimics much genetic programming of the social insects.

We see the extreme power of the tendency to reciprocate disfavors in some wars, wherein it increases hatred to a level causing very brutal conduct. For long stretches in many wars, no prisoners were taken; the only acceptable enemy being a dead one. And sometimes that was not enough, as in the case of Genghis Khan, who was not satisfied with corpses. He insisted on their being hacked into pieces.

One interesting mental exercise is to compare Genghis Khan, who exercised extreme, lethal hostility toward other men, with ants that display extreme, lethal hostility toward members of their own species that are not part of their breeding colony. Genghis looks sweetly lovable when compared to the ants. The ants are more disposed to fight and fight with more extreme cruelty. Indeed, E. O. Wilson once waggishly suggested that if ants were suddenly to get atom bombs, all ants would be dead within eighteen hours. What both human and ant history suggest is (1) that nature has no general algorithm making intraspecies, turn-the-other-cheek behavior a booster of species survival, (2) that it is not clear that a country would have good prospects were it to abandon all reciprocate-disfavor tendency directed at outsiders, and (3) if turn-the-other-cheek behavior is a good idea for a country as it deals with outsiders, man's culture is going to have to do a lot of heavy lifting because his genes won't be of much help.

I next turn to man's reciprocated hostility that falls well short of war. Peacetime hostility can be pretty extreme, as in many modern cases of "road rage" or injury-producing temper tantrums on athletic fields.

The standard antidote to one's overactive hostility is to train oneself to defer reaction. As my smart friend Tom Murphy so frequently says, "You can always tell the man off tomorrow, if it is such a good idea."

Of course, the tendency to reciprocate favor for favor is also very intense, so much so that it occasionally reverses the course of reciprocated hostility. Weird pauses in fighting have sometimes occurred right in the middle of wars, triggered by some minor courtesy or favor on the part of one side, followed by favor reciprocation from the other side, and so on, until fighting stopped for a considerable period. This happened more than once in the trench warfare of World War I, over big stretches of the front and much to the dismay of the generals.

It is obvious that commercial trade, a fundamental cause of modern prosperity, is enormously facilitated by man's innate tendency to reciprocate favors. In trade, enlightened self-interest joining with Reciprocation Tendency results in constructive conduct. Daily interchange in marriage is also assisted by Reciprocation Tendency, without which marriage would lose much of its allure.

And Reciprocation Tendency, insomuch as it causes good results, does not join forces only with the superpower of incentives. It also joins Inconsistency-Avoidance Tendency in helping cause (1) the fulfillment of promises made as part of a bargain, including loyalty promises in marriage ceremonies, and (2) correct behavior expected from persons serving as priests, shoemakers, physicians, and all else.

Like other psychological tendencies, and also man's ability to turn somersaults, reciprocate-favor tendency operates to a very considerable degree at a subconscious level. This helps make the tendency a strong force that can sometimes be used by some men to mislead others, which happens all the time.

For instance, when an automobile salesman graciously steers you into a comfortable place to sit and gives you a cup of coffee, you are very likely being tricked, by this small courtesy alone, into parting with an extra five hundred dollars. This is far from the most extreme case of sales success that is rooted in a salesman dispensing minor favors. However, in this scenario of buying a car, you are going to be disadvantaged by parting with an extra five hundred dollars of your own money. This potential loss will protect you to some extent.

But suppose you are the purchasing agent of someone else—a rich employer, for instance. Now the minor favor you receive from the salesman is less opposed by the threat of extra cost to you because someone else is paying the extra cost. Under such circumstances, the salesman is often able to maximize his advantage, particularly when government is the purchaser.

Wise employers, therefore, try to oppose reciprocate-favor tendencies of employees engaged in purchasing. The simplest antidote works best: Don't let them accept any favors from vendors. Sam Walton agreed with this idea of absolute prohibition. He wouldn't let purchasing agents accept so much as a hot dog from a vendor. Given the subconscious level at which much Reciprocation Tendency operates, this policy of Walton's was profoundly correct. If I controlled the Defense Department, its policies would mimic Walton's.

In a famous psychology experiment, Cialdini brilliantly demonstrated the power of "compliance practitioners" to mislead people by triggering their subconscious Reciprocation Tendency.

Carrying out this experiment, Cialdini caused his "compliance practitioners" to wander around his campus and ask strangers to supervise a bunch of juvenile delinquents on a trip to a zoo. Because this happed on a campus, one person in six out of a large sample actually agreed to do this. After accumulating this one-in-six statistic, Cialdini changed his procedure. His practitioners next wandered around the campus asking strangers to devote a big chunk of time every week for two years to the supervision of juvenile delinquents. This ridiculous request got him a one hundred percent rejection rate. But the practitioner had a follow-up question: "Will you at least spend one afternoon taking juvenile delinquents to a zoo?" This raised Ciladini's former acceptance rate of 1/6 to 1/2—a tripling.

What Cialdini's "compliance practitioners" had done was make a small concession, which was reciprocated by a small concession from the other side. This subconscious reciprocation of a concession by Cialdini's experimental subjects actually caused a much increased percentage of them to end up irrationally agreeing to go to a zoo with juvenile delinquents. Now, a professor who can invent an experiment like that, which so powerfully demonstrates something so important, deserves much recognition in the wider world, which he indeed got to the credit of many universities that learned a great deal from Cialdini.

Why is Reciprocation Tendency so important? Well, consider the folly of having law students graduate, and go out in the world representing clients in negotiations, not knowing the nature of the subconscious processes of the mind as exhibited in Cialdini's experiment. Yet such folly was prevalent in the law schools of the world for decades, in fact, generations. The correct name for that is educational malpractice. The law schools didn't know, or care to teach, what Sam Walton so well knew.

The importance and power of reciprocate-favor tendency was also demonstrated in Cialdini's explanation of the foolish decision of the attorney general of the United States to authorize the Watergate burglary. There, an aggressive subordinate made some extreme proposal for advancing Republican interests through use of some combination of whores and a gigantic yacht. When this ridiculous request was rejected, the subordinate backed off, in gracious concession, to merely asking for consent to a burglary, and the attorney general went along. Cialdini believes that subconscious Reciprocation Tendency thus became one important cause of the resignation of a United States president in the Watergate debacle, and so do I. Reciprocation Tendency subtly causes many extreme and dangerous consequences, not just on rare occasions but pretty much all the time.

Man's belief in reciprocate-favor tendency, following eons of his practicing it, has done some queer and bad things in religions. The ritualized murder of the Phoenicians and the Aztecs, in which they sacrificed human victims to their gods, was a particularly egregious example. And we should not forget that as late as the Punic Wars, the civilized Romans, out of fear of defeat, returned in a few instances to the practice of human sacrifice. On the other hand, the reciprocity-based, religion-boosting idea of obtaining help from God in reciprocation for good human behavior has probably been vastly constructive.

Overall, both inside and outside religions, it seems clear to me that Reciprocation Tendency's constructive contributions to man far outweigh its destructive effects. In cases of psychological tendencies being used to counter or prevent bad results from one or more other psychological tendencies—for instance, in the case of interventions to end chemical dependency—you will usually find Reciprocation Tendency performing strongly on the constructive side.

And the very best part of human life probably lies in relationships of affection wherein parties are more interested in pleasing than being pleased—a not uncommon outcome in display of reciprocate-favor tendency.

Before we leave reciprocate-favor tendency, the final phenomenon we will consider is widespread human misery from feelings of guilt. To the extent the feeling of guilt has an evolutionary base, I believe the most plausible cause is the mental conflict triggered in one direction by reciprocate-favor tendency and in the opposite direction by reward superresponse tendency pushing one to enjoy one hundred percent of some good thing. Of course, human culture has often greatly boosted the genetic tendency to suffer from feelings of

guilt. Most especially, religious culture has imposed hard-to-follow ethical and devotional demands on people. There is a charming Irish Catholic priest in my neighborhood who, with rough accuracy, often says, "The old Jews may have invented guilt, but we Catholics perfected it." And if you, like me and this priest, believe that, averaged out, feelings of guilt do more good than harm, you may join in my special gratitude for reciprocate-favor tendency, no matter how unpleasant you find feelings of guilt.

Ten:
Influence-from-Mere-Association Tendency

In the standard conditioned reflexes studied by Skinner and most common in the world, responsive behavior, creating a new habit, is directly triggered by rewards previously bestowed. For instance, a man buys a can of branded shoe polish, has a good experience with it when shining his shoes, and because of this "reward," buys the same shoe polish when he needs another can.

But there is another type of conditioned reflex wherein mere association triggers a response. For instance, consider the case of many men who have been trained by their previous experience in life to believe that when several similar items are presented for purchase, the one with the highest price will have the highest quality. Knowing this, some seller of an ordinary industrial product will often change his product's trade dress and raise its price significantly hoping that quality-seeking buyers will be tricked into becoming purchasers by mere association of his product and its high price. This industrial practice frequently is effective in driving up sales and even more so in driving up profits. For instance, it worked wonderfully with high-priced power tools for a long time. And it would work better yet with high-priced pumps at the bottom of oil wells. With luxury goods, the process works with a special boost because buyers who pay high prices often gain extra status from thus demonstrating both their good taste and their ability to pay.

Even association that appears to be trivial, if carefully planned, can have extreme and peculiar effects on purchasers of products. The target purchaser of shoe polish may like pretty girls. And so he chooses the polish with the pretty girl on the can or the one with the pretty girl in the last ad for shoe polish that he saw.

Advertisers know about the power of mere association. You won't see Coke advertised alongside some account of the death of a child. Instead, Coke ads picture life as happier than reality.

Similarly, it is not from mere chance that military bands play such impressive music. That kind of music, appearing in mere association with military service, helps to attract soldiers and keep them in the army. Most armies have learned to use mere association in this successful way.

However, the most damaging miscalculations from mere association do not ordinarily come from advertisers and music providers.

Some of the most important miscalculations come from what is accidentally associated with one's past success, or one's liking and loving, or one's disliking and hating, which includes a natural hatred for bad news.

To avoid being misled by the mere association of some fact with past success, use this memory clue. Think of Napoleon and Hitler when they invaded Russia after using their armies with much success elsewhere. And there are plenty of mundane examples of results like those of Napoleon and Hitler. For instance, a man foolishly gambles in a casino and yet wins. This unlikely correlation causes him to try the casino again, or again and again, to his horrid detriment. Or a man gets lucky in an odds-against venture headed by an untalented friend. So influenced, he tries again what worked before—with terrible results.

The proper antidotes to being made such a patsy by past success are (1) to carefully examine each past success, looking for accidental, non-causative factors associated with such success that will tend to mislead as one appraises odds implicit in a proposed new undertaking and (2) to look for dangerous aspects of the new undertaking that were not present when past success occurred.

The damage to the mind that can come from liking and loving was once demonstrated by obviously false testimony given by an otherwise very admirable woman, the wife of a party in a jury case. The famous opposing counsel wanted to minimize his attack on such an admirable woman yet destroy the credibility of her testimony. And so, in his closing argument, he came to her testimony last. He then shook his head sadly and said, "What are we to make of such testimony? The answer lies in the old rhyme:

'As the husband is,
So the wife is.
She is married to a clown,
And the grossness of his nature
Drags her down.'"

The jury disbelieved the woman's testimony. They easily recognized the strong misinfluence of love on her cognition. And we now often see even stronger misinfluence from love as tearful mothers, with heartfelt conviction, declare before TV cameras the innocence of their obviously guilty sons.

People disagree about how much blindness should accompany the association called love. In *Poor Richard's Almanack* Franklin counseled: "Keep your eyes wide open before marriage and half shut thereafter." Perhaps this "eyes-half-shut" solution is about right, but I favor a tougher prescription: "See it like it is and love anyway."

Hating and disliking also cause miscalculation triggered by mere association. In business, I commonly see people underappraise both the competency and morals of competitors they dislike. This is a dangerous practice, usually disguised because it occurs on a subconscious basis.

Another common bad effect from the mere association of a person and a hated outcome is displayed in "Persian Messenger Syndrome." Ancient Persians actually killed some messengers whose sole fault was that they brought home truthful bad news, say, of a battle lost. It was actually safer for the messenger to run away and hide, instead of doing his job as a wiser boss would have wanted it done.

And Persian Messenger Syndrome is alive and well in modern life, albeit in less lethal versions. It is actually dangerous in many careers to be a carrier of unwelcome news. Union negotiators and employer representatives often know this, and it leads to many tragedies in labor relations. Sometimes lawyers, knowing their clients will hate them if they recommend an unwelcome but wise settlement, will carry on to disaster. Even in places well known for high cognition, one will sometimes find Persian Messenger Syndrome. For instance, years ago, two major oil companies litigated in a Texas trial court over some ambiguity in an operating agreement covering one of the largest oil reservoirs in the Western hemisphere. My guess is that the cause of the trial was some general counsel's unwillingness to carry bad news to a strong-minded CEO.

CBS, in its late heyday, was famous for occurrence of Persian Messenger Syndrome because Chairman Paley was hostile to people who brought him bad news. The result was that Paley lived in a cocoon of unreality, from which he made one bad deal after another, even exchanging a large share of CBS for a company that had to be liquidated shortly thereafter.

The proper antidote to creating Persian Messenger Syndrome and its bad effects, like those at CBS, is to develop, through exercise of will, a habit of welcoming bad news. At Berkshire, there is a common injunction: "Always tell us the bad news promptly. It is only the good news that can wait." It also helps to be so wise and informed that people fear not telling you bad news because you are so likely to get it elsewhere.

Influence-from-Mere-Association Tendency often has a shocking effect that helps swamp the normal tendency to return favor for favor. Sometimes, when one receives a favor, his condition is unpleasant, due to poverty, sickness, subjugation, or something else. In addition, the favor may trigger an envy-driven dislike for the person who was in so favorable a state that he could easily be a favor giver. Under such circumstances, the favor receiver, prompted partly by mere association of the favor giver with past pain, will not only dislike the man who helped him but also try to injure him.

This accounts for a famous response, sometimes dubiously attributed to Henry Ford: "Why does that man hate me so? I never did anything for him." I have a friend, whom I will now call "Glotz," who had an amusing experience in favor-giving. Glotz owned an apartment building that he had bought because he wanted, eventually, to use the land in different development. Pending this outcome, Glotz was very lenient in collecting below-market rents from tenants. When, at last, there was a public hearing on Glotz's proposal to tear down the building, one tenant who was far behind in his rent payments was particularly angry and hostile. He came to the public hearing and said, "This proposal is outrageous. Glotz doesn't need any more money. I know this because I was supported in college by Glotz fellowships."

A final serious clump of bad thinking caused by mere association lies in the common use of classification stereotypes. Because Pete knows that Joe is ninety years old and that most ninety-year-old persons don't think very well, Pete appraises old Joe as a thinking klutz even if old Joe still thinks very well. Or, because Jane is a white-haired woman, and Pete knows no old women good at higher math, Pete appraises Jane as no good at it even if Jane is a whiz. This sort of wrong thinking is both natural and common. Pete's antidote is not to believe that, on average, ninety-year-olds think as well as forty-year-olds or that there are as many females as males among Ph. D.'s in math. Instead, just as he must learn that trend does not always correctly predict destiny, he must learn that the average dimension in some group will not reliably guide him to the dimension of some specific item. Otherwise Pete will make many errors, like that of the fellow who drowned in a river that averaged out only eighteen inches deep.

Eleven:
Simple, Pain-Avoiding Psychological Denial

This phenomenon first hit me hard in World War II when the superathlete, superstudent son of a family friend flew off over the Atlantic Ocean and never came back. His mother, who was a very sane woman, then refused to believe he was dead. That's Simple, Pain-Avoiding Psychological Denial. The reality is too painful to bear, so one distorts the facts until they become bearable. We all do that to some extent, often causing terrible problems. The tendency's most extreme outcomes are usually mixed up with love, death, and chemical dependency.

Where denial is used to make dying easier, the conduct meets almost no criticism. Who would begrudge a fellow man such help at such a time? But some people hope to leave life hewing to the iron prescription, "It is not necessary to hope in order to persevere." And there is something admirable in anyone able to do this.

In chemical dependency, wherein morals usually break down horribly, addicted persons tend to believe that they remain in respectable condition, with respectable prospects. They thus display an extremely unrealistic denial of reality as they go deeper and deeper into deterioration. In my youth, Freudian remedies failed utterly in reversing chemical dependency, but nowadays Alcoholics Anonymous routinely achieves a fifty percent cure rate by causing several psychological tendencies to act together to counter addiction. However, the cure process is typically difficult and draining, and a fifty percent success rate implies a fifty percent failure rate. One should stay far away from any conduct at all likely to drift into chemical dependency. Even a small chance of suffering so great a damage should be avoided.

Twelve:
Excessive Self-Regard Tendency

We all commonly observe the excessive self-regard of man. He mostly misappraises himself on the high side, like the ninety percent of Swedish drivers that judge themselves to be above average. Such misappraisals also apply to a person's major "possessions." One spouse usually overappraises the other spouse. And a man's children are likewise appraised higher by him than they are likely to be in a more objective view. Even man's minor possessions tend to be overappraised. Once owned, they suddenly become worth more to him than he would pay if they were offered for sale to him and he didn't already own them. There is a name in psychology for this overappraise-your-own-possessions phenomenon: the "endowment effect." And all man's decisions are suddenly regarded by him as better than would have been the case just before he made them.

Man's excess of self-regard typically makes him strongly prefer people like himself. Psychology professors have had much fun demonstrating this effect in "lost-wallet" experiments. Their experiments all show that the finder of a lost wallet containing identity clues will be most likely to return the wallet when the owner most closely resembles the finder. Given this quality in psychological nature, cliquish groups of similar persons will always be a very influential part of human culture, even after we wisely try to dampen the worst effects.

Some of the worst consequences in modern life come when dysfunctional groups of cliquish persons, dominated by Excessive Self-Regard Tendency, select as new members of their organizations persons who are very much like themselves. Thus if the English department at an elite university becomes mentally dysfunctional or the sales department of a brokerage firm slips into routine fraud, the problem will have a natural tendency to get worse and to be quite resistant to change for the better. So also with a police department or prison-guard unit or political group gone sour and countless other places mired in evil and folly,

such as the worst of our big-city teachers' unions that harm our children by preventing discharge of ineffective teachers. Therefore, some of the most useful members of our civilization are those who are willing to "clean house" when they find a mess under their ambit of control.

Well, naturally, all forms of excess of self-regard cause much error. How could it be otherwise?

Let us consider some foolish gambling decisions. In lotteries, the play is much lower when numbers are distributed randomly than it is when the player picks his own number. This is quite irrational. The odds are almost exactly the same and much against the player. Because state lotteries take advantage of man's irrational love of self-picked numbers, modern man buys more lottery tickets than he otherwise would have, with each purchase foolish.

Intensify man's love of his own conclusions by adding the possessory wallop from the "endowment effect," and you will find that a man who has already bought a pork-belly future on a commodity exchange now foolishly believes, even more strongly than before, in the merits of his speculative bet.

And foolish sports betting, by people who love sports and think they know a lot about relative merits of teams, is a lot more addictive than race track betting—partly because of man's automatic overappraisal of his own complicated conclusions.

Also extremely counterproductive is man's tendency to bet, time after time, in games of skill, like golf or poker, against people who are obviously much better players. Excessive Self-Regard Tendency diminishes the foolish bettor's accuracy in appraising his relative degree of talent.

More counterproductive yet are man's appraisals, typically excessive, of the quality of the future service he is to provide to his business. His overappraisal of these prospective contributions will frequently cause disaster.

Excesses of self-regard often cause bad hiring decisions because employers grossly overappraise the worth of their own conclusions that rely on impressions in face-to-face contact. The correct antidote to this sort of folly is to underweigh face-to-face impressions and overweigh the applicant's past record.

I once chose exactly this course of action while I served as chairman of an academic search committee. I convinced fellow committee members to stop all further interviews and simply appoint a person whose achievement record was much better than that of any other applicant. And when it was suggested to me that I wasn't giving "academic due process," I replied that I was the one being true to academic values because I was using academic research showing poor predictive value of impressions from face-to-face interviews.

Because man is likely to be overinfluenced by face-to-face impressions that by definition involve his active participation, a job candidate who is a marvelous "presenter" often causes great danger under modern executive-search practice. In my opinion, Hewlett-Packard faced just such a danger when it interviewed the articulate, dynamic Carly Fiorina in its search for a new CEO. And I believe (1) that Hewlett-Packard made a bad decision when it chose Ms. Fiorina and (2) that this bad decision would not have been made if Hewlett-Packard had taken the methodological precautions it would have taken if it knew more psychology.

There is a famous passage somewhere in Tolstoy that illuminates the power of Excessive Self-Regard Tendency. According to Tolstoy, the worst criminals don't appraise themselves as all that bad. They come to believe either (1) that they didn't commit their crimes or (2) that, considering the pressures and disadvantages of their lives, it is understandable and forgivable that they behaved as they did and became what they became.

The second half of the "Tolstoy effect", where the man makes excuses for his fixable poor performance, instead of providing the fix, is enormously important. Because a majority of mankind will try to get along by making way too many unreasonable excuses for fixable poor performance, it is very important to have personal and institutional antidotes limiting the ravages of such folly. On the personal level a man should try to face the two simple facts: (1) fixable but unfixed bad performance is bad character and tends to create more of itself, causing more damage to the excuse giver with each tolerated instance, and (2) in demanding places, like athletic teams and General Electric, you are almost sure to be discarded in due course if you keep giving excuses instead of behaving as you should. The main institutional antidotes to this part of the "Tolstoy effect" are (1) a fair, meritocratic, demanding culture plus personnel handling methods that build up morale and (2) severance of the worst offenders. Of course, when you can't sever, as in the case of your own child, you must try to fix the child as best you can. I once heard of a child-teaching method so effective that the child remembered the learning experience over fifty years later. The child later became Dean of the USC School of Music and then related to me what his father said when he saw his child taking candy from the stock of his employer with the excuse that he intended to replace it later. The father said, "Son, it would be better for you to simply take all you want and call yourself a thief every time you do it."

The best antidote to folly from an excess of self-regard is to force yourself to be more objective when you are thinking about yourself, your family and friends, your property, and the value of your past and future activity. This isn't easy to do well and won't work perfectly, but it will work much better than simply letting psychological nature take its normal course.

While an excess of self-regard is often counterproductive in its effects on cognition, it can cause some weird successes from overconfidence that happens to cause success. This factor accounts for the adage: "Never underestimate the man who overestimates himself."

Of course, some high self-appraisals are correct and serve better than false modesty. Moreover, self-regard in the form of a justified pride in a job well done, or a life well lived, is a large constructive force. Without such justified pride, many more airplanes would crash. "Pride" is another word generally left out of psychology textbooks, and this omission is not a good idea. It is also not a good idea to construe the bible's parable about the Pharisee and the Publican as condemning all pride.

Of all forms of useful pride, perhaps the most desirable is a justified pride in being trustworthy. Moreover, the trustworthy man, even after allowing for the inconveniences of his chosen course, ordinarily has a life that averages out better than he would have if he provided less reliability.

Thirteen:
Overoptimism Tendency

About three centuries before the birth of Christ, Demosthenes, the most famous Greek orator, said, "What a man wishes, that also will he believe."

Demosthenes, parsed out, was thus saying that man displays not only Simple, Pain-Avoiding Psychological Denial but also an excess of optimism even when he is already doing well.

The Greek orator was clearly right about an excess of optimism being the normal human condition, even when pain or the threat of pain is absent. Witness happy people buying lottery tickets or believing that credit-furnishing, delivery-making grocery stores were going to displace a great many superefficient cash-and-carry supermarkets.

One standard antidote to foolish optimism is trained, habitual use of the simple probability math of Fermat and Pascal, taught in my youth to high school sophomores. The mental rules of thumb that evolution gives you to deal with risk are not adequate. They resemble the dysfunctional golf grip you would have if you relied on a grip driven by evolution instead of golf lessons.

Fourteen:
Deprival-Superreaction Tendency

The quantity of man's pleasure from a ten-dollar gain does not exactly match the quantity of his displeasure from a ten-dollar loss. That is, the loss seems to hurt much more than the gain seems to help. Moreover, if a man almost gets something he greatly wants and has it jerked away from him at the last moment, he will react much as if he had long owned the reward and had it jerked away. I

include the natural human reactions to both kinds of loss experience—the loss of the possessed reward and the loss of the almost-possessed reward—under one description, Deprival-Superreaction Tendency.

In displaying Deprival-Superreaction Tendency, man frequently incurs disadvantage by misframing his problems. He will often compare what is near instead of what really matters. For instance, a man with $10 million in his brokerage account will often be extremely irritated by the accidental loss of $100 out of the $300 in his wallet.

The Mungers once owned a tame and good-natured dog that displayed the canine version of Deprival-Superreaction Tendency. There was only one way to get bitten by this dog. And that was to try and take some food away from him after he already had it in his mouth. If you did that, this friendly dog would automatically bite. He couldn't help it. Nothing could be more stupid than for the dog to bite his master. But the dog couldn't help being foolish. He had an automatic Deprival-Superreaction Tendency in his nature.

Humans are much the same as this Munger dog. A man ordinarily reacts with irrational intensity to even a small loss, or threatened loss, of property, love, friendship, dominated territory, opportunity, status, or any other valued thing. As a natural result, bureaucratic infighting over the threatened loss of dominated territory often causes immense damage to an institution as a whole. This factor, among others, accounts for much of the wisdom of Jack Welch's long fight against bureaucratic ills at General Electric. Few business leaders have ever conducted wiser campaigns.

Deprival-Superreaction Tendency often protects ideological or religious views by triggering dislike and hatred directed toward vocal nonbelievers. This happens, in part, because the ideas of the nonbelievers, if they spread, will diminish the influence of views that are now supported by a comfortable environment including a strong belief-maintenance system. University liberal arts departments, law schools, and business organizations all display plenty of such ideology-based groupthink that rejects almost all conflicting inputs. When the vocal critic is a former believer, hostility is often boosted both by (1) a concept of betrayal that triggers additional Deprival-Superreaction Tendency because a colleague is lost and (2) fears that conflicting views will have extra persuasive power when they come from a former colleague. The foregoing considerations help account for the old idea of heresy, which for centuries justified much killing of heretics, frequently after torture and frequently accomplished by burning the victim alive.

It is almost everywhere the case that extremes of ideology are maintained with great intensity and with great antipathy to non-believers, causing extremes of cognitive dysfunction. This happens, I believe, because two psychological tendencies are usually acting concurrently toward this same sad result: (1) Inconsistency-Avoidance Tendency, plus (2) Deprival-Superreaction Tendency.

One antidote to intense, deliberate maintenance of groupthink is an extreme culture of courtesy, kept in place despite ideological differences, like the behavior of the justices now serving on the U.S. Supreme Court. Another antidote is to deliberately bring in able and articulate disbelievers of incumbent groupthink. Successful corrective measures to evil examples of groupthink maintenance have included actions like that of Derek Bok when, as president of Harvard, he started disapproving tenure appointments proposed by ideologues at Harvard Law School.

Even a one-degree loss from a 180-degree view will sometime create enough Deprival-Superreaction Tendency to turn a neighbor into an enemy, as I once observed when I bought a house from one of two neighbors locked into hatred by a tiny tree newly installed by one of them.

As the case of these two neighbors illustrated, the clamor of almost any group of neighbors displaying irrational, extreme deprival-superreaction over some trifle in a zoning hearing is not a pretty thing to watch. Such bad behavior drives some people from the zoning field. I once bought some golf clubs from an artisan who was formerly a lawyer. When I asked him what kind of law he had practiced, I expected to hear him say, "divorce law." But his answer was, "zoning law."

Deprival-Superreaction Tendency has ghastly effects in labor relations. Most of the deaths in the labor strife that occurred before World War I came when employers tried to reduce wages. Nowadays, we see fewer deaths and more occasions when whole companies disappear, as competition requires either takeaways from labor—which it will not consent to—or death of the business. Deprival-Superreaction Tendency causes much of this labor resistance, often in cases where it would be in labor's interest to make a different decision.

In contexts other than labor relations, takeaways are also difficult to get. Many tragedies, therefore, occur that would have been avoided had there been more rationality and less subconscious heed of the imperative from Deprival-Superreaction Tendency.

Deprival-Superreaction Tendency is also a huge contributor to ruin from compulsion to gamble. First, it causes the gambler to have a passion to get even once he has suffered loss, and the passion grows with the loss. Second, the most addictive forms of gambling provide a lot of near misses and each one triggers Deprival-Superreaction Tendency. Some slot machine creators are vicious in exploiting this weakness of man. Electronic machines enable these creators to produce a lot of meaningless bar-bar-lemon results that greatly increase play by fools who think they have very nearly won large rewards.

Deprival-Superreaction Tendency often does much damage to man in open-outcry auctions. The "social proof" that we will next consider tends to convince man that the last price from another bidder was reasonable, and then Deprival-Super-reaction Tendency prompts him strongly to top the last bid. The best antidote to being thus triggered into paying foolish prices at open-outcry auctions is the simple Buffett practice: Don't go to such auctions.

Deprival-Superaction Tendency and Inconsistency-Avoidance Tendency often join to cause one form of business failure. In this form of ruin, a man gradually uses up all his good assets in a fruitless attempt to rescue a big venture going bad. One of the best antidotes to this folly is good poker skill learned young. The teaching value of poker demonstrates that not all effective teaching occurs on a standard academic path.

I myself, the would-be instructor here, many decades ago made a big mistake caused in part by subconscious operation of my Deprival-Superreaction Tendency. A friendly broker called and offered me 300 shares of ridiculously underpriced, very thinly traded Belridge Oil at $115 per share, which I purchased using cash I had on hand. The next day, he offered me 1,500 more shares at the same price, which I declined to buy partly because I could only have made the purchase had I sold something or borrowed the required $173,000. This was a very irrational decision. I was a well-to-do man with no debt; there was no risk of loss; and similar no-risk opportunities were not likely to come along. Within two years, Belridge Oil sold out to Shell at a price of about $3,700 per share, which made me about $5.4 million poorer than I would have been had I then been psychologically acute. As this tale demonstrates, psychological ignorance can be very expensive.

Some people may question my defining Deprival-Superreaction Tendency to include reaction to profit barely missed, as in the well-documented responses of slot machine players. However, I believe that I haven't defined the tendency as broadly as I should. My reason for suggesting an even broader definition is that many Berkshire Hathaway shareholders I know never sell or give away a single share after immense gains in market value have occurred. Some of this reaction is caused by rational calculation, and some is, no doubt, attributable to some combination of (1) reward superresponse, (2) "status quo bias" from Inconsistency-Avoidance Tendency, and (3) "the endowment effect" from Excessive Self-Regard Tendency. But I believe the single strongest irrational explanation is a form of Deprival-Super-reaction Tendency. Many of these shareholders simply can't stand the idea of having their Berkshire Hathaway holdings smaller. Partly they dislike facing what they consider an impairment of identity, but mostly they fear missing out on future gains from stock sold or given away.

Fifteen:
Social-Proof Tendency

The otherwise complex behavior of man is much simplified when he automatically thinks and does what he observes to be thought and done around him. And such followership often works fine. For instance, what simpler way could there be to find out how to walk to a big football game in a strange city than by following the flow of the crowd. For some such reason, man's evolution left him with Social-Proof Tendency, an automatic tendency to think and act as he sees others around him thinking and acting.

Psychology professors love Social-Proof Tendency because in their experiments it causes ridiculous results. For instance, if a professor arranges for some stranger to enter an elevator wherein ten "compliance practitioners" are all silently standing so that they face the rear of the elevator, the stranger will often turn around and do the same. The psychology professors can also use Social-Proof Tendency to cause people to make large and ridiculous measurement errors.

And, of course, teenagers' parents usually learn more than they would like about teenagers' cognitive errors from Social-Proof Tendency. This phenomenon was recently involved in a break-through by Judith Rich Harris who demonstrated that superrespect by young people for their peers, rather than for parents or other adults, is ordained to some considerable extent by the genes of the young people. This makes it wise for parents to rely more on manipulating the quality of the peers than on exhortations to their own offspring. A person like Ms. Harris, who can provide an insight of this quality and utility, backed by new reasons, has not lived in vain.

And in the highest reaches of business, it is not all uncommon to find leaders who display followership akin to that of teenagers. If one oil company foolishly buys a mine, other oil companies often quickly join in buying mines. So also if the purchased company makes fertilizer. Both of these oil company buying fads actually bloomed, with bad results.

Of course, it is difficult to identify and correctly weigh all the possible ways to deploy the cash flow of an oil company. So oil company executives, like everyone else, have made many bad decisions that were quickly triggered by discomfort from doubt. Going along with social proof provided by the action of other oil companies ends this discomfort in a natural way.

When will Social-Proof Tendency be most easily triggered? Here the answer is clear from many experiments: Triggering most readily occurs in the presence of puzzlement or stress, and particularly when both exist.

Because stress intensifies Social-Proof Tendency, disreputable sales organizations, engaged, for instance, in such action as selling swampland to schoolteachers, manipulate targets into situations combining isolation and stress. The isolation strengthens the social proof provided by both the knaves and the people who buy first, and the stress, often increased by fatigue, augments the targets' susceptibility to the social proof. And, of course, the techniques of our worst "religious" cults imitate those of the knavish salesmen. One cult even used rattlesnakes to heighten the stress felt by conversion targets.

Because both bad and good behavior are made contagious by Social-Proof Tendency, it is highly important that human societies (1) stop any bad behavior before it spreads and (2) foster and display all good behavior.

My father once told me that just after commencing law practice in Omaha, he went with a large group from Nebraska to South Dakota to hunt pheasants. A South Dakota hunting license was, say, $2 for South Dakota residents and $5 for nonresidents. All the Nebraska residents, one by one, signed up for South Dakota licenses with phony South Dakota addresses until it was my father's turn. Then, according to him, he barely prevented himself from doing what the others were doing, which was some sort of criminal offense.

Not everyone so resists the social contagion of bad behavior. And, therefore, we often get "Serpico Syndrome," named to commemorate the state of a near-totally corrupt New York police division joined by Frank Serpico. He was then nearly murdered by gunfire because of his resistance to going along with the corruption in the division. Such corruption was being driven by social proof plus incentives, the combination that creates Serpico Syndrome. The Serpico story should be taught more than it now is because the didactic power of its horror is aimed at a very important evil, driven substantially by a very important force: social proof.

In social proof, it is not only action by others that misleads but also their inaction. In the presence of doubt, inaction by others becomes social proof that inaction is the right course. Thus, the inaction of a great many bystanders led to the death of Kitty Genovese in a famous incident much discussed in introductory psychology courses.

In the ambit of social proof, the outside directors on a corporate board usually display the near ultimate form of inaction. They fail to object to anything much short of an axe murder until some public embarrassment of the board finally causes their intervention. A typical board-of-directors' culture was once well described by my friend, Joe Rosenfield, as he said, "They asked me if I wanted to become a director of Northwest Bell, and it was the last thing they ever asked me."

In advertising and sales promotion, Social-Proof Tendency is about as strong a factor as one could imagine. "Monkey-see, monkey-do" is the old phrase that reminds one of how strongly John will often wish to do something, or have something, just because Joe does or has it. One interesting consequence is that an advertiser will pay a lot to have its soup can, instead of someone else's, in a movie scene involving soup consumption only in a peripheral way.

Social-Proof Tendency often interacts in a perverse way with Envy/Jealousy and Deprival-Superreaction Tendency. One such interaction amused my family for years as people recalled the time when my cousin Russ and I, at ages three and four, fought and howled over a single surplus shingle while surrounded by a virtual sea of surplus shingles.

But the adult versions of this occasion, boosted by psychological tendencies preserving ideologies, are not funny and can bring down whole civilizations. The Middle East now presents just such a threat. By now the resources spent by Jews, Arabs and all others over a small amount of disputed land if divided arbitrarily among land claimants, would have made every one better off, even before taking into account any benefit from reduced threat of war, possibly nuclear.

Outside domestic relations it is rare now to try to resolve disputes by techniques including discussion of impacts from psychological tendencies. Considering the implications of childishness that would be raised by such inclusion, and the defects of psychology as now taught, this result may be sound. But, given the nuclear stakes now involved and the many failures in important negotiations lasting decades, I often wonder if some day, in some way, more use of psychological insight will eventually improve outcomes. If so, correct teaching of psychology matters a lot. And, if old psychology professors are even less likely than old physics professors to learn new ways, which seems nearly certain, then we may, as Max Planck predicted, need a new generation of psychology professors who have grown up to think in a different way.

If only one lesson is to be chosen from a package of lessons involving Social-Proof Tendency, and used in self improvement, my favorite would be: Learn how to ignore the examples from others when they are wrong, because few skills are more worth having.

Sixteen:
Contrast-Misreaction Tendency

Because the nervous system of man does not naturally measure in absolute scientific units, it must instead rely on something simpler. The eyes have a solution that limits their programming needs: the contrast in what is seen is registered. And as in sight, so does it go, largely, in the other senses. Moreover, as perception goes, so goes cognition. The result is man's Contrast-Misreaction Tendency.

Few psychological tendencies do more damage to correct thinking. Small-scale damages involve instances such as man's buying an overpriced $1,000 leather dashboard merely because the price is so low compared to his concurrent purchase of a $65,000 car. Large- scale damages often ruin lives, as when a wonderful woman having terrible parents marries a man who would be judged satisfactory only in comparison to her parents. Or as when a man takes wife number two who would be appraised as all right only in comparison to wife number one.

A particularly reprehensible form of sales practice occurs in the offices of some real estate brokers. A buyer from out of the city, perhaps needing to shift his family there, visits the office with little time available. The salesman deliberately shows the customer three awful houses at ridiculously high prices. Then he shows him a merely bad house at a price only moderately too high. And, boom, the broker often makes an easy sale.

Contrast-Misreaction Tendency is routinely used to cause disadvantage for customers buying merchandise and services. To make an ordinary price seem low, the vendor will very frequently create a highly artificial price that is much higher than the price always sought, then advertise his standard price as a big reduction from his phony price. Even when people know that this sort of customer manipulation is being attempted, it will often work to trigger buying. This phenomenon accounts in part for much advertising in newspapers. It also demonstrates that being aware of psychological ploys is not a perfect defense.

When a man's steps are consecutively taken toward disaster, with each step being very small, the brain's Contrast-Misreaction Tendency will often let the man go too far toward disaster to be able to avoid it. This happens because each step presents so small a contrast from his present position.

A bridge-playing pal of mine once told me that a frog tossed into very hot water would jump out, but that the same frog would end up dying if placed in room-temperature water that was later heated at a very slow rate. My few shreds of physiological knowledge make me doubt this account. But no matter because many businesses die in just the manner claimed by my friend for the frog. Cognition, misled by tiny changes involving low contrast, will often miss a trend that is destiny.

One of Ben Franklin's best-remembered and most useful aphorisms is "A small leak will sink a great ship." The utility of the aphorism is large precisely because the brain so often misses the functional equivalent of a small leak in a great ship.

Seventeen:
Stress-Influence Tendency

Everyone recognizes that sudden stress, for instance from a threat, will cause a rush of adrenaline in the human body, prompting faster and more extreme reaction. And everyone who has taken Psych 101 knows that stress makes Social-Proof Tendency more powerful.

In a phenomenon less well recognized but still widely known, light stress can slightly improve performance—say, in examinations—whereas heavy stress causes dysfunction.

But few people know more about really heavy stress than that it can cause depression. For instance, most people know that an "acute stress depression" makes thinking dysfunctional because it causes an extreme of pessimism, often extended in length and usually accompanied by activity-stopping fatigue. Fortunately, as most people also know, such a depression is one of mankind's more reversible ailments. Even before modern drugs were available, many people afflicted by depression, such as Winston Churchill and Samuel Johnson, gained great achievement in life.

Most people know very little about nonde-pressive mental breakdowns influenced by heavy stress. But there is at least one exception, involving the work of Pavlov when he was in his seventies and eighties. Pavlov had won a Nobel Prize early in life by using dogs to work out the physiology of digestion. Then he became world-famous by working out mere-association responses in dogs, initially salivating dogs—so much so that changes in behavior triggered by mere-association, like those caused by much modern advertisement, are today often said to come from "Pavlovian" conditioning.

What happened to cause Pavlov's last work was especially interesting. During the great Leningrad Flood of the 1920s, Pavlov had many dogs in cages.

Their habits had been transformed, by a combination of his "Pavlovian conditioning" plus standard reward responses, into distinct and different patterns. As the waters of the flood came up and receded, many dogs reached a point where they had almost no airspace between their noses and the tops of their cages. This subjected them to maximum stress. Immediately thereafter, Pavlov noticed that many of the dogs were no longer behaving as they had. The dog that formerly had liked his trainer now disliked him, for example. This result reminds one of modern cognition reversals in which a person's love of his parents suddenly becomes hate, as new love has been shifted suddenly to a cult. The unanticipated, extreme changes in Pavlov's dogs would have driven any good experimental scientist into a near-frenzy of curiosity. That was indeed Pavlov's reaction. But not many scientists would have done what Pavlov next did.

And that was to spend the rest of his long life giving stress-induced nervous breakdowns to dogs, after which he would try to reverse the breakdowns, all the while keeping careful experimental records. He found (1) that he could classify dogs so as to predict how easily a particular dog would breakdown; (2) that the dogs hardest to break down were also the hardest to return to their pre-breakdown state; (3) that any dog could be broken down; and (4) that he couldn't reverse a breakdown except by reimposing stress.

Now, practically everyone is revolted by such experimental treatment of man's friend, the dog.

Moreover, Pavlov was Russian and did his last work under the Communists. And maybe those facts account for the present extreme, widespread ignorance of Pavlov's last work. The two Freudian psychiatrists with whom I tried many years ago to discuss this work had never heard of it. And the dean of a major medical school actually asked me, several years ago, if any of Pavlov's experiments were "repeatable" in experiments of other researchers. Obviously, Pavlov is now a sort of forgotten hero in medical science.

I first found a description of Pavlov's last work in a popular paperback, written by some Rockefeller-financed psychiatrist, when I was trying to figure out (1) how cults worked their horrible mischief and (2) what should the law say about what parents could do to "deprogram" children who had become brainwashed zombies. Naturally, mainstream law objected to the zombies being physically captured by their parents and next subjected to stress that would help to deprogram the effects of the stress they had endured in cult conversions.

I never wanted to get into the legal controversy that existed about this subject. But I did conclude that the controversy couldn't be handled with maximized rationality without considering whether, as Pavlov's last work suggests, the heavy-handed imposition of stress might be the only reversal method that would work to remedy one of the worst evils imaginable: a stolen mind. I have included this discussion of Pavlov (1) partly out of general antagonism toward taboos, (2) partly to make my talk reasonably complete as it considers stress and (3) partly because I hope some listener may continue my inquiry with more success.

Eighteen:
Availability-Misweighing Tendency

This mental tendency echoes the words of the song: "When I'm not near the girl I love, I love the girl I'm near." Man's imperfect, limited-capacity brain easily drifts into working with what's easily available to it. And the brain can't use what it can't remember or what it is blocked from recognizing because it is heavily influenced by one or more psychological tendencies bearing strongly on it, as the fellow is influenced by the nearby girl in the song. And so the mind overweighs what is easily available and thus displays Availability-Misweighing Tendency.

The main antidote to miscues from Availability-Misweighing Tendency often involve procedures, including use of checklists, which are almost always helpful.

Another antidote is to behave somewhat like Darwin did when he emphasized disconfirming evidence. What should be done is to especially emphasize factors that don't produce reams of easily available numbers, instead of drifting mostly or entirely into considering factors that do produce such numbers. Still another antidote is to find and hire some skeptical, articulate people with far-reaching minds to act as advocates for notions that are opposite to the incumbent notions.

One consequence of this tendency is that extra-vivid evidence, being so memorable and thus more available in cognition, should often consciously be underweighed while less vivid evidence should be overweighed.

Still, the special strength of extra-vivid images in influencing the mind can be constructively used (1) in persuading someone else to reach a correct conclusion or (2) as a device for improving one's own memory by attaching vivid images, one after the other, to many items one doesn't want to forget. Indeed, such use of vivid images as memory boosters is what enabled the great orators of classical Greece and Rome to give such long, organized speeches without using notes.

The great algorithm to remember in dealing with this tendency is simple: An idea or a fact is not worth more merely because it is easily available to you.

Nineteen:
Use-It-or-Lose-It Tendency

All skills attenuate with disuse. I was a whiz at calculus until age twenty, after which the skill was soon obliterated by total nonuse. The right antidote to such a loss is to make use of the functional equivalent of the aircraft simulator employed in pilot training. This allows a pilot to continuously practice all of the rarely used skills that he can't afford to lose.

Throughout his life, a wise man engages in practice of all his useful, rarely used skills, many of them outside his discipline, as a sort of duty to his better self. If he reduces the number of skills he practices and, therefore, the number of skills he retains, he will naturally drift into error from man with a hammer tendency. His learning capacity will also shrink as he creates gaps in the latticework of theory he needs as a framework for understanding new experience. It is also essential for a thinking man to assemble his skills into a checklist that he routinely uses. Any other mode of operation will cause him to miss much that is important.

Skills of a very high order can be maintained only with daily practice. The pianist Paderewski once said that if he failed to practice for a single day, he could notice his performance deterioration and that, after a week's gap in practice, the audience could notice it as well.

The hard rule of Use-It-or-Lose-It Tendency tempers its harshness for the diligent. If a skill is raised to fluency, instead of merely being crammed in briefly to enable one to pass some test, then the skill (1) will be lost more slowly and (2) will come back faster when refreshed with new learning. These are not minor advantages, and a wise man engaged in learning some important skill will not stop until he is really fluent in it.

Twenty:
Drug-Misinfluence Tendency

This tendency's destructive power is so widely known to be intense, with frequent tragic consequences for cognition and the outcome of life, that it needs no discussion here to supplement that previously given under "Simple, Pain-Avoiding Psychological Denial."

Twenty-One:
Senescence-Misinfluence Tendency

With advanced age, there comes a natural cognitive decay, differing among individuals in the earliness of its arrival and the speed of its progression. Practically no one is good at learning complex new skills when very old. But some people remain pretty good in maintaining intensely practiced old skills until late in life, as one can notice in many a bridge tournament.

Old people like me get pretty skilled, without working at it, at disguising age-related deterioration because social convention, like clothing, hides much decline.

Continuous thinking and learning, done with joy, can somewhat help delay what is inevitable.

Twenty-Two:
Authority-Misinfluence Tendency

Living in dominance hierarchies as he does, like all his ancestors before him, man was born mostly to follow leaders, with only a few people doing the leading. And so, human society is formally organized into dominance hierarchies, with their culture augmenting the natural follow-the-leader tendency of man.

But automatic as most human reactions are, with the tendency to follow leaders being no exception, man is often destined to suffer greatly when the leader is wrong or when his leader's ideas don't get through properly in the bustle of life and are misunderstood. And so, we find much miscognition from man's Authority-Misinfluence Tendency.

Some of the misinfluences are amusing, as in a case described by Cialdini. A physician left a written order for a nurse treating an earache, as follows: "Two drops, twice a day, 'r. ear.'" The nurse then directed the patient to turn over and put the eardrops in his anus.

Other versions of confused instructions from authority figures are tragic. In World War II, a new pilot for a general, who sat beside him in the copilot's seat, was so anxious to please his boss that he misinterpreted some minor shift in the general's position as a direction to do some foolish thing. The pilot crashed the plane and became a paraplegic.

Well, naturally, cases like this one get the attention of careful thinkers like Boss Buffett, who always acts like an overquiet mouse around his pilots.

Such cases are also given attention in the simulator training of copilots who have to learn to ignore certain really foolish orders from boss pilots because boss pilots will sometimes err disastrously. Even after going through such a training regime, however, copilots in simulator exercises will too often allow the simulated plane to crash because of some extreme and perfectly obvious simulated error of the chief pilot.

After Corporal Hitler had risen to dominate Germany, leading a bunch of believing Lutherans and Catholics into orgies of genocide and other mass destruction, one clever psychology professor, Stanley Milgram, decided to do an experiment to determine exactly how far authority figures could lead ordinary people into gross misbehavior. In this experiment, a man posing as an authority figure, namely a professor governing a respectable experiment, was able to trick a great many ordinary people into giving what they had every reason to believe were massive electric shocks that inflicted heavy torture on innocent fellow citizens. This experiment did demonstrate a terrible result contributed to by Authority-Misinfluence Tendency, but it also demonstrated extreme ignorance in the psychology professoriate right after World War II.

Almost any intelligent person with my checklist of psychological tendencies in his hand would, by simply going down the checklist, have seen that Milgram's experiment involved about six powerful psychological tendencies acting in confluence to bring about his extreme experimental result. For instance, the person pushing Milgram's shock lever was given much social proof from presence of inactive bystanders whose silence communicated that his behavior was okay. Yet it took over a thousand psychological papers, published before I got to Milgram, for the professoriate to get his experiment only about ninety percent as well understood as it would have immediately been by any intelligent person who used (1) any sensible organization of psychology along the lines of this talk, plus (2) a checklist procedure. This outcome displaying the dysfunctional thinking of long-dead professors deserves a better explanation. I will later deal with the subject in a very hesitant fashion.

We can be pleased that the psychology professoriate of a former era wasn't quite as dysfunctional as the angler in my next-to-last illustration of Authority-Misinfluence Tendency.

When I once fished in the Rio Colorado in Costa Rica, my guide, in a state of shock, told me a story about an angler who'd earlier come to the river without ever having fished for tarpon. A fishing guide like the one I had runs the boat and gives fishing advice, establishing himself in this context as the ultimate authority figure. In the case of this guide, his native language was Spanish, while the angler's native language was English. The angler got a big tarpon on and began submitting to many directions from this authority figure called a guide: tip up, tip down, reel in, etc. Finally, when it was necessary to put more pressure on the fish by causing more bending of the angler's rod, the guide said in English: "Give him the rod, give him the rod." Well, the angler threw his expensive rod at the fish, and when last seen, it was going down the Rio Colorado toward the ocean. This example shows how powerful is the tendency to go along with an authority figure and how it can turn one's brain into mush.

My final example comes from business. A psychology Ph. D. once became a CEO of a major company and went wild, creating an expensive new headquarters, with a great wine cellar, at an isolated site. At some point, his underlings remonstrated that money was running short. "Take the money out of the depreciation reserves," said the CEO. Not too easy because a depreciation reserve is a liability account.

So strong is undue respect for authority that this CEO, and many even worse examples, have actually been allowed to remain in control of important business institutions for long periods after it was clear they should be removed. The obvious implication: Be careful whom you appoint to power because a dominant authority figure will often be hard to remove, aided as he will be by Authority-Misinfluence Tendency.

Twenty-Three:
Twaddle Tendency

Man, as a social animal who has the gift of language, is born to prattle and to pour out twaddle that does much damage when serious work is being attempted. Some people produce copious amounts of twaddle and others very little.

A trouble from the honeybee version of twaddle was once demonstrated in an interesting experiment. A honeybee normally goes out and finds nectar and then comes back and does a dance that communicates to the other bees where the nectar is. The other bees then go out and get it. Well some scientist—clever, like B. F. Skinner—decided to see how well a honeybee would do with a handicap. He put the nectar straight up. Way up. Well, in a natural setting, there is no nectar a long way straight up, and the poor honeybee doesn't have a genetic program that is adequate to handle what she now has to communicate. You might guess that this honeybee would come back to the hive and slink into a corner, but she doesn't. She comes into the hive and does an incoherent dance. Well, all my life I've been dealing with the human equivalent of that honeybee. And it's a very important part of wise administration to keep prattling people, pouring out twaddle, far away from the serious work. A rightly famous Caltech engineering professor, exhibiting more insight than tact, once expressed his version of this idea as follows: "The principal job of an academic administration is to keep the people who don't matter from interfering with the work of the people that do." I include this quotation partly because I long suffered from backlash caused by my version of this professor's conversational manner. After much effort, I was able to improve only slightly, so one of my reasons for supplying the quotation is my hope that, at least in comparison, I will appear tactful.

Twenty-Four:
Reason-Respecting Tendency

There is in man, particularly one in an advanced culture, a natural love of accurate cognition and a joy in its exercise. This accounts for the widespread popularity of crossword puzzles, other puzzles, and bridge and chess columns, as well as all games requiring mental skill.

This tendency has an obvious implication. It makes man especially prone to learn well when a would-be teacher gives correct reasons for what is taught, instead of simply laying out the desired belief ex cathedra with no reasons given. Few practices, therefore, are wiser than not only thinking through reasons before giving orders but also communicating these reasons to the recipient of the order.

No one knew this better than Carl Braun, who designed oil refineries with spectacular skill and integrity. He had a very simple rule, one of many in his large, Teutonic company: You had to tell Who was to do What, Where, When, and Why. And if you wrote a communication leaving out your explanation of why the addressee was to do what was ordered, Braun was likely to fire you because Braun well knew that ideas got through best when reasons for the ideas were meticulously laid out.

In general, learning is most easily assimilated and used when, life long, people consistently hang their experience, actual and vicarious, on a latticework of theory answering the question: Why? Indeed, the question "Why?" is a sort of Rosetta stone opening up the major potentiality of mental life.

Unfortunately, Reason-Respecting Tendency is so strong that even a person's giving of meaningless or incorrect reasons will increase compliance with his orders and requests. This has been demonstrated in psychology experiments wherein "compliance practitioners" successfully jump to the head of the lines in front of copying machines by explaining their reason: "I have to make some copies." This sort of unfortunate byproduct of Reason-Respecting Tendency is a conditioned reflex, based on a widespread appreciation of the importance of reasons. And, naturally, the practice of laying out various claptrap reasons is much used by commercial and cult "compliance practitioners" to help them get what they don't deserve.

Twenty-Five:
Lollapalooza Tendency—The Tendency to Get Extreme Consequences from Confluences of Psychological Tendencies Acting in Favor of a Particular Outcome

This tendency was not in any of the psychology texts I once examined, at least in any coherent fashion, yet it dominates life. It accounts for the extreme result in the Milgram experiment and the extreme success of some cults that have stumbled through practice evolution into bringing pressure from many psychological tendencies to bear at the same time on conversion targets. The targets vary in susceptibility, like the dogs Pavlov worked with in his old age, but some of the minds that are targeted simply snap into zombiedom under cult pressure. Indeed, that is one cult's name for the conversion phenomenon: snapping.

What are we to make of the extreme ignorance of the psychology textbook writers of yesteryear? How could anyone who had taken a freshman course in physics or chemistry not be driven to consider, above all, how psychological tendencies combine and with what effects? Why would anyone think his study of psychology was adequate without his having endured the complexity involved in dealing with intertwined psychological tendencies? What could be more ironic than professors using oversimplified notions while studying bad cognitive effects grounded in the mind's tendency to use oversimplified algorithms?

I will make a few tentative suggestions. Maybe many of the long-dead professors wanted to create a whole science from one narrow type of repeatable psychology experiment that was conductible in a university setting and that aimed at one psychological tendency at a time. If so, these early psychology professors made a massive error in so restricting their approach to their subject. It would be like physics ignoring (1) astrophysics because it couldn't happen in a physics lab, plus (2) all compound effects. What psychological tendencies could account for early psychology professors adopting an over-restricted approach to their own subject matter? One candidate would be Availability-Misweighing Tendency grounded in a preference for easy-to-control data. And then the restrictions would eventually create an extreme case of man with a hammer tendency. Another candidate might be envy/jealousy Tendency through which early psychology professors displayed some weird form of envy of a physics that was misunderstood. And this possibility tends to demonstrate that leaving envy/jealousy out of academic psychology was never a good idea.

I now quitclaim all these historical mysteries to my betters.

Well, that ends my brief description of psychological tendencies.

Questions and Answers:

Now, as promised, I will ask and answer a few general questions.

My first is a compound question: Isn't this list of psychological tendencies tautological to some extent compared to the system of Euclid? That is, aren't there overlaps in the tendencies? And couldn't the system be laid out just as plausibly in a somewhat different way? The answers are yes, yes, and yes, but this matters only moderately. Further refinement of these tendencies, while desirable, has a limited practical potential because a significant amount of messiness is unfixable in a soft science like psychology.

My second question is: Can you supply a real-world model, instead of a Milgram-type controlled psychology experiment, that uses your system to illustrate multiple psychological tendencies interacting in a plausibly diagnosable way? The answer is yes. One of my favorite cases involves the McDonnell Douglas airliner evacuation test. Before a new airliner can be sold, the government requires that it pass an evacuation test, during which a full load of passengers must get out in some short period of time. The government directs that the test be realistic. So you can't pass by evacuating only twenty-year-old athletes. So McDonnell Douglas scheduled such a test in a darkened hangar using a lot of old people as evacuees. The passenger cabin was, say, twenty feet above the concrete floor of the hangar and was to be evacuated through moderately flimsy rubber chutes. The first test was made in the morning. There were about twenty very serious injuries, and the evacuation took so long it flunked the time test. So what did McDonnell Douglas next do? It repeated the test in the afternoon, and this time there was another failure, with about twenty more serious injuries, including one case of permanent paralysis.

What psychological tendencies contributed to this terrible result? Well, using my tendency list as a checklist, I come up with the following explanation. Reward-Superresponse Tendency drove McDonnell Douglas to act fast. It couldn't sell its airliner until it passed the test. Also pushing the company was Doubt-Avoidance Tendency with its natural drive to arrive at a decision and run with it. Then the government's direction that the test be realistic drove Authority-Misinfluence Tendency into the mischief of causing McDonnell Douglas to overreact by using what was obviously too dangerous a test method. By now the course of action had been decided, so Inconsistency-Avoidance Tendency helped preserve the near-idiotic plan. When all the old people got to the dark hangar, with its high airline cabin and concrete floor, the situation must have made McDonnell Douglas employees very queasy, but they saw other employees and supervisors not objecting. Social-Proof Tendency, therefore, swamped the queasi-

ness. And this allowed continued action as planned, a continuation that was aided by more Authority-Misinfluence Tendency. Then came the disaster of the morning test with its failure, plus serious injuries. McDonnell Douglas ignored the strong disconfirming evidence from the failure of the first test because confirmation bias, aided by the triggering of strong Deprival-Superreaction Tendency, favored maintaining the original plan. McDonnell Douglas' Deprival-Superreaction Tendency was now like that which causes a gambler, bent on getting even after a huge loss, to make his final big bet. After all, McDonnell Douglas was going to lose a lot if it didn't pass its test as scheduled. More psychology-based explanation can probably be made, but the foregoing discussion is complete enough to demonstrate the utility of my system when used in a checklist mode.

My third question is also compound: In the practical world, what good is the thought system laid out in this list of tendencies? Isn't practical benefit prevented because these psychological tendencies are so thoroughly programmed into the human mind by broad evolution [the combination of genetic and cultural evolution] that we can't get rid of them? Well, the answer is that the tendencies are probably much more good than bad. Otherwise, they wouldn't be there, working pretty well for man, given his condition and his limited brain capacity. So the tendencies can't be simply washed out automatically, and shouldn't be. Nevertheless, the psychological thought system described, when properly understood and used, enables the spread of wisdom and good conduct and facilitates the avoidance of disaster. Tendency is not always destiny, and knowing the tendencies and their antidotes can often help prevent trouble that would otherwise occur. Here is a short list of examples reminding us of the great utility of elementary psychological knowledge:

One: Carl Braun's communication practices.

Two: The use of simulators in pilot training.

Three: The system of Alcoholics Anonymous.

Four: Clinical training methods in medical schools.

Five: The rules of the U.S. Constitutional Convention: totally secret meetings, no recorded vote by name until the final vote, votes reversible at any time before the end of the convention, then just one vote on the whole Constitution. These are very clever psychology-respecting rules. If the founders had used a different procedure, many people would have been pushed by various psychological tendencies into inconsistent, hardened positions. The elite founders got our Constitution through by a whisker only because they were psychologically acute.

Six: The use of Granny's incentive-driven rule to manipulate oneself toward better performance of one's duties.

Seven: The Harvard Business School's emphasis on decision trees. When I was young and foolish I used to laugh at the Harvard Business School. I said, "They're teaching twenty-eight-year-old people that high school algebra works in real life?" But later, I wised up and realized that it was very important that they do that to counter some bad effects from psychological tendencies. Better late than never.

Eight: The use of autopsy equivalents at Johnson & Johnson. At most corporations, if you make an acquisition and it turns out to be a disaster, all the people, paperwork, and presentations that caused the foolish acquisition are quickly forgotten. Nobody wants to be associated with the poor outcome by mentioning it. But at Johnson & Johnson, the rules make everybody revisit old acquisitions, comparing predictions with outcomes. That is a very smart thing to do.

Nine: The great example of Charles Darwin as he avoided confirmation bias, which has morphed into the extreme anti-confirmation-bias method of the "double blind" studies wisely required in drug research by the F.D.A.

Ten: The Warren Buffett rule for open-outcry auctions: Don't go.

My fourth question is: What special knowledge problems lie buried in the thought system demonstrated by your list?

Well, one answer is paradox. In social psychology, the more people learn about the system the less it is true, and this is what gives the system its great value as a preventer of bad outcomes and a driver of good outcomes. This result is paradoxical, and doesn't remind one of elementary physics, but so what. One can't get all the paradox out of pure math, so why should psychology be shocked by some paradox?

There is also some paradox in cognition change that works even when the manipulated person knows he is being manipulated. This creates a sort of paradox in a paradox, but, again, so what. I once much enjoyed an occasion of this sort. I drew this beautiful woman as my dinner partner many years ago. I'd never seen her before. She was married to a prominent Los Angeles man. She sat down next to me, turned her beautiful face up, and said, "Charlie, what one word accounts for your remarkable success in life?" I knew I was being manipulated by a practiced routine, and I just loved it. I never see this woman without a little lift in my spirits. And, by the way, I told her I was rational. You'll have to judge yourself whether that's true. I may be demonstrating some psychological tendency I hadn't planned on demonstrating.

My fifth question is: Don't we need more reconciliation of psychology and economics? My answer is yes, and I suspect that some slight progress is being made. I have heard of one such example. Colin Camerer of Caltech, who works in "experi-mental economics," devised an interesting experiment in which he caused high I.Q. students, playing for real money, to pay price A+B for a "security" they knew would turn into A dollars at the end of the day. This foolish action occurred because the students were allowed to trade with each other in a liquid market for the security. And some students then paid price A+B because they hoped to unload on other students at a higher price before the day was over. What I will now confidently predict is that, despite Camerer's experimental outcome, most economics and corporate finance professors who still believe in the "hard-form efficient market hypothesis" will retain their original belief. If so, this will be one more indication of how irrational smart people can be when influenced by psychological tendencies.

My sixth question is: Don't moral and prudential problems come with knowledge of these psychological tendencies? The answer is yes. For instance, psychological knowledge improves persuasive power and, like other power, it can be used for good or ill. Captain Cook once played a psychology-based trick on his seamen to cause them to eat sauerkraut and avoid scurvy. In my opinion, this action was both ethical and wise under the circumstances, despite the deliberate manipulation involved. But ordinarily, when you try to use your knowledge of psychological tendencies in the artful manipulation of someone whose trust you need, you will be making both a moral and prudential error.

The moral error is obvious. The prudential error comes because many intelligent people, targeted for conscious manipulation, are likely to figure out what you are trying to do and resent your action.

My final question is: Aren't there factual and reasoning errors in this talk? The answer is yes, almost surely yes. The final revision was made from memory over about fifty hours by a man eighty-one years old, who never took a course in psychology and has read none of it, except one book on developmental psychology, for nearly fifteen years. Even so, I think the totality of my talk will stand up very well, and I hope all my descendants and friends will carefully consider what I have said. I even hope that more psychology professors will join me in: (1) making heavy use of inversion; (2) driving for a complete description of the psychological system so that it works better as a checklist; and (3) especially emphasizing effects from combinations of psychological tendencies.

Well that ends my talk. If in considering what I have said you had ten percent the fun I had saying it, you were lucky recipients.

"Peter, you and Warren sucked me into rewriting this thing, and it's taken over my life." (February 2005)

Talk Four Revisited

Talk Four contains the most extreme-sounding message I ever delivered. It claims nothing less than (1) that academic psychology is hugely important; (2) that, even so, it is usually ill-thought-out and ill-presented by its Ph.D. denizens; and (3) that my way of presenting psychology has a large superiority in practical utility, compared to most textbooks.

Naturally, I believe these extreme claims are correct. After all, I assembled the material contained in Talk Four as sort of a check list to help me succeed in practical thinking and not to gain reputational advantage by making public any would-be-clever notions.

If I am even partly right, the world will eventually see much more psychology in roughly the form of Talk Four. If so, I confidently predict that the change will improve general competency.

"And with that,
I have nothing more to add."

Charles T. Munger

October 10, 2005

Charlie Munger's Recommended Books

"In my whole life, I have known no wise people (over a broad subject matter area) who didn't read all the time—none, zero. You'd be amazed at how much Warren reads—and at how much I read. My children laugh at me. They think I'm a book with a couple of legs sticking out."

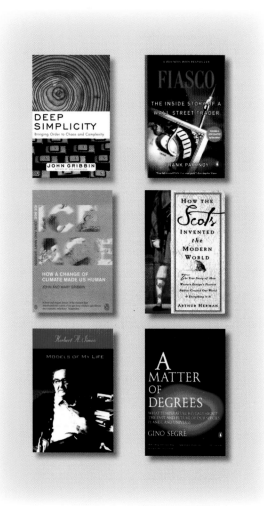

■ *Deep Simplicity: Bringing Order to Chaos and Complexity*
John Gribbin, Random House (2005)

■ *F.I.A.S.C.O.: The Inside Story of a Wall Street Trader*
Frank Partnoy, Penguin Books (1999)

■ *Ice Age*
John & Mary Gribbin, Barnes & Noble (2002)

■ *How the Scots Invented the Modern World: The True Story of How Western Europe's Poorest Nation Created Our World & Everything in It*
Arthur Herman, Three Rivers Press (2002)

■ *Models of My Life*
Herbert A. Simon, The MIT Press (1996)

■ *A Matter of Degrees: What Temperature Reveals About the Past and Future of Our Species, Planet, and Universe*
Gino Segre, Viking Books (2002)

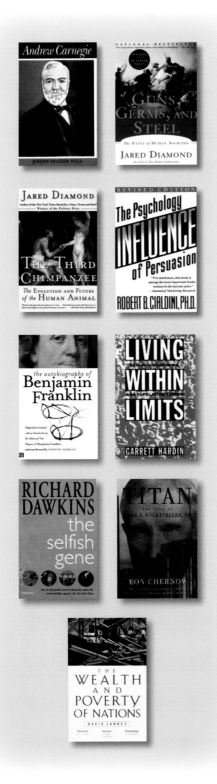

- *Andrew Carnegie*
  Joseph Frazier Wall,
  Oxford University Press
  (1970)

- *Guns, Germs, and Steel:*
  The Fates of Human
  Societies
  Jared M. Diamond, W.
  W. Norton & Company
  (1999)

- *The Third Chimpanzee:*
  The Evolution and Future of the Human Animal
  Jared M. Diamond, Perennial (1992)

- *Influence:*
  The Psychology of Persuasion
  Robert B. Cialdini, Perennial Currents (1998)

- *The Autobiography of Benjamin Franklin*
  Benjamin Franklin, Yale Nota Bene (2003)

- *Living Within Limits:*
  Ecology, Economics, and Population Taboos
  Garrett Hardin, Oxford University Press (1995)

- *The Selfish Gene*
  Richard Dawkins, Oxford University Press (1990)

- *Titan:*
  The Life of John D. Rockefeller, Sr.
  Ron Chernow, Vintage (2004)

- *The Wealth and Poverty of Nations:*
  Why Some Are So Rich and Some So Poor
  David S. Landes, W. W. Norton & Company (1998)

- **The Warren Buffett Portfolio:**
  Mastering the Power of the Focus Investment Strategy
  Robert G. Hagstrom, Wiley (2000)

- **Genome:**
  The Autobiography of a Species in 23 Chapters
  Matt Ridley, HarperCollins Publishers (2000)

- **Getting to Yes:**
  Negotiating Agreement Without Giving In
  Roger Fisher, William Ury, and Bruce Patton, Penguin Books (1991)

- **Three Scientists and Their Gods:**
  Looking for Meaning in an Age of Information
  Robert Wright, HarperCollins Publishers (1989)

- **Only the Paranoid Survive**
  Andy Grove, Currency (1996)

And a few from your editor...

- **Les Schwab:**
  Pride in Performance
  Les Schwab, Pacific Northwest Books (1986)

- **Men and Rubber:**
  The Story of Business
  Harvey S. Firestone, Kessinger Publishing (2003)

- **Men to Match My Mountains:**
  The Opening of the Far West, 1840–1900
  Irving Stone, Book Sales (2001)

"Warren likes the game, I like the game, and even in the periods that look tough to other people, it's been a lot of fun, a lot of fun...."

Acknowledgments

Poor Charlie's Almanack is a survey of Charles T. Munger: his approach to learning, decision making, investing, his speeches, his "zingers," and more. The impetus for the book came from the many people who, over the years, have said they wished one existed—and have done so with ever-increasing vigor at Berkshire and Wesco shareholder meetings, at dinner parties, on message boards, and many other places. Hearing this clamor, your editor, Peter Kaufman, suggested to Warren Buffett that a book be done and was encouraged to take it upon himself to make it happen.

Illustrator and caricature artist Ed Wexler has made caricature drawings of each contributor to the project and has also produced several dozen other illustrations throughout the book. We hope you enjoy all of his work as much as we do. Special recognition is also due Whitney Tilson, who compiled the Mungerisms section (unabridged edition); Michael Broggie, the author of our biographical portrait of Charlie (unabridged edition); and Carol Loomis, who edited certain sections of the book (and on multiple occasions saved the editor from himself.)

The design, production, and editorial team included, from left to right (back row), Travis Gallup, Carl Foote, Scott Rule, Dwight Tompkins, Michael Broggie, Steve Mull, (middle row) Pamela Koch, Eric Hartman-Birge, Paul Hartman, Charles Belser, Ed Wexler, (front row) Whitney Tilson, Marcus Kaufman, Peter Kaufman, Carol Loomis, Debbie Bosanek, and Doerthe Obert.

Finally, if you enjoy reading *Poor Charlie's Almanack Abridged* half as much as we enjoyed putting it together, we will consider our efforts a distinct success. In every respect, but particularly in our interactions with Charlie, his family, and the Mungers' wide circle of friends and associates, we have been favored with calm skies and smooth sailing in the production of this book. We hope our efforts have proven worthy of our subject, a good and admirable man.

Index

Other Acknowledgments

We also wish to express our appreciation for document submittal, preparation and editing by the following individuals: Sharon Broggie, Robert Denham, Dick Esbenshade, Elaine Fong, Joseph Hsiung, Stefaan Marien, Pat McGee, Jeff Moore, Nancy Munger, Sandra Shatto, Nancy Stepanovich, Stephen Sweeney, Sherwin Tieng, and Christopher Toomey.

For our abridged edition, we wish to recognize the efforts of Russell O. Wiese and KimMarie Zamot of Davis Advisors who were a joy to work with in every respect, writer Steve Goldberg and editor Fred Frailey of *Kiplinger Personal Finance Magazine* for their September 2005 interview of Charlie, and the research assistance of William N. Thorndike, Jr. and Aleem Choudhry in connection with the Henry Singleton and Teledyne sidebar.

And a special thank you from the Editor to Warren Buffett for the encouragement and support that made *Poor Charlie's Almanack* a reality.

December 10, 2004, with the first mockup of *Poor Charlie's Almanack*.

Charles T. Munger—Chronology

1924   Charles Thomas Munger born January 1 in Omaha, Nebraska, to Al and Toody Munger.

1941–42   Charlie attends the University of Michigan as a math major. Does not graduate.

1943   Charlie joins the U.S. Army Air Corps and serves as a meteorological officer.

1943–44   While serving in the Army Air Corps, Charlie attends the California Institute of Technology in Pasadena, California.

1946   Charlie marries Nancy Huggins.

1948   Charlie graduates from Harvard Law School, magna cum laude. He begins practicing law in Los Angeles at Wright & Garrett, which later became Musick Peeler & Garrett.

1949   Charlie admitted to the California Bar.

1950   Charlie builds a relationship with Ed Hoskins and eventually joins him in ownership and operation of Transformer Engineers Company.

1953   Charlie and Nancy Huggins divorce.

1955   Charlie's son Teddy dies of leukemia.

1956   Charlie marries Nancy Barry Borthwick, his wife of forty-nine years.

1959   Warren Buffett and Charlie meet at a dinner in Omaha hosted by children of their mutual friend Dr. Edwin Davis.

1960   Charlie demolishes a family mansion on two lots in the Hancock Park area of Los Angeles. He sells one lot to finance the project and moves his family into a house he builds on the other lot.

1961   Charlie and partner Ed Hoskins sell Transformer Engineers Company. Otis Booth and Charlie begin their first real estate development.

1962   On February 1, Wheeler, Munger & Company, a limited partnership, is established in Los Angeles, with Charlie and Jack Wheeler as partners. The law firm of Munger, Tolles is launched with seven attorneys, including Roy Tolles, Roderick Hills, who later became chairman of the SEC, and his wife, Carla Anderson Hills, who among other top government posts, became U.S. Trade Representative. Warren starts buying shares in Berkshire Hathaway, later acquiring control of the beleaguered New Bedford, Massachusetts, textile manufacturer.

1965   Charlie steps down as an active member of Munger, Tolles & Olson, ceasing his practice of law. Charlie, Warren, and Rick Guerin begin buying shares in Blue Chip Stamps. Warren accumulates enough shares of Berkshire to take control of the company.

1967   Charlie and Warren go to New York to buy Associated Cotton Shops. Warren has earlier acquired National Indemnity Company and National Fire and Marine Insurance Company for $8.6 million.

1968   Warren convenes a group of friends and fellow investors, including Charlie, to travel to Coronado, California, to meet with Benjamin Graham and discuss the flagging stock market. Warren starts to liquidate Berkshire's assets and restructure it as a holding company.

1969   Charlie and Warren provide financial and legal support for the appeal to the California Supreme Court of Dr. Belous, a physician who referred a patient to an abortion clinic. Charlie becomes a trustee of Harvard School in Los Angeles, which later merged with Westlake School. The one-hundred-member Buffett Partnership is terminated at the end of the year. Investors had multiple choices—take cash, take shares in Berkshire, or follow Warren's recommendation to invest in the Sequoia Fund. Previously, Berkshire has purchased the Illinois National Bank.

1972   Through Blue Chip Stamps, Warren and Charlie buy See's Candy for $25 million. Rick Guerin and Charlie acquire controlling interest in the New America Fund.

1973   Berkshire's *Omaha Sun* newspaper, under the direction of Stan Lipsey, wins a Pulitzer Prize for its exposé of Boys Town. Berkshire begins investing in The Washington Post Company, becoming the largest shareholder outside the family of Katharine Graham.

1974   Charlie becomes chairman of the board of Harvard School, serving until 1979. Warren and Charlie buy Wesco Financial, the parent company of a Pasadena savings and loan association.

1975   Charlie steps down as head of Wheeler, Munger & Company, and the partnership is liquidated in 1976. Its compounded annual growth rate from 1962 to 1975 was 19.8 percent vs. 5.0 percent for the Dow.

1976   The Securities and Exchange Commission completes an investigation of the relationship of Blue Chip Stamps, Wesco Financial, and Berkshire, Blue Chip Stamps settles. Warren and Charlie settle without claiming innocence or admitting guilt and pays $115,000 to Wesco shareholders who may have been damaged by their business practices. Charlie becomes chairman of Blue Chip Stamps.

1977   Through Blue Chip Stamps, Warren and Charlie purchase the *Buffalo Evening News* for $32 million. Berkshire's equity interest in Blue Chip Stamps increases to 36.5 percent by the end of the year. Berkshire invests $10.9 million in Capital Cities Communications.

1978   Charlie becomes Berkshire's vice chairman. Berkshire's stake in Blue Chip Stamps increases to fifty-eight percent, requiring that the company be fully consolidated into Berkshire's financial statements. Charlie's vision problems begin.